Praise for *Java Application Arch*

MW00845704

"The fundamentals never go out of style, and in this book Kirk returns us to the fundamentals of architecting economically interesting software-intensive systems of quality. You'll find this work to be well-written, timely, and full of pragmatic ideas."

—Grady Booch, IBM Fellow

"Along with GOF's *Design Patterns*, Kirk Knoernschild's *Java Application Architecture* is a must-own for every enterprise developer and architect and on the required reading list for all Paremus engineers."

—Richard Nicholson, Paremus CEO, President of the OSGi Alliance

"In writing this book, Kirk has done the software community a great service: He's captured much of the received wisdom about modularity in a form that can be understood by newcomers, taught in computer science courses, and referred to by experienced programmers. I hope this book finds the wide audience it deserves."

—Glyn Normington, Eclipse Virgo Project Lead

"Our industry needs to start thinking in terms of modules—it needs this book!"

—Chris Chedgey, Founder and CEO, Structure 101

"In this book, Kirk Knoernschild provides us with the design patterns we need to make modular software development work in the real world. While it's true that modularity can help us manage complexity and create more maintainable software, there's no free lunch. If you want to achieve the benefits modularity has to offer, buy this book."

—Patrick Paulin, Consultant and Trainer, Modular Mind

"Kirk has expertly documented the best practices for using OSGi and Eclipse runtime technology. A book any senior Java developer needs to read to better understand how to create great software."

—Mike Milinkovich, Executive Director, Eclipse Foundation

Java Application Architecture

The Robert C. Martin Series

Visit **informit.com/martinseries** for a complete list of available publications.

The Robert C. Martin Series is directed at software developers, team-leaders, business analysts, and managers who want to increase their skills and proficiency to the level of a Master Craftsman. The series contains books that guide software professionals in the principles, patterns, and practices of programming, software project management, requirements gathering, design, analysis, testing and others.

Java Application Architecture

MODULARITY PATTERNS WITH EXAMPLES USING OSGI

Kirk Knoernschild

PRENTICE
HALL

Upper Saddle River, NJ • Boston • Indianapolis • San Francisco
New York • Toronto • Montreal • London • Munich • Paris • Madrid
Capetown • Sydney • Tokyo • Singapore • Mexico City

Many of the designations used by manufacturers and sellers to distinguish their products are claimed as trademarks. Where those designations appear in this book, and the publisher was aware of a trademark claim, the designations have been printed with initial capital letters or in all capitals.

The author and publisher have taken care in the preparation of this book, but make no expressed or implied warranty of any kind and assume no responsibility for errors or omissions. No liability is assumed for incidental or consequential damages in connection with or arising out of the use of the information or programs contained herein.

The publisher offers excellent discounts on this book when ordered in quantity for bulk purchases or special sales, which may include electronic versions and/or custom covers and content particular to your business, training goals, marketing focus, and branding interests. For more information, please contact:

U.S. Corporate and Government Sales
(800) 382-3419
corpsales@pearsontechgroup.com

For sales outside the United States, please contact:

International Sales
international@pearson.com

Visit us on the Web: informit.com/ph

Library of Congress Cataloging-in-Publication Data
Knoernschild, Kirk.
  Java application architecture : modularity patterns with examples using OSGi / Kirk Knoernschild.
       p.   cm.
  Includes index.
  ISBN 978-0-321-24713-1 (pbk. : alk. paper)
  1. Java (Computer program language) 2. Application software—Development.
3. Software architecture. 4. Component software. I. Title.
  QA76.73.J38K563 2012
  005.13'3—dc23

                                                                    2011051434

ISBN-13: 978-0-321-24713-1
ISBN-10:   0-321-24713-2
Text printed in the United States on recycled paper at RR Donnelley in Crawfordsville, Indiana.
First printing, March 2012

Tammy,
My wife, best friend, and soul mate . . . forever!
Thank you for all that you do.
I love you.

Cory,
Fly high.

Cody,
Play ball.

Izi,
Cheer loud.

Chloe,
Dream big.

CONTENTS

FOREWORD BY ROBERT C. MARTIN

I'm dancing! By God I'm dancing on the walls. I'm dancing on the ceiling. I'm ecstatic. I'm overjoyed. I'm really, really pleased.

"Why?" you ask. Well, I'll tell you why—since you asked. I'm happy because *somebody finally read John Lakos's book!*

Way back in the 1990s, John Lakos wrote a book entitled *Large-Scale C++ Software Design*. The book was brilliant. The book was groundbreaking. The book made the case for large-scale application architecture and made it well.

There was just one problem with John's book. The book had "C++" in the title and was published just as the software community was leaping to Java. And so the people who really needed to read that book didn't read it.

Ah, but then the people doing Java back then weren't reading *any* books on software design, because they were all 22 years old, sitting in Herman-Miller office chairs, hacking Java, day trading, and dreaming of being billionaires by the time they were 23. Oh, God, they were such hot stuff!

So, here we are, more than a decade later. We've matured a bit. And we've failed a bit. And our failures have winnowed and seasoned us. We now look back at the wasteland of Java architectures we created and grimace. How could we have been so naïve? How could we have lost sight of the principles of Jacobson, Booch, Rumbaugh, Fowler, and Lakos? Where did we go wrong?

I'll tell you where we went wrong. The Web bamboozled us. We all got Twitterpated. We thought the Web was revolutionary. We thought the

Web changed everything. We thought the Web made all the old rules irrelevant. We thought the Web was so new, so revolutionary, and so game-changing that we ignored the rules of the game.

And we paid. Oh, God, how we paid. We paid with huge, unmanageable designs. We paid with tangled, messy code. We paid with misguided directionless architectures. We paid with failed projects, bankrupt companies, and broken dreams. We paid, and we paid, and we paid.

It took 15 years, and we've just begun to realize why. We've just begun to see that the game hasn't changed at all. We've begun to see that the Web is just another delivery mechanism, no different from all the others—a reincarnation of the old IBM green-screen request/response technology. It was just plain old software after all, and we should never have abandoned the rules of the game.

Now we can see that we should have stuck to the wisdom of Parnas, Weinberg, Page-Jones, and DeMarco all along. We should never have walked away from the teachings of Jacobson and Booch. *And we should have read that damn book by Lakos!*

Well, somebody *did* read that book. And he must have read a few others, too, because he's written a book that states the rules of the Java architecture game better than I've seen them stated before. You're holding that book in your hands right now. The man who wrote it is named Kirk Knoernschild.

In this book Kirk has gone beyond Lakos, beyond Jacobson, beyond Booch. He's taken the principles of those past masters and created a brilliant new synthesis of principles, rules, guidelines, and patterns. *This is how you build a Java application, people.*

Go ahead and flip through the pages. Notice something? Yeah, no fluff! It's all hard-core. It's all right to the point. It's all pragmatic, useful, necessary! It's all about the nuts and bolts architecture of Java applications—the way it *should* be: modular, decoupled, levelized, independently deployable, and smart.

If you are a Java programmer, if you are a tech lead or a team lead, if you are an architect, if you are someone who wants and needs to make a difference on your software development team, *read this book*. If you want to avoid repeating the tragedy of the last 15 years, *read this book*. If you want to learn what software architecture is really all about, *read this book!*
Nuff said.

—Uncle Bob
35,000 feet over the Atlantic
October 1, 2011

FOREWORD BY PETER KRIENS

About two years ago (January 2010) I got an e-mail from Kirk Knoerns-child, soliciting feedback for his almost-ready book. Looking back at the heated discussion that ensued—50 or more lengthy mails—I cannot but wonder that some resentment must have formed on his side. I am pretty sure our conversations caused heavy delays in his initial schedule. I was therefore pleasantly surprised when Kirk asked me to write a foreword for this book; it takes a strong man to let an opponent write a foreword for the book he put so much effort into.

Now, I do agree with most of what Kirk says in this book. We are both intrigued by the magic of modularity, and we see eye to eye on most of the fundamental concepts. However, as is so often the case, the most heated debates are between people who agree on the principles but differ on the details. It was not until the OSGi Community Event in Darmstadt, Germany (two days before the deadline of this foreword), that I suddenly understood Kirk's resistance.

At this event Graham Charters (IBM) presented the "Modularity Maturity Model," which he derived from IBM's SOA Maturity Model, which of course came from the original SEI Capability Maturity Model (CMM). This was an insightful presentation that made me understand that my perspective of system design is very much tainted by more than 13 years of living modularity.

One of the key lessons of the CMM was that it is impossible to skip a step. If your company is on level 1 of CMM (chaotic), then it is not a good idea to make plans to move to level 4 (managed) in one giant step. Companies have tried and failed spectacularly. Transitions through each of the intermediate stages are required to help organizations understand the intricacies of the different levels. Every level has its own set of problems that are solved by the next level.

After Graham's presentation, it became clear to me that I basically look down from level 5, and Kirk is trying to make people look up from level 1. The particular issues that we were disagreeing on are about the challenges you will encounter when designing modular software. These challenges seem perfectly sensible after you've reached level 2 or 3 but tend not to make a lot of sense on level 1. Our brains are wired in such a way that we can understand a solution only once we experience the corresponding problem. I was trying to beat Kirk into discussing those solutions before his readers had experienced and understood the problems of the prior levels.

In my Modularity Maturity Model (Graham's was a bit different), I see the following levels:

1. Unmanaged/chaos
2. Managing dependencies
3. Proper isolation
4. Modifying the code base to minimize coupling
5. Service-oriented architectures

In the first level, applications are based on the class path, a linear list of JARs. Applications consist of a set of JARs or directories with classes that form the classpath. In this level there is no modularity whatsoever. Problems on this level are missing classes or mixing versions.

The second level is when you get module identity and specify dependencies on other modules. Modules get a name and can be versioned. They still are linearly searched, and many of the problems from level 1 exist, but the system is more maintainable and the results more repeatable. Problems on this level mainly circulate around "downloading the Internet" because of excessive transitive dependencies. This is the level Maven is currently at.

The third stage is to truly isolate the modules from each other with a very distinct set of exported, imported, and private packages. Dependencies can now be expressed on packages, reducing the need to "download the Internet." This isolation provides an internal namespace for a module that is truly local to the module, and it allows multiple namespaces so that different versions of a package can be supported in the same system. The problems at this level are usually caused by popular Java patterns based on dynamic class loading that are rarely compatible with module boundaries and multiple namespaces.

The fourth level starts when the code base is modified only for the purpose of maximizing cohesion and minimizing coupling. There is increased awareness that a single line in the code can actually cause an excessive amount of dependencies. Combining or separating functions can have a significant influence on how the system behaves during deployment. At this level the existing Java patterns become painful to use because they often require central configuration, while the solutions seem to indicate a more equal peer-to-peer model. In OSGi, μServices become very attractive since they solve many problems.

At level 5, the last level, the modules become less important than the μServices they provide. Design and dependency resolution is now completely by μServices; modules are just containers that consume and provide μServices.

In the past 13 years I've lived and breathed level 5 as it is implemented in OSGi. This sometimes makes it hard to empathize with people who have used only the classpath and simple JARs. Looking at Graham Charter's presentation, I realized that Kirk's ambition is to help people understand the importance of modular design principles and move them from level 1 to level 2, ultimately giving them a solid foundation to achieve even greater maturity with OSGi. I realize that I often tried to drag the book straight to level 5, foregoing several important lessons that are necessary to design modular software. That book is still critical and is one I hope to write myself someday.

Kirk's book is so important now because it provides patterns to get started with modular thinking and allows you to begin your journey in building modular software using the platforms, frameworks, and languages most widely used today. Yes, I do believe there are better solutions to some of the problems in this book, but I also realize that better is often the enemy of good.

This is therefore an excellent book if you build Java applications using Spring, Guice, or other popular dependency injection frameworks but continue to experience the pain of brittle and rigid software that is difficult and expensive to maintain. The global coupling of your code makes it hard to add new functionality or change the existing code base. This book teaches you many of the fundamental lessons of modularity and will give you a view into the magic of modularity.

That said, I also hope you pay special attention to the examples throughout the book that use OSGi. The first is at the end of Chapter 4 and demonstrates how OSGi helps you achieve proper isolation and minimize coupling using μServices. As much value as this book provides, I am convinced that following its advice will help you build software with greater architectural integrity and will lead you on the correct migration path toward OSGi. OSGi is by far the most mature modularity solution around.

Kirk has been a more than worthy opponent; he has taught me more about my own ideas than almost anybody else in the last few years by forcing me to put them into words. I do hope you will have as much fun reading this book as I had discussing this book with him over the last two years.

—Peter Kriens
 Technical Director, OSGi Alliance
 Beaulieu, England
 September 2011

ACKNOWLEDGMENTS

The inspiration for this book comes from several sources, and the help I've received over the past several years is tremendous. However, I owe a very special thanks to seven individuals. It is their ideas that have guided my work over the past two decades, the development of these patterns over the past ten years, and the completion of this book over the past two years. They include the following:

Robert C. Martin (*Uncle Bob*): Bob's work on object-oriented design principles (i.e., the SOLID principles) is a cornerstone of many of the techniques discussed throughout this book. In fact, this book is part of his series, and Appendix A provides an overview of several of the principles.

Clemens Szyperski: Clemens's *Component Software: Beyond Object Oriented Programming* served as the building block upon which the definition of *module* is used throughout this book.

John Lakos: Johns's *Large Scale C++ Software Design* is the only book I'm aware of that discusses physical design. The ideas in John's book served as inspiration and increased my interest in physical design, allowing me, over the past ten years, to apply and refine techniques that have resulted in the modularity patterns.

Ralph Johnson, John Vlissides, Erich Gamma, and Richard Helm ("the GOF" or "the Gang of Four"): Aside from providing the pattern template I use throughout this book, *Design Patterns* helped cement my understanding of object-oriented concepts.

Additionally, I want to thank the following individuals whose feedback has served me tremendously in helping improve the book's message.

Notably, Peter Kriens, technology director of the OSGi Alliance: Peter provided enough feedback that I should have probably listed him as a coauthor.

I'd also like to thank Brad Appleton, Kevin Bodie, Alex Buckley, Robert Bogetti, Chris Chedgey, Michael Haupt, Richard Nicholson, Glyn Normington, Patrick Paulin, John Pantone, and Vineet Sinha for providing thoughtful reviews and valuable feedback that helped me clarify certain areas of the text and provide alternative views on the discussion. Of course, along this journey, several others have influenced my work. Sadly, I'm sure I've neglected to mention a few of them. You know who you are. Thank you!

Of course, the Prentice Hall team helped make it all happen. Chris Guzikowski, my editor, gave me more chances over the past several years to complete this book than I probably deserved. Sheri Cain, my development editor, provided valuable formatting advice, answered several of my silly questions, and helped me structure and refine a very rough manuscript. Olivia Basegio and Raina Chrobak, the editorial assistants, helped guide me through the entire process. Anna Popick, the project editor, saw it through to completion. And Kim Wimpsett, my copy editor, helped polish the final manuscript.

Finally, I want to thank my family. Without their love, few things are possible, and nothing is worthwhile. Mom and Dad, for their gentle guidance along life's journey. I'm sure there were many times they wondered where I was headed. Grandma Maude, the greatest teacher there ever was. My children, Cory, Cody, Izi, and Chloe, who make sure there is never a dull moment. And of course, my wife, Tammy. My best friend whose encouragement inspired me to dust off an old copy of the manuscript and start writing again. Thank you. All of you!

About the Author

Kirk Knoernschild is a software developer who has filled most roles on a software development team. Kirk is the author of *Java Design: Objects, UML, and Process* (Addison-Wesley, 2002), and he contributed to *No Fluff Just Stuff 2006 Anthology* (Pragmatic Bookshelf, 2006). Kirk is an open source contributor, has written numerous articles, and is a frequent conference speaker. He has trained and mentored thousands of software professionals on topics including Java/J2EE, modeling, software architecture and design, component-based development, service-oriented architecture, and software process. You can visit his website at http://techdistrict .kirkk.com.

Introduction

In 1995, design patterns were all the rage. Today, I find the exact opposite. Patterns have become commonplace, and most developers use patterns on a daily basis without giving it much thought. New patterns rarely emerge today that have the same impact of the Gang of Four (GOF) patterns.[1] In fact, the industry has largely moved past the patterns movement. Patterns are no longer fashionable. They are simply part of a developer's arsenal of tools that help them design software systems.

But, the role design patterns have played over the past decade should not be diminished. They were a catalyst that propelled object-oriented development into the mainstream. They helped legions of developers understand the real value of inheritance and how to use it effectively. Patterns provided insight into how to construct flexible and resilient software systems. With nuggets of wisdom, such as "Favor object composition over class inheritance" and "Program to an interface, not an implementation" (Gamma 1995), patterns helped a generation of software developers adopt a new programming paradigm.

Patterns are still widely used today, but for many developers, they are instinctive. No longer do developers debate the merits of using the Strategy pattern. Nor must they constantly reference the GOF book to identify

---

1. The patterns in the book *Design Patterns: Elements of Reusable Object-Oriented Software* are affectionately referred to as the GOF patterns. GOF stands for the Gang of Four, in reference to the four authors.

which pattern might best fit their current need. Instead, good developers now instinctively design object-oriented software systems.

Many patterns are also timeless. That is, they are not tied to a specific platform, programming language, nor era of programming. With some slight modification and attention to detail, a pattern is molded to a form appropriate given the context. Many things dictate context, including platform, language, and the intricacies of the problem you're trying to solve. As we learn more about patterns, we offer samples that show how to use patterns in a specific language. We call these *idioms*.

I'd like to think the modularity patterns in this book are also timeless. They are not tied to a specific platform or language. Whether you're using Java or .NET, OSGi,[2] or Jigsaw[3] or you want to build more modular software, the patterns in this book help you do that. I'd also like to think that over time, we'll see idioms emerge that illustrate how to apply these patterns on platforms that support modularity and that tools will emerge that help us refactor our software systems using these patterns. I'm hopeful that when these tools emerge, they will continue to evolve and aid the development of modular software. But most important, I hope that with your help, these patterns will evolve and morph into a pattern language that will help us design better software—software that realizes the advantages of modularity. Time will tell.

OBJECT-ORIENTED DESIGN

SOLID principles, 319 Over the past several years, a number of object-oriented design principles have emerged. Many of these design principles are embodied within design patterns. The SOLID design principles espoused by Uncle Bob are prime examples. Further analysis of the GOF patterns reveals that many of them adhere to these principles.

For all the knowledge shared, and advancements made, that help guide object-oriented development, creating very large software systems is still inherently difficult. These large systems are still difficult to maintain, extend, and manage. The current principles and patterns of object-oriented development fail in helping manage the complexity of large software

---

2. OSGi is the dynamic module system for the Java platform. It is a specification managed by the OSGi Alliance. For more, see www.osgi.org.

3. Jigsaw is the proposed module system for Java SE 8.

systems because they address a different problem. They help address problems related to logical design but do not help address the challenges of physical design.

LOGICAL VERSUS PHYSICAL DESIGN

Almost all principles and patterns that aid in software design and architecture address logical design.[4] Logical design pertains to language constructs such as classes, operators, methods, and packages. Identifying the methods of a class, relationships between classes, and a system package structure are all logical design issues.

It's no surprise that because most principles and patterns emphasize logical design, the majority of developers spend their time dealing with logical design issues. When designing classes and their methods, you are defining the system's logical design. Deciding whether a class should be a Singleton is a logical design issue. So is determining whether an operation should be abstract or deciding whether you should inherit from a class versus contain it. Developers live in the code and are constantly dealing with logical design issues.

Making good use of object-oriented design principles and patterns is important. Accommodating the complex behaviors required by most business applications is a challenging task, and failing to create a flexible class structure can have a negative impact on future growth and extensibility. But logical design is not the focus of this book. Numerous other books and articles provide the guiding wisdom necessary to create good logical designs. Logical design is just one piece of the software design and architecture challenge. The other piece of the challenge is physical design. If you don't consider the physical design of your system, then your logical design, no matter how beautiful, may not provide you with the benefits you believe it does. In other words, logical design without physical design may not really matter all that much.

Physical design represents the physical entities of your software system. Determining how a software system is packaged into its deployable units is a physical design issue. Determining which classes belong in

---

4. One exception is the excellent book by John Lakos, *Large-Scale C++ Software Design*. Here, Lakos presents several principles of logical and physical design to aid development of software programs written using C++.

which deployable units is also a physical design issue. Managing the relationships between the deployable entities is also a physical design issue. Physical design is equally as, if not more important than, logical design.

For example, defining an interface to decouple clients from all classes implementing the interface is a logical design issue. Decoupling in this fashion certainly allows you to create new implementations of the interface without impacting clients. However, the allocation of the interface and its implementing classes to their physical entities is a physical design issue. If the interface has several different implementations and each of those implementation classes has underlying dependencies, the placement of the interface and implementation has a tremendous impact on the overall quality of the system's software architecture. Placing the interface and implementation in the same module introduces the risk of undesirable deployment dependencies. If one of the implementations is dependent upon a complex underlying structure, then you'll be forced to include this dependent structure in all deployments, regardless of which implementation you choose to use. Regardless of the quality of the logical design, the dependencies between the physical entities will inhibit reusability, maintainability, and many other benefits you hope to achieve with your design.

Unfortunately, although many teams spend a good share of time on logical design, few teams devote effort to their physical design. Physical design is about how we partition the software system into a system of modules. Physical design is about software modularity.

MODULARITY

Large software systems are inherently more complex to develop and maintain than smaller systems. Modularity involves breaking a large system into separate physical entities that ultimately makes the system easier to understand. By understanding the behaviors contained within a module and the dependencies that exist between modules, it's easier to identify and assess the ramification of change.

For instance, software modules with few incoming dependencies are easier to change than software modules with many incoming dependencies. Likewise, software modules with few outgoing dependencies are much easier to reuse than software modules with many outgoing dependencies. Reuse and maintainability are important factors to consider when designing software modules, and dependencies play an important factor. But dependencies aren't the only factor.

Module cohesion also plays an important role in designing high-quality software modules. A module with too little behavior doesn't do enough to be useful to other modules using it and therefore provides minimal value. Contrarily, a module that does too much is difficult to reuse because it provides more behavior than other modules desire. When designing modules, identifying the right level of granularity is important. Modules that are too fine-grained provide minimal value and may also require other modules to be useful. Modules that are too coarse-grained are difficult to reuse.

The principles in this book provide guidance on designing modular software. They examine ways that you can minimize dependencies between modules while maximizing a module's reuse potential. Many of these principles would not be possible without the principles and patterns of object-oriented design. As you'll discover, the physical design decisions you make to modularize the system will often dictate the logical design decisions.

UNIT OF MODULARITY: THE JAR FILE

Physical design on the Java platform is done by carefully designing the relationships and behavior of Java JAR files. On the Java platform, the unit of modularity is the JAR file. Although these principles can be applied to any other unit, such as packages, they shine when using them to design JAR files.

module defined, 17

OSGI

The OSGi Service Platform is the dynamic module system for Java. In OSGi parlance, a module is known as a *bundle*. OSGi provides a framework for managing bundles that are packaged as regular Java JAR files with an accompanying manifest. The manifest contains important metadata that describes the bundles and its dependencies to the OSGi framework.

OSGi, 273

You'll find examples leveraging OSGi throughout this book. However, OSGi is not a prerequisite for using the modularity patterns. OSGi simply provides a runtime environment that enables and enforces modularity on the Java platform. OSGi offers the following capabilities:

- **Modularity**: Enables and enforces a modular approach to architecture on the Java platform.
- **Versioning**: Supports multiple versions of the same software module deployed within the same Java Virtual Machine (JVM) instance.

- **Hot deployments**: Permits modules to be deployed and updated within a running system without restarting the application or the JVM.
- **Encapsulation**: Allows modules to hide their implementation details from consuming modules.
- **Service orientation**: Encourages service-oriented design principles in a more granular level within the JVM. To accomplish this, OSGi uses µServices.
- **Dependency management**: Requires explicit declaration of dependencies between modules.

WHO THIS BOOK IS FOR

This book is for the software developer or architect responsible for developing software applications. If you're interested in improving the design of the systems you create, this book is for you.

This book is not exclusively for individuals who are using a platform that provides native support for modularity. For instance, if you're using OSGi, this book helps you leverage OSGi to design more modular software. But if you're not using OSGi, the techniques discussed in this book are still valuable in helping you apply techniques that increase the modularity of your software systems. Nor is this book exclusively for Java developers. Although the examples throughout this book use Java, the techniques discussed can be applied to other platforms, such as .NET, with relative ease.

If you want to understand more deeply the benefits of modularity and start designing modular software systems, this book is for you! This book provides answers to the following questions:

- What are the benefits of modularity and why is it important?
- How can I convince other developers of the importance of modularity?
- What techniques can I apply to increase the modularity of my software systems?
- How can I start using modularity now, even if I'm not developing on a platform with native support for modularity, such as OSGi?
- How can I migrate large-scale monolithic applications to applications with a modular architecture?

HOW THIS BOOK IS ORGANIZED

This book is divided into three parts. Part I presents the case for modularity. Here, you explore the important role that software modularity plays in designing software systems and learn why you want to design modular software. Part II is a catalog of 18 patterns that help you design more modular software. These patterns rely heavily on the ideas discussed in Part I. Part III introduces OSGi and demonstrates how a software system designed using the patterns in this book is well positioned to take advantage of platform support for modularity. Part III relies heavily on code examples to demonstrate the points made.

Naturally, I suggest reading the book cover to cover. But, you might also want to explore the book by jumping from chapter to chapter. Feel free! Throughout this book, in the margin, you'll notice several forward and backward references to the topics relevant to the current topic. This helps you navigate and consume the ideas more easily. The following is a summary of each chapter.

PART I: THE CASE FOR MODULARITY

Part I presents the reasons why modularity is important. It is the case for modularity. A brief synopsis of each chapter in Part I follows:

- **Chapter 1, "Module Defined":** This chapter introduces modularity and formally defines and identifies the characteristics of a software module. I encourage everyone to read this short chapter.

- **Chapter 2, "The Two Facets of Modularity":** There are two aspects to modularity: the runtime model and the development model. Much emphasis has been placed on providing runtime support for modularity. As more platforms provide runtime support for modularity, the importance of the development model will take center stage. The development model consists of the programming model and the design paradigm.

- **Chapter 3, "Architecture and Modularity":** Modularity plays a critical role in software architecture. It fills a gap that has existed since teams began developing enterprise software systems. This chapter examines the goal of software architecture and explores the important role modularity plays in realizing that goal.

- **Chapter 4, "Taming the Beast Named Complexity":** Enterprise software systems are fraught with complexity. Teams are challenged by technical debt, and systems are crumbling from rotting design. This chapter explains how modularity helps us tame the increasing complexity of software systems.

- **Chapter 5, "Realizing Reuse":** Reuse is the panacea of software development. Unfortunately, few organizations are able to realize high rates of reuse. This chapter examines the roadblocks that prevent organizations from realizing reuse and explores how modularity increases the chance of success.

- **Chapter 6, "Modularity and SOA":** Modularity and SOA are complementary in many ways. This chapter explores how modularity and SOA are a powerful combination.

- **Chapter 7, "Reference Implementation":** It's important to provide some decent samples that illustrate the concepts discussed. The reference implementation serves two purposes. First, it ties together the material in the first six chapters so you can see how these concepts are applied. Second, it lays the foundation for many of the patterns discussed in Part II.

PART II: THE PATTERNS

The patterns are a collection of modularity patterns. They are divided into five separate categories, each with a slightly different purpose. There is some tension between the different categories. For instance, the usability patterns aim to make it easy to use a module while the extensibility patterns make it easier to reuse modules. This tension between use and reuse is further discussed in Chapter 5.

- **Chapter 8, "Base Patterns":** The base patterns are the fundamental elements upon which many of the other patterns exist. They establish the conscientious thought process that go into designing systems with a modular architecture. They focus on modules as the unit of reuse, dependency management, and cohesion. All are important elements of well-designed modular software systems.

- **Chapter 9, "Dependency Patterns":** I've personally found it fascinating that development teams spend so much time designing class relationships but spend so little time creating a supporting physical structure. Here, you find some guidance that helps you create a physical structure that emphasizes low coupling between modules. You'll also find some discussion exploring how module design impacts deployment.

- **Chapter 10, "Usability Patterns":** Although coupling is an important measurement, cohesion is equally important. It's easy to create and manage module dependencies if I throw all of my classes in a couple of JAR files. But in doing so, I've introduced a maintenance nightmare. In this chapter, we see patterns that help ensure our modules are cohesive units. It's interesting that you'll find some contention between the dependency patterns and usability patterns. I talk about this contention and what you can do to manage it.

- **Chapter 11, "Extensibility Patterns":** A goal in designing software systems is the ability to extend the system without making modifications to the existing codebase. Abstraction plays a central role in accomplishing this goal, but simply adding new functionality to an existing system is only part of the battle. We also want to be able to deploy those new additions without redeploying the entire application. The extensibility patterns focus on helping us achieve this goal.

- **Chapter 12, "Utility Patterns":** The utility patterns aid modular development. Unlike the other patterns, they don't emphasize reuse, extensibility, or usability. Instead, they discuss ways that modularity can be enforced and that help address quality-related issues.

Part III: POMA and OSGi

Standard Java gives you everything you need to begin using the patterns in this book. Undoubtedly, though, you want to see the patterns in the context of an environment that provides first-class support for modularity. In this section, we do just that and use the OSGi framework to illustrate this through example.

- **Chapter 13, "Introducing OSGi":** This chapter provides a brief introduction to OSGi, including its capabilities and benefits. This chapter isn't meant as a tutorial and assumes some cursory knowledge of OSGi. We talk about OSGi and modularity, including µServices and the Blueprint specification. Additionally, you'll see how the dynamism of OSGi brings modularity to the runtime environment. Finally, we wrap up by exploring how the patterns relate to development in OSGi. We point out how OSGi makes it easier to use some of the modularity patterns in their purest form.

- **Chapter 14, "The Loan Sample and OSGi":** As you read through the pattern discussions, you'll notice a common example we use is a loan system. In this chapter, we again use the loan system but refactor the application so that it runs in an OSGi environment. You'll be surprised that once you have a modular architecture, OSGi is just a simple step away.

- **Chapter 15, "OSGi and Scala":** The Java platform supports multiple languages, and OSGi doesn't inhibit you from using alternative languages on the Java platform. In this section, we show how we can create a Scala module and plug it into a system. You'll see two simple advantages. First, the modular architecture makes it easy to add code without making modifications to any other code in the system. Second, it clearly illustrates the dynamism of OSGi.

- **Chapter 16, "OSGi and Groovy":** Like the Scala example in Chapter 15, we develop another module using the Groovy programming language to further illustrate the flexibility and dynamicity of a runtime environment that supports modularity.

- **Chapter 17, "Future of OSGi":** What's the future of modularity and OSGi? How might it transform how we currently think about large enterprise software systems? In this chapter, we explore that future with a provocative look at what's in store for modularity and OSGi.

PATTERN FORM

Each pattern is consistent in structure to help maximize its readability. Each is also accompanied by an example that illustrates how the underlying principles it captures are applied. Not all sections appear for all patterns. In some cases, certain sections are omitted when a previous discussion can be referenced. The general structure of each pattern resembles the Gang of Four (GOF) format, which is the format used in the book *Design Patterns: Elements of Reusable Object-Oriented Software*, structured as follows:

PATTERN NAME

First, the name of the pattern is presented. The name is important, because it helps establish a common vocabulary among developers.

PATTERN STATEMENT

The pattern statement is a summary that describes the pattern. This statement helps establish the intent of the pattern.

SKETCH

A sketch is a visual representation that shows the general structure of the pattern. Usually, the Unified Modeling Language (UML) is used here.

DESCRIPTION

The description offers a more detailed explanation of the problem that the pattern solves. The description establishes the motivation behind the pattern.

IMPLEMENTATION VARIATIONS

As with any pattern, subtle implementation details quickly arise when applying the pattern to a real-world problem. "Implementation Variations" discusses some of the more significant alternatives you should consider when applying the pattern.

CONSEQUENCES

All design decisions have advantages and disadvantages, and like most advice on software design, the use of these patterns must be judicious. While they offer a great deal of flexibility, that flexibility comes with a price. The "Consequences" section discusses some of the interesting things you'll likely encounter when applying the pattern and some of the probable outcomes should you decide to ignore the pattern. After reading through the consequences, you should have a better idea of when you'll want to apply the pattern and when you may want to consider using an alternative approach. Boiled down, this section represents the advantages and disadvantages of using the pattern, the price you'll pay, and the benefits you should realize.

SAMPLE

It's usually easier to understand a pattern when you can see a focused example. In this section, we walk through a sample that illustrates how the pattern can be applied. Sometimes, we work through some code, and other times, some simple visuals clearly convey the message. Most important though is that the sample won't exist in a vacuum. When we apply patterns in the real world, patterns are often used in conjunction with each other to create a more flexible tailored solution. In cases where it makes sense, the sample builds on previous samples illustrated in other patterns. The result is insight into how you can pragmatically apply the pattern in your work.

WRAPPING UP

This section offers a few closing thoughts on the pattern.

PATTERN CATALOG

The following are the modularity patterns:

- **Base Patterns**
  - Manage Relationships: Design module relationships.
  - Module Reuse: Emphasize reusability at the module level.
  - Cohesive Modules: Module behavior should serve a singular purpose.
- **Dependency Patterns**
  - Acyclic Relationships: Module relationships must be acyclic.
  - Levelize Modules: Module relationships should be levelized.
  - Physical Layers: Module relationships should not violate the conceptual layers.
  - Container Independence: Modules should be independent of the runtime container.

- Independent Deployment: Modules should be independently deployable units.
- **Usability Patterns**
  - Published Interface: Make a module's published interface well known.
  - External Configuration: Modules should be externally configurable.
  - Default Implementation: Provide modules with a default implementation.
  - Module Facade: Create a facade serving as a coarse-grained entry point to another fine-grained module's underlying implementation.
- **Extensibility Patterns**
  - Abstract Module: Depend upon the abstract elements of a module.
  - Implementation Factory: Use factories to create a module's implementation classes.
  - Separate Abstractions: Place abstractions and the classes that implement them in separate modules.
- **Utility Patterns**
  - Colocate Exceptions: Exceptions should be close to the class or interface that throws them.
  - Levelize Build: Execute the build in accordance with module levelization.
  - Test Module: Each module should have a corresponding test module.

THE CODE

Numerous examples are spread throughout this book, and many of these samples include code. All pattern samples for this book can be found in the following GitHub repository: https://github.com/pragkirk/poma.

If you're interested in running the code on your machine but are unfamiliar with Git, see the Git documentation at http://git-scm.com/documentation.

The sample code in Chapter 7 can be found in a Google Code Subversion repository at http://code.google.com/p/kcode/source/browse/#svn/trunk/billpayevolution/billpay.

I encourage everyone to download the code from these repositories and use the code while reading each pattern's "Sample" section. Although code is included with many of the patterns, it's not possible to include all the code for each sample. The code you find in this book helps guide you through the discussion and provides an overview of how the pattern can be applied. But, you gain far greater insight to the intricacies of the pattern by downloading and reviewing the code.

AN OPENING THOUGHT ON THE MODULARITY PATTERNS

There was some debate surrounding the modularity patterns as I wrote this book. Some suggested they would be more aptly referred to as principles, while others preferred laws. Some even suggested referring to them as heuristics, guidelines, idioms, recipes, or rules. At the end of the day, however, all reviewers said they loved this book's content and approach. So, in the end, I stuck with patterns. Instead of trying to decide whether you feel these should be patterns, principles, heuristics, or something else, I encourage you to focus on the topic of discussion for each pattern. The idea! That's what's important.

REFERENCE

Gamma, Erich, et al. 1995. *Design Patterns: Elements of Reusable Object-Oriented Software*. Reading, MA: Addison-Wesley.

THE CASE FOR MODULARITY

There is no shortage of books on software design. Numerous books are available that will teach you fundamental and advanced concepts of object-oriented design. You can find a similar number that will teach you basic and advanced concepts of service-oriented architecture. However, there is a missing ingredient: modularity. Rarely do you see thoughtful discussions that tie together architecture at the highest levels of the system with the code that lives in the bowels of the system.

In this first part of the book, we begin by establishing a common understanding of the term *module*. We quickly move on to discuss the different facets of modularity—the runtime model and the development model. From there, we examine how modularity helps us "architect all the way down" by allowing us to tie together important high-level architectural constructs with more detailed implementations. We also explore the role of modularity in helping us tame the beast we call *complexity* and achieve the panacea we call *reuse*. Finally, before we move on to the modularity patterns, we walk through a sample exercise that illustrates the benefits of modularity. Throughout, we make a strong case for modularity.

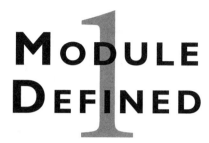

MODULE DEFINED

First, we need to answer a simple question:

What is a software module on the Java platform?

1.1 DEFINING A MODULE

A module is simply a "chunk of software." Unfortunately, that's not concise enough to differentiate a module from other software chunks, such as classes, packages, components, services, or even applications. So, we need to focus on this definition:

A software module is a deployable, manageable, natively reusable, composable, stateless unit of software that provides a concise interface to consumers.

That's a mouthful, and I feel bad about dumping this on you in the very first chapter. But, after some explanation, you're sure to grasp what a module is. Figure 1.1 illustrates this definition. Next, you explore the individual elements of a module.

1.1.1 DEPLOYABLE

Modules are a unit of deployment. Unlike other software entities, such as classes and packages, a module is a discrete unit of deployment that can go

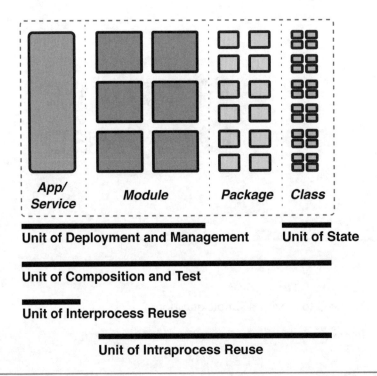

Figure 1.1 Defining a module

alongside other software modules. In this sense, modules represent something more physical and coarse-grained than classes or packages, which are intangible software entities. Examples of deployable units of software include EAR, WAR, and JAR files.

1.1.2 MANAGEABLE

Modules are a unit of management. In the presence of a runtime module system, software modules can be installed, uninstalled, and refreshed. During development, partitioning a system into modules helps ease a number of otherwise complicated activities. This includes improving build efficiency, allowing developers to independently develop autonomous modules, and planning the development effort along module boundaries. Examples of software entities that comply with this segment of the definition include EAR, WAR, and JAR files.

1.1.3 TESTABLE

A module is a unit of testability. Like a class can be independently tested using test-driven development, a module can also be independently tested. Examples of software entities that comply with this segment of the definition include classes, packages, and JAR files.

Test Module pattern, 263

1.1.4 NATIVELY REUSABLE

Modules are a unit of intraprocess reuse. Unlike applications or services, modules are not a distributed computing technology, although service-oriented architecture (SOA) principles can be used to design software modules. Instead, modularity is a way to organize units of deployment in a way that they can be reused across applications, but a module is always invoked natively. That is, the operations exposed by a module are invoked by calling the method directly.

reuse, 61

The way we reuse modules is also different from how we reuse services. Typically, a service is deployed only a single time and invoked by multiple consumers. Because modules are used intraprocess, a module is deployed with each process that intends to reuse its functionality. Examples of software entities that comply with this segment of the definition include classes, packages, and JAR files.

1.1.5 COMPOSABLE

Modules are a unit of composition. Modules can be composed of other modules. Typically, this involves coarse-grained modules being a composition of finer-grained modules.

granularity, 63

1.1.6 STATELESS

Modules are stateless. There exists only a single instance of a specific version of a module. We don't instantiate software modules, although we do instantiate instances of the classes within software modules, and these classes may maintain state. However, the module itself does not. Examples of software entities that adhere to this segment of the definition include WAR, EAR, and JAR files.

1.2 Succinct Definition of a Software Module

Before we get too far, here's a more succinct definition of a software module. Upon applying each segment of the definition, we can more clearly state the following:

> The best candidate as the unit of modularity on the Java platform is the JAR file!

1.3 Conclusion

To differentiate a software module on the Java platform from other "chunks of software," it's important to agree upon a concise definition of *module*. Throughout the remainder of this book, when we refer to a module, we are referring to a JAR file on the Java platform that possesses each of the attributes discussed in this chapter.

THE TWO FACETS
OF MODULARITY

Modularity consists of two aspects: the runtime model and the development model. Today, emphasis is on the runtime model, with frameworks emerging that provide runtime support for modularity. But eventually, as the runtime model gains adoption, the importance of the development model will take center stage. The patterns in this book focus on an aspect of the development model referred to as the *design paradigm*.

2.1 THE RUNTIME MODEL

The runtime model focuses on how to manage modular software systems at runtime. The de facto standard module system on the Java platform is OSGi, and many application platforms leverage OSGi to take advantage of the runtime capabilities resulting from increased modularity. To an extent, this allows the enterprise to realize the advantages of OSGi without knowing much about it. Faster application start-up times and platform adaptability are two advantages organizations will realize as vendors bake OSGi into their products.

more runtime benefits, 274

Until recently, however, many of the most widely used platforms encapsulated OSGi and chose to keep it hidden from enterprise developers. Because of this, developers were unable to build applications that took advantage of the modular runtime. However, this is changing as the platforms are exposing the virtues of OSGi and allowing developers to tap into its powerful runtime capabilities. No longer will we be subject to classpath hell and the monolithic applications that plague us today. Instead, modules will be able to discover other modules at runtime, and the artificial walls that separate applications will no longer exist.

Eventually, as support for modularity is baked into the platform, enterprise developers will be able to leverage the frameworks and technologies that aid them in developing more modular software systems. When this happens, the development model will become very relevant.

2.2 THE DEVELOPMENT MODEL

The development model deals with how developers use the framework to build their software applications. The development model can be further broken down into two categories: the programming model and the design paradigm. Each is important in helping developers build more modular software applications.

2.2.1 THE PROGRAMMING MODEL

weight, 64 Taking advantage of the runtime module system demands that programmers have the ability to interact with the module system's application programming interface (API). However, dependencies on the API result in heavyweight modules that are difficult to test and execute outside of the runtime system. To reduce the dependency on the module system API, frameworks and technologies must provide levels of abstraction so that our code doesn't depend directly upon the framework's API. Examples of these frameworks and technologies include OSGi Blueprint Services, Declarative Services, Spring Dynamic Modules, and iPojo.

Developers can leverage these frameworks and tools to tap into the capabilities of the runtime module system without worrying about the programming model. These frameworks encapsulate dependencies on the API so your code doesn't have to talk directly to the API. The separation of concerns achieved through these frameworks ensures Java classes remain plan old Java objects (POJOs) that aren't dependent on the module system's framework. This makes programming and testing much easier.

2.2.2 THE DESIGN PARADIGM

There are other challenges in developing modular software that extend beyond the runtime model and programming model. The design paradigm must also be addressed. How does an organization create a more modular architecture? What is the right granularity for a module? How heavily dependent should modules be on each other? How do we minimize module dependencies? How do we break apart larger modules into a smaller set of more cohesive modules? How do we modularize an existing monolithic software system? When do we do this? These questions—and others—are the important architectural and design questions that surround modularity in enterprise software development. The patterns in this book emphasize the design paradigm.

To understand the importance of the design paradigm, we can learn important lessons by examining the history of a few other technologies. Let's look at two different examples of technologies that prove the pending relevance of the module design paradigm: object-oriented (OO) programming and Enterprise JavaBeans (EJB).

2.2.2.1 Object Orientation

In the early 1990s, the object-oriented paradigm was touted as the savior. Development teams would be able to build systems by composing reusable objects. The object-oriented paradigm promised significantly reduced time-to-market and higher-quality software. The promises were not met, and the benefits of the object-oriented paradigm were never fully realized. There are a few reasons why development teams failed to realize the benefits. Classes are too granular to serve as the foundation of reuse. Developments teams also had difficulty grasping and applying object-oriented concepts correctly. Deep inheritance hierarchies laden with base classes rich in functionality contributed to poorly designed and brittle software systems. In general, object-oriented development was an early failure.

The runtime capabilities of object-oriented programming languages provided features such as polymorphism and dynamic binding, and developers were able to easily understand many aspects of the programming model. Using dot notation to invoke methods and defining private member variables were trivial concepts. But it took a long time for us to understand how to design good programs using object-oriented design techniques. In other words, we struggled with the design paradigm. What we accept today as simple truths surrounding object-oriented design ("favor object composition over object inheritance" and "program to an interface, not an implementation")[1] were unknown, or at least a mystery to us, 15 years ago. Even now, we continue to learn new ways to design better software systems using object technology.

2.2.2.2 Enterprise JavaBeans

Enterprise JavaBeans (EJB), and especially entity beans, were presented as a way to componentize business applications developed using Java. The runtime capabilities of EJB were alluring—transactions, persistence, security, transparency, and so on—and baked directly into the platform. Unfortunately, there were two glaring problems: The development model was complex, and it was not well understood.

It was several years ago, but I still vividly recall my first experience with EJB. I arrived on the team midway through its development effort. At that point, the team had more than 100 entity beans, the local development environment took more than four hours to start, and problems were rampant. I stuck around for three weeks before I voluntarily left the project. The project ended up being canceled shortly thereafter. The problem with EJB was not the runtime model or the programming model. There were excellent tools available to make each easy to work with. The runtime model fulfilled many of its promises, and the code generation wizards accompanying many tools made working with the programming model relatively straightforward. Frameworks even emerged that allowed developers to decouple their code from the EJB programming model and focus on designing simpler POJOs. However, EJB was a new technology, and many developers lacked the design wisdom to leverage the technology effectively. Again, understanding the design paradigm surrounding EJB proved to be its death knell.

2.2.2.3 Lessons Learned

Object-oriented programming and EJB were two promising technologies that, arguably, failed to live up to their initial hype. The problems were not with object-oriented programming languages or with the platform implementations of the EJB specification but with how we chose to design

---

1. These timeless statements can be found in the GOF book *Design Patterns: Elements of Reusable Object-Oriented Software.*

our applications using these technologies. The most significant challenges were centered around the design paradigm.

These lessons serve as examples of the difficult road that lies ahead for OSGi and, specifically, modularity on the Java platform. If the design paradigm isn't understood, with principles and patterns that guide how developers leverage the technology, the benefits of the runtime model will not be realized. Modularity is a key element of designing software systems with a flexible and adaptable architecture. There is a need for modularity on the Java platform, especially in developing large enterprise software systems. But if we do not begin to understand how to design more modular applications today, we'll face significant challenges when platform support for modularity arrives.

OSGi, 273

2.3 MODULARITY TODAY

It might appear that the runtime model and development model are inextricably linked. A runtime module system makes designing modular software easier but is not required to design modular software. In fact, given the significant advantages of modularity discussed throughout the remainder of Part I, it's a good idea for development teams to start modularizing their applications right now, even if they aren't deploying to a platform with runtime module system support. If you're using a platform that supports modularity, good for you. But if not, you might be wondering how you can design modular software today.

We know a lot about the OSGi runtime model, and details on Jigsaw are emerging.[2] It's likely the platform we're using is leveraging the OSGi runtime model internally, even if it's not exposed to us right now. We know the unit of modularity is the JAR file, and we can start modularizing our applications today by emphasizing the JAR file as the unit of modularity and using the patterns in this book. In Chapter 7, "Reference Implementation," we see firsthand how we can take a system and modularize it by emphasizing the JAR file as the unit of modularity, even in the absence of a runtime module system. The sample for many of the patterns intentionally avoid using OSGi, though we discuss how the pattern can be implemented when using OSGi where it helps offer further clarification.

---

2. Again, OSGi is the de facto standard module system for the Java platform. Jigsaw is the module system in Java SE 8.

In some cases, we include a sample that leverages OSGi to illustrate its advantages.

Even when OSGi hits your platform, it's pertinent to remember that the intent of modularizing our applications is not only to develop applications that leverage OSGi. The real value is the modular architecture that results.

2.3.1 BEWARE

module dependencies, 48

It's critical to keep in mind that modularizing a software system without runtime module support will be challenging. In the absence of a runtime system, the tools you'll use are critical. Visualization tools that help you understand your structure, build tools that help enforce the structure, and dependency management tools that help you manage dependencies are a necessity. For many of the examples throughout this book, we use JarAnalyzer to help us manage the dependencies between modules.

Levelize Build pattern, 253

Additionally, the patterns in this book help you modularize a system. For instance, the Levelize Build pattern helps you enforce your module relationships at compile time. With good tools and strong discipline, modular architecture is something you can achieve. Furthermore, after your modular architecture is in place, you can take advantage of runtime support once it's available. However, without runtime support, you are simply unable to accomplish some things. A runtime module system often provides support for the following:

example of encapsulation, 37

- **Encapsulation**[3]: In standard Java, any public class in a package found on the classpath is available to anything else on the classpath. In other words, there is no way to hide implementation details. Everything is global, which impedes modular design. A runtime module system provides the ability to hide implementation details. For instance, OSGi uses μServices that expose an interface to the underlying implementation details.
- **Dynamic deployment**: In standard Java, updating the software typically involves restarting the JVM. A runtime module system supports hot deploys.

---

3. Encapsulation and μServices are a powerful combination whose value cannot be stressed enough. They enable you to enforce your modular design. In standard Java, you cannot enforce modularity. We will revisit this idea in several sections throughout this book.

- **Versioning**: In standard Java, it's not possible to deploy multiple versions of a class. A module system allows for multiple versions to be deployed.

- **Dependency management**: In standard Java, there is no way to enforce the dependency structure of the modules. Build tools such as Maven attempt to solve this problem through repositories of JAR files that describe their dependencies. A runtime module system enforces runtime dependency management.

2.4 CONCLUSION

There are two facets to modularity: the runtime model and the development model. The development model is comprised of the programming model and the design paradigm. All facets are important, but failing to understand how to design modular software will detract from the benefits of using a modular runtime or framework. The discussions throughout this book primarily address the design paradigm.

ARCHITECTURE AND MODULARITY

Modularity plays an important role in software architecture. It fills a gap that has existed since we began developing enterprise software systems in Java. This chapter discusses that gap and explores how modularity is an important intermediary technology that fills that gap.

3.1 DEFINING ARCHITECTURE

There are numerous definitions of *architecture*. But within each lies a common theme and some key phrases. Here are a few of the definitions. From Booch, Rumbaugh, and Jacobson (1999):

> An architecture is the set of **significant decisions about the organization of a software system**, the selection of **the structural elements and their interfaces** by which the system is composed, **together with their behavior** as specified in the collaborations among those elements, the **composition of these structural elements and behavioral elements into progressively larger subsystems**, and the architecture style that guides this organization — these elements and their interfaces, their collaborations, and their composition.

Now, from the ANSI/IEEE Std 1471-2000 (the Open Group):

> The **fundamental organization of a system**, embodied in its **components,** their **relationships** to each other and the environment, and the **principles governing its design and evolution**.

In the Open Group Architecture Framework (TOGAF), *architecture* has two meanings depending on context (the Open Group):

1) A **formal description of a system**, or a **detailed plan of the system at component level** to guide its implementation

2) The **structure of components**, their **inter-relationships**, and the **principles and guidelines governing their design and evolution over time**

Examining these definitions reveals many common keywords, which I've made bold in the various definitions. Important underlying currents are embodied by these keywords. But, these keywords lead to some important questions that must be answered to more fully understand architecture. What makes a decision architecturally significant? What are the elements of composition? How do we accommodate evolution of architecture? What does this have to do with modularity? As we delve into these questions, I want to start with a story on software architecture.

3.2 A SOFTWARE ARCHITECTURE STORY

The story of software architecture reminds me of the following story (Hawking 1998):

> A well-known scientist (some say it was Bertrand Russell) once gave a public lecture on astronomy. He described how the earth orbits around the sun and how the sun, in turn, orbits around the center of a vast collection of stars called our galaxy. At the end of the lecture, a little old lady at the back of the room got up and said: "What you have told us is rubbish. The world is really a flat plate supported on the back of a giant tortoise." The scientist gave a superior smile before replying, "What is the tortoise standing on?" "You're very clever, young man, very clever," said the old lady. "But it's turtles all the way down!"
>
> —*A Brief History of Time* by Stephen Hawking

Software architecture is "turtles all the way down." How? This section discusses these ideas.

3.2.1 THE IVORY TOWER

Many of us can relate to the ivory tower. In dysfunctional organizations, architects and developers fail to communicate effectively. The result is a

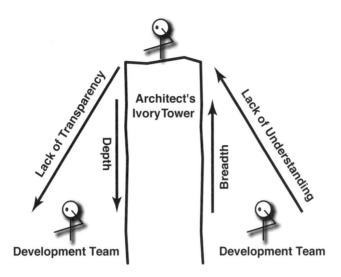

Adapted from http://www.rendell.org/jam/upload/2009/1/tower-12054835.jpg

Figure 3.1 The ivory tower (the Open Group)

lack of transparency and a lack of understanding by both sides. As shown in Figure 3.1, architects bestow their wisdom upon developers who are unable to translate high-level concepts into concrete implementations. The failure often occurs (although I recognize there are other causes) because architecture is about breadth and development is about depth. Each group has disparate views of software architecture, and although both are warranted, there's a gap between these views. The architect might focus on applications and services, while the developer focuses on the code. Sadly, there is a lot in between that no one focuses on. This gap between breadth and depth contributes to ivory tower architecture.

3.2.2 TURTLES AND THE TOWER

Without question, the ivory tower is dysfunctional, and systems lacking architectural integrity are a symptom of ivory tower architecture. So, assuming good intent on the part of the architect and the developer, how can we bridge the gap between breadth and depth? How can we more effectively communicate? How do we increase understanding and transparency?

Let's revisit the definition of software architecture by exploring another definition. My favorite definition of software architecture was offered by Ralph Johnson in an article by Martin Fowler (2003). He states:

> In most successful software projects, the expert developers working on that project have a shared understanding of the system design. This shared understanding is called "architecture." This understanding includes how the system is divided into components and how the components interact through interfaces. These components are usually composed of smaller components, but the architecture only includes the components and interfaces that are understood by all the developers . . . Architecture is about the important stuff. Whatever that is.

The key aspect of this definition that differentiates it from the earlier definitions in this chapter is that of "shared understanding," which implies that there is a social aspect to software architecture. We must have a shared understanding of how the system is divided into components and how they interact. Architecture isn't just some technical concept; it's also a social construct. Through this social aspect of architecture, we can break down the divide between architects and developers.

architecture all the way down, 69 To ensure shared understanding, we have to architect "all the way down." Architects cannot worry only about services, and developers cannot worry only about code. Each group must also focus on a huge middle ground, as illustrated in Figure 3.2.

Focusing exclusively on top-level abstractions is not enough. Emphasizing only code quality is not enough either. We must bridge the gap through other means, including module and package design. Often, when I speak at various conferences, I ask the audience to raise their hands if they devote effort to service design. Many hands raise. I also ask them to raise their hand if they spend time on class design and code quality. Again, many hands go up. But when I ask if they also devote effort to package and module design, only a small percentage leave their hands raised.

This is unfortunate, because module and package design are equally as important as service and class design. But somewhere along the way, with our emphasis on services and code quality, we've lost sight of what lies in between. Within each application or service awaits a rotting design, and atop even the most flexible code sits a suite of applications or services riddled with duplication and lack of understanding. A resilient package structure and corresponding software modules help bridge the divide between services and code. Modularity is an important intermediate

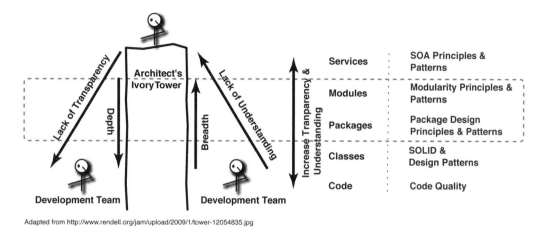

Adapted from http://www.rendell.org/jam/upload/2009/1/tower-12054835.jpg

Figure 3.2 Architecture all the way down

technology that helps us architect all the way down and is the conduit that fills the gap between breadth and depth.

We need to focus on modularity to ensure a consistent architecture story is told. It is the glue that binds. It's the piece that helps bridge low-level class design with higher-level service design. It's the piece that helps bring down the ivory tower, enhance communication, increase transparency, ensure understanding, and verify consistency at multiple levels. It is the piece that allows us to "architect all the way down" and allows us to realize the goal of architecture.

3.3 THE GOAL OF ARCHITECTURE

Modularity helps address the social aspect of software architecture, but it also helps us design more flexible software systems—that is, systems with resilient, adaptable, and maintainable architectures. Examining the earlier definitions of architecture leads us to the goal of architecture. The Johnson definition of architecture as quoted by Fowler makes it apparent that architecture is about the important stuff. In the following statement, Booch makes it clear that something is architecturally significant if it's difficult to change (2006):

All architecture is design but not all design is architecture. Architecture represents the significant design decisions that shape a system, where significant is measured by cost of change.

Based on these statements, it's fair to conclude that the goal of software architecture must be to eliminate the impact and cost of change, thereby eliminating architectural significance. We attempt to make something architecturally insignificant by creating flexible solutions that can be changed easily, as illustrated in Figure 3.3. But herein lies a paradox.

3.3.1 THE PARADOX

The idea behind eliminating architecture isn't new. In fact, Fowler mentions "getting rid of software architecture" in his article "Who Needs an Architect?" (2003). The way to eliminate architecture by minimizing the impact of cost and change is through flexibility. The more flexible the system, the more likely that the system can adapt and evolve as necessary. But herein lies the paradox, and a statement by Ralph Johnson presents and supports the idea (Fowler 2003):

> *. . . making everything easy to change makes the entire system very complex . . .*

complexity, 46   As flexibility increases, so does the complexity. And complexity is the beast we are trying to tame because complex things are more difficult to deal with than simple things. It's a battle for which there is no clear path to victory, for sure. But, what if we were able to tame complexity while increasing flexibility, as illustrated in Figure 3.4? Let's explore the possibility of designing flexible software without increasing complexity. Is it even possible? In other words, how do we eliminate architecture?

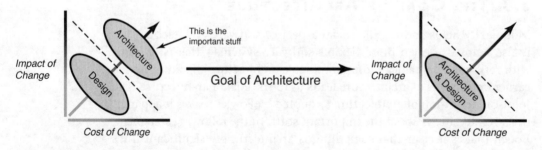

Figure 3.3 The goal of architecture

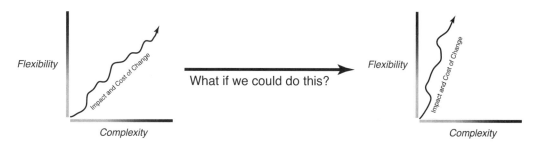

Figure 3.4 Maximizing flexibility, managing complexity

3.3.2 ELIMINATING ARCHITECTURE

As the Johnson quote clearly points out, it's not feasible to design an infinitely flexible system. Therefore, it's imperative that we recognize where flexibility is necessary to reduce the impact and cost of change. The challenge is that we don't always know early in the project what might eventually change, so it's impossible to create a flexible solution to something we can't know about. This is the problem with Big Architecture Up Front (BAUF), and it's why we must make architectural decisions temporally. In other words, we should try to defer commitment to specific architectural decisions that would lock us to a specific solution until we have the requisite knowledge that will allow us to make the most informed decision.

It's also why we must take great care in insulating and isolating decisions we're unsure of and ensuring that these initial decisions are easy to change as answers to the unknown emerge. For this, modularity is a missing ingredient that helps minimize the impact and cost of change, and it's a motivating force behind why we should design software systems with a modular architecture. In the UML User Guide (page 163), Booch talks about "modeling the seams in a system." He states (1999):

> *Identifying the seams in a system involves identifying clear lines of demarcation in your architecture. On either side of those lines, you'll find components that may change independently, without affecting the components on the other side, as long as the components on both sides conform to the contract specified by that interface.*

Where Booch talks about components, we talk about modules. Where Booch talks about seams, we'll talk about joints. Modularity, combined with design patterns and SOLID principles, represents our best hope to

SOLID principles, 319

joints, 56

minimize the impact and cost of change, thereby eliminating the architectural significance of change.

3.4 MODULARITY: THE MISSING INGREDIENT

*module
definition, 17*

Two of the key elements of the architectural definitions are component and composition. Yet there is no standard and agreed-upon definition of *component*[1] (reminding me of architecture, actually), and most use the term loosely to mean "a chunk of code." But, that doesn't work, and in the context of OSGi, it's clear that a module is a software component. Developing a system with an adaptive, flexible, and maintainable architecture requires modularity because we must be able to design a flexible system that allows us to make temporal decisions based on shifts that occur throughout development. Modularity has been a missing piece that allows us to more easily accommodate these shifts, as well as focus on specific areas of the system that demand the most flexibility, as illustrated in Figure 3.5. It's easier to change a design encapsulated within a module than it is to make a change to the design than spans several modules.

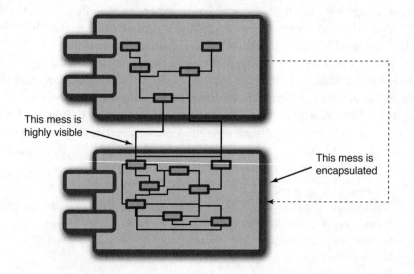

Figure 3.5 Encapsulating design

---

1. In his book *Component Software: Beyond Object-Oriented Programming*, Clemens Szyperski makes one of the few attempts I've seen to formally define the term *component*. He did a fine job, too.

3.4.1 IS IT REALLY ENCAPSULATED?

In standard Java, there is no way to enforce encapsulation of design details to a module because Java provides no way to define packages or classes that are module scope. As a result, classes in one module will always have access to the implementation details of another module. This is where a module framework, such as OSGi, shines because it allows you to forcefully encapsulate implementation details within a module through its explicit import package and export package manifest headers. Even public classes within a package cannot be accessed by another module unless the package is explicitly exported. The difference is subtle, although profound. We see several examples of this in the patterns throughout this book, and I point it out as it occurs. For now, let's explore a simple example.

modularizing without a runtime module, 26

3.4.1.1 Standard Java: No Encapsulation

Figure 3.6 illustrates a `Client` class that depends upon `Inter`, an interface, with `Impl` providing the implementation. The `Client` class is packaged in the `client.jar` module, and `Inter` and `Impl` are packaged in the `provider.jar` module. This is a good example of a modular system but demonstrates how we cannot encapsulate implementation details in standard Java because there is no way to prevent access to `Impl`. Classes

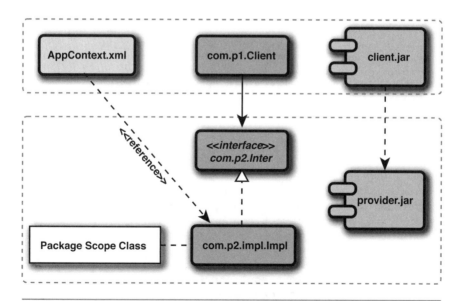

Figure 3.6 Standard Java can't encapsulate design details in a module.

outside of the `provider.jar` module can still reach the `Impl` class to instantiate and use it directly.

In fact, the `Impl` class is defined as a package scope class, as shown in Listing 3.1. However, the `AppContext.xml` Spring XML configuration file, which is deployed in the `client.jar` module, is still able to create the `Impl` instance at runtime and inject it into `Client`. The `AppContext.xml` and `Client` class are shown in Listing 3.2 and Listing 3.3, respectively. The key element is that the `AppContext.xml` is deployed in the `client.jar` module and the `Impl` class it creates is deployed in the `provider.jar` module. As shown in Listing 3.2, the `AppContext.xml` file deployed in the `client.jar` file violates encapsulation by referencing an implementation detail of the `provider.jar` module. Because the Spring configuration is a global configuration, the result is a violation of encapsulation.

Listing 3.1 Impl Class

```
package com.p2.impl;

import com.p2.*;

class Impl implements Inter {
        public void doIt() { . . . /* any implementation */ }
}
```

Listing 3.2 AppContext.xml Spring Configuration

```
<beans>
    <bean id="inter" class="com.p2.impl.Impl"/>
</beans>
```

Listing 3.3 Client Class

```
package com.p1;

import com.p2.*;
import org.springframework.context.*;
import org.springframework.context.support.*;

public class Client {
   public static void main(String args[]) {
      ApplicationContext appContext = new
      FileSystemXmlApplicationContext(
         "com/p1/AppContext.xml");
```

```
        Inter i = (Inter) appContext.getBean("inter");
        i.doIt();
    }
}
```

3.4.1.2 OSGi and Encapsulation

Now let's look at the same example using OSGi. Here, the `Impl` class in *OSGi, 273*
the `provider.jar` module is tightly encapsulated, and no class in any
other module is able to see the `Impl` class. The `Impl` class and `Inter`
interface remain the same as in the previous examples; no changes are
required. Instead, we've taken the existing application and simply set it up
to work with the OSGi framework, which enforces encapsulation of module implementation details and provides an intermodule communication
mechanism.

Figure 3.7 demonstrates the new structure. It's actually an exam- *Abstract Modules*
ple of the Abstract Modules pattern. Here, I separated the Spring XML *pattern, 222*

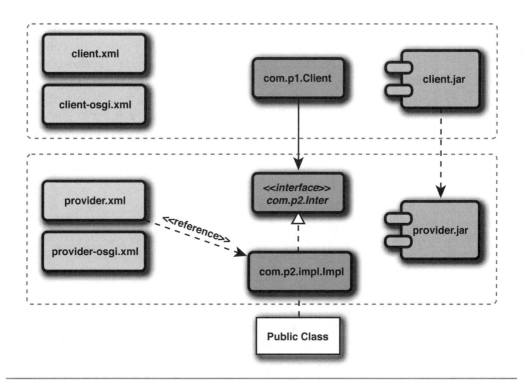

Figure 3.7 Encapsulating design with OSGi

configuration into four different files. I could have easily used only two configuration files, but I want to keep the standard Java and OSGi framework configurations separate for each module. The `provider.jar` module is responsible for the configuration itself and exposing its capabilities when it's installed. Before we describe the approach, here is a brief description of each configuration file:

- **client.xml**: Standard Spring configuration file that describes how the application should be launched by the OSGi framework
- **client-osgi.xml**: Spring configuration file that allows the Client class to consume an OSGi μService
- **provider.xml**: Spring configuration with the `provider.jar` module bean definition
- **provider-osgi.xml**: Spring configuration that exposes the bean definition in `provider.xml` as an OSGi μService

Before we look at how the two modules are wired together, let's look at the `provider.jar` module, which contains the `Inter` interface, `Impl` implementation, and two configuration files. Again, `Inter` and `Impl` remain the same as in the previous example, so let's look at the configuration files. The `provider.xml` file defines the standard Spring bean configuration and is what was previously shown in the `AppContext.xml` file in Figure 3.7. Listing 3.4 shows the `provider.xml` file. The key is that this configuration is deployed with the `provider.jar` module. Attempting to instantiate the `Impl` class outside of the `provider.jar` module will not work. Because OSGi enforces encapsulation, any attempt to reach the implementation details of a module will result in a runtime error, such as a `ClassNotFoundException`.

Listing 3.4 provider.xml Configuration File

```
<beans>
        <bean id="inter" class="com.p2.impl.Impl"/>
</beans>
```

How does OSGi prevent other classes from instantiating the `Impl` class directly? The `Manifest.mf` file included in the `provider.jar` module exposes classes only in the `com.p2` package, not the `com.p2.impl` package. So, the `Inter` interface registered as an OSGi μService is accessible by other modules but not by the `Impl` class. Listing 3.5 shows the section of the `Manifest.mf` illustrating the package export.

Listing 3.5 provider.xml Configuration File

```
Export-Package: com.p2
```

The `provider-osgi.xml` file is where things get very interesting, and it is where we expose the behavior of the `provider.jar` module as an OSGi μService that serves as the contract between the `Client` and `Impl` classes. The configuration for the `provider.jar` module lives within the `provider.jar` module, so no violation of encapsulation occurs.

Listing 3.6 shows the configuration. The name of the μService we are registering with the OSGi framework is called `interService`, and it references the `Impl` bean defined in Listing 3.4, exposing its behavior as type `Inter`. At this point, the `provider.jar` module has a `interService` OSGi μService that can be consumed by another module. This service is made available by the `provider.jar` module after it is installed and activated in the OSGi framework.

Listing 3.6 provider.xml Configuration File

```
<osgi:service id="interService" ref="inter"
       interface="com.p2.Inter"/>
```

Now, let's look at the `client.jar` module. The `client.xml` file configures the `Client` class. It effectively replaces the `main` method on the `Client` class in Listing 3.3 with the `run` method, and the OSGi framework instantiates the `Client` class, configures it with an `Inter` type, and invokes the `run` method. Listing 3.7 shows the `client.xml` file, and Listing 3.8 shows the `Client` class. This is the mechanism that initiates the process and replaces the `main` method in the `Client` class of the previous example.

Listing 3.7 Client.xml Configuration File

```
<beans>
     <bean name="client" class="com.p1.impl.Client"
     init-method="run">
                   <property name="inter"
                    ref="interService"/>
     </bean>
</beans>
```

Listing 3.8 The Client Class

```
package com.p1.impl;
import com.p2.*;
import com.p1.*;
public class Client {
      private Inter i;
      public void setInter(Inter i) {
            this.i = i;
      }

      public void run() throws Exception {
            i.doIt();
      }
}
```

The `Inter` type that is injected into the client class is done through the `client-osgi.xml` configuration file. Here, we specify that we want to use a µService of type `Inter`, as shown in Listing 3.9.

Listing 3.9 Client.xml Configuration File

```
<osgi:reference id="interService"
  interface="com.p2.Inter"/>
```

The `Manifest.mf` file for the `client.jar` module imports the `com.p2` packages, which gives it access to the `Inter` µService. Listing 3.10 shows the section of `Manifest.mf` showing the package imports and exports for the `client.jar` module.

Listing 3.10 Client.xml Configuration File

```
Import-Package: com.p2
```

Independent Deployment pattern, 178

This simple example has several interesting design aspects.[2] The `provider.jar` module is independently deployable. It has no dependencies on any other module, and it exposes its set of behaviors as a µService. No other module in the system needs to know these details.

---

2. Although this example builds upon the OSGi Blueprint Specification, some of you may not be huge fans of XML. If that's the case, Peter Kriens has an implementation that uses OSGi Declarative Services. The sample can be found at http://bit.ly/OSGiExamples in the aQute. poma.basic directory.

The design could have also been made even more flexible by packaging the `Impl` class and `Inter` interface in separate modules. By separating the interface from the implementation, we bring a great deal of flexibility to the system, especially with OSGi managing our modules.

Separate Abstractions pattern, 237

At first glance, it might also appear to contradict the External Configuration pattern. When defining the external configuration for a module, we still want to ensure implementation details are encapsulated. External configuration is more about allowing clients to configure a module to its environmental context and not about exposing implementation details of the module.

External Configuration pattern, 200

The key takeaway from this simple demonstration is that the classes in the `provider.jar` module are tightly encapsulated because the OSGi framework enforces type visibility. We expose only the public classes in the packages that a module exports, and the μService is the mechanism that allows modules to communicate in a very flexible manner. The μService spans the joints of the system, and because OSGi is dynamic, so too are the dependencies on μServices. Implementations of the μService can come and go at runtime, and the system can bind to new instances as they appear.

joints, 56

Again, we'll see several more examples of this throughout the remainder of the discussion. Even though you can't enforce encapsulation of module implementation using standard Java, it's still imperative to begin designing more modular software systems. As we'll see, by applying several of the techniques we discuss in this book, we put ourselves in an excellent position to take advantage of a runtime module system.

3.5 ANSWERING OUR QUESTIONS

Earlier, this chapter posed the following questions after introducing the three definitions of software architecture. Through explanation, we answered each question. But to be clear, let's offer concise answers:

What makes a decision architecturally significant? A decision is architecturally significant if the impact and cost of change is significant.

What are the elements of composition? The elements of composition include classes, modules, and services.

How do we accommodate evolution of architecture? Evolution is realized by designing flexible solutions that can adapt to change. But flexibility breeds complexity, and we must be careful to build flexibility in the right areas of the system.

3.6 CONCLUSION

The goal of architecture is to minimize the impact and cost of change. Modularity helps us realize this goal by filling in a gap that exists between top-level architectural constructs and lower-level code. Modularity is the important intermediate that helps increase architectural agility. It fills a gap that exists between architects and developers. It allows us to create a software architecture that can accommodate shifts. Modularity helps us architect all the way down.

3.7 REFERENCES

Booch, Grady, James Rumbaugh, and Ivar Jacobson. 1999. *The Unified Modeling Language User Guide*. Reading, MA: Addison-Wesley.

The Open Group. *The Open Group Architecture Framework*. www.open-group.org/architecture/togaf8-doc/arch/chap01.html

Hawking, Stephen. 1998. *A Brief History of Time*. Bantam.

Fowler, Martin. 2003. "Who Needs an Architect?" IEEE Software.

Booch, Grady. 2006. *On Design*. www.handbookofsoftwarearchitecture.com/index.jsp?page=Blog&part=All

TAMING THE BEAST
NAMED COMPLEXITY

Modularity is not a new concept. In his 1972 paper "On the Criteria to Be Used in Decomposing Systems into Modules," David Parnas cited the work of Gouthier and Pont as the first lucid statement of modular programming (1972):

> *A well-defined segmentation of the project effort ensures system modularity. Each task forms a separate, distinct program module. At implementation time each module and its inputs and outputs are well-defined, there is no confusion in the intended interface with other system modules. At checkout time the integrity of the module is tested independently; there are few scheduling problems in synchronizing the completion of several tasks before checkout can begin. Finally, the system is maintained in modular fashion; system errors and deficiencies can be traced to specific system modules, thus limiting the scope of detailed error searching.*

Parnas went on to discuss the important decisions developers must make when modularizing their software systems. Encapsulating design decisions within autonomous modules allowed for modules to evolve independently and reveal little about their inner workings. The designs were encapsulated, shielding other developers from this unnecessary complexity, and helping them to more easily understand the software system.

Although much has changed since the Parnas paper was first published, one constant remains: Software is still incredibly difficult to design and develop. Unfortunately, in the decades since modular programming was introduced, these ideas were lost. Today, few development teams consciously decompose software systems into modules. Fortunately, we have the luxury of using a platform with an excellent unit of modularity built in, and it's time we start using it.

4.1 ENTERPRISE COMPLEXITY

Most software systems don't begin their life as complex entities but grow complex over time. Lehman's 2nd Law summarizes this phenomenon (1980):

> *As a system evolves, its complexity increases unless work is done to maintain or reduce it.*

Lehman chose to use the evolution of IBM's OS/360 for his work by examining the growth of the system over a series of releases. His findings revealed that for each release, the size of the software system increased. The logical conclusion? As software system size increases, so does the complexity.

Many of us have experienced this phenomenon. In almost every way, larger software systems are inherently more difficult to design, build, and manage than are smaller software systems. Examining more modern evidence of Lehman's Law, we turn to the evolution of the Spring framework. Figure 4.1 illustrates this evolution between release 0.9.1 and release 2.5. Since the earliest releases of the framework dating back to 2003, we've seen almost a sixfold increase in the size of the code. Examining other projects such as Linux, Tomcat, and Firefox reveals similar growth.

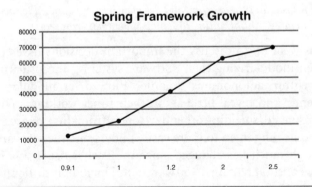

Figure 4.1 Evolutionary growth of Spring framework in lines of code

Such phenomenal growth is not only expected but desired. We can only hope that the systems we create are in such high demand that we have the opportunity to grow them with new features and functionality over time. A software system that doesn't change dies. In fact, studies (Koskinen 2010) suggest that the cost to maintain software and manage its evolution exceeds 90 percent of the total cost of a system. Evolution is a big deal!

Not only is evolution expected, but it's desirable. It's in our best interests to encourage change in software systems. But, as we've seen, change breeds complexity. What is the cause of all this complexity, and what can we do to manage it?

4.2 Technical Debt

Software tends to rot over time. When you establish your initial vision for the software's design and architecture, you imagine a system that is easy to modify, extend, and maintain. Unfortunately, as time passes, changes trickle in that exercise your design in unexpected ways. Each change begins to resemble nothing more than another hack, until finally the system becomes a tangled web of code that few developers care to venture through. Sadly, design rot is self-inflicted, and technical debt describes the effect of rotting design.

Technical debt is a metaphor developed by Ward Cunningham to describe the design trade-offs made in order to meet schedules and customer expectations. Martin Fowler offers the following analogy when comparing technical debt to financial debt (2009):

> Like a financial debt, the technical debt incurs interest payments, which come in the form of the extra effort that we have to do in future development because of the quick and dirty design choice. We can choose to continue paying the interest, or we can pay down the principal by refactoring the quick and dirty design into the better design. Although it costs to pay down the principal, we gain by reduced interest payments in the future.

There are situations where leveraging suboptimal designs, thereby incurring technical debt, is warranted to meet short-term demands. For instance, the schedule may not allow longer-term designs to be used. However, if we ignore this debt, it continues to build over time, and incurring too much debt leads to significant inefficiencies surrounding our ability to effectively change the software system. Lehman's Law in action, for sure.

At some point, we hit a wall where we are no longer able to afford the interest payments. It's imperative that we manage technical debt to ensure long-term survivability of our software system. Too much debt will cause the system to crumble. At some point, we must deal with the technical debt we've incurred. If we don't, our design will continue to rot!

4.3 DESIGN ROT

The most common cause of rotting software is tightly coupled code with excessive dependencies. Of course, any interesting software system must have dependencies for it to do anything. Yet, for large teams and large applications, managing dependencies is especially important. Excessive dependencies increase technical debt and cause numerous problems. As Lehman's Law suggests, the problems will persist and continue to increase unless work is done to maintain it. What exactly are the problems with excessive dependencies?

4.3.1 HINDER MAINTENANCE

Dependencies hinder the maintenance effort. When you're working on a system with heavy dependencies, you typically find that changes in one area of the application trickle to many other areas of the application. In some cases, this cannot be avoided. For instance, when you add a column to a database table that must be displayed on the user interface, you're forced to modify at least the data access and user interface layers. Such a scenario is mostly inevitable. However, applications with a well-thought-out dependency structure make change easier since developers have a more complete understanding of the impact of change.

4.3.2 PREVENT EXTENSIBILITY

Dependencies prevent extensibility. The goal of flexible software architecture is to remain open for extension but closed to modification. The desire is to add new functionality to the system by extending existing abstractions and plugging these extensions into the existing system without making rampant modifications. One reason for heavy dependencies is the improper use of abstraction, and those cases where abstractions are not present are areas that are difficult to extend. Abstraction aids teams by exposing well-defined extension points, as well as encapsulating implementation complexity.

4.3.3 INHIBIT REUSABILITY

Dependencies inhibit reusability. Reuse is often touted as a fundamental advantage of well-designed object-oriented software. Unfortunately, few applications realize this benefit. Too often, we emphasize class-level reuse. To achieve higher levels of reuse, careful consideration must also be given to the package structure and module structure. Software with complex package and module dependencies minimize the likelihood of achieving higher degrees of reuse.

4.3.4 RESTRICT TESTABILITY

Dependencies restrict testability. Tight coupling between classes eliminates the ability to test classes independently. Unit testing is a fundamental principle that should be employed by all developers. Tests provide you with the courage to improve your designs, knowing flaws will be caught by unit tests. They also help you design proactively and discourage undesirable dependencies. Heavy dependencies do not allow you to test software modules independently. Teams with few tests cannot respond to change easily because of the inability to access the impact of change.

4.3.5 HAMPER INTEGRATION

Dependencies hamper integration. It's easy for separate teams to plow forward, usually under tremendous pressure from looming deadlines. They operate under the false assumption that if they can simply reach the final feature destination, they can quickly pull things together toward the end of a project. This Big Bang approach to integration does not work. As individual modules are pulled together, common issues that surface include degradation of overall system performance, incorrect levels of behavioral granularity provided by system modules, and transactional incompatibilities. More frequent integration brings many of these issues to the forefront earlier in the project.

4.3.6 LIMIT UNDERSTANDING

Dependencies limit understanding. When working on a software system, it's important that you understand the system's structural architecture and design constructs. A structure with complex dependencies is inherently more difficult to understand. Clear and concise dependencies that are well-thought-out allow teams to more easily access the impact of change.

4.4 CYCLIC DEPENDENCIES—THE DEATH KNELL

Acyclic Relationships pattern, 146 Excessive dependencies are bad. But, cyclic dependencies are especially bad. Cyclic dependencies are manifest in various ways at different levels within a system. It's also possible that acyclic relationships at one level cause cycles at another. For more information on cyclic and acyclic dependencies, check out the Acyclic Relationships pattern.

4.4.1 TYPES OF CYCLES

Cycles exist across a variety of entities, notably classes, packages, and modules. Class cycles exist when two classes, such as `Customer` and `Bill` (shown in Figure 4.2), each reference the other. In this example, assume a `Customer` has a list of `Bill` instances, and `Bill` references the `Customer` to calculate a discount amount. This is also known as a *bidirectional association*. It's a maintenance and testing issue, because you can't do anything to either class without affecting the other.

Listing 4.1 shows the `Customer` class, while Listing 4.2 shows the `Bill` class. (Certain portions of each class are omitted for clarity.) The bidirectional relationship can be clearly identified.

Figure 4.2 Cyclic dependency between classes

Listing 4.1 The Customer Class

```
package com.kirkk.cust;
import java.util.*;
import java.math.BigDecimal;
import com.kirkk.bill.*;

public class Customer {
    private List bills;
```

```java
//Derivation of the discount depends on the number of
//bills for a specific Customer.
public BigDecimal getDiscountAmount() {
   if (bills.size() > 5) {
      return new BigDecimal(0.1);
   } else {
      return new BigDecimal(0.03);
   }
}

public void createBill() {
   Bill bill = new Bill(this);
   if (bills == null) {
      bills = new ArrayList();
   }
   bills.add(bill);
}
}
```

Listing 4.2 The Bill Class

```java
package com.kirkk.bill;
import com.kirkk.cust.*;
import java.math.BigDecimal;

public class Bill {
   private Customer customer;

   public Bill(Customer customer) {
      this.customer = customer;
   }

   public BigDecimal pay() {
      BigDecimal discount = new BigDecimal(1).subtract(
         this.customer.getDiscountAmount()).setScale(2,
         BigDecimal.ROUND_HALF_UP);
      //Apply the discount and make the payment...
      return paidAmount;
   }
}
```

Class cycles can be broken a few different ways, one of which is to introduce an abstraction that breaks the cycle, as shown in Figure 4.3. Now, the Bill class can easily be tested with a mock DiscountCalculator.

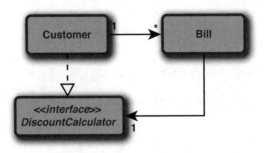

Figure 4.3 Breaking the cycle

Testing `Customer`, of course, still requires the presence of `Bill`. This is not a cyclic issue; it's a different type of coupling issue because `Bill` is a concrete class and is fodder for a separate discussion, which we'll tackle in Chapter 8. Clearly, introducing `DiscountCalculator` has broken the cycle between `Customer` and `Bill`. But, has it broken all cycles, including those that might exist between modules?

Manage Relationships pattern, 116

Listing 4.3 shows the modified `Customer` class that implements the `DiscountCalculator` interface, which is shown in Listing 4.4.

Listing 4.3 The Modified Customer Class

```
package com.kirkk.cust;

import java.util.*;
import java.math.BigDecimal;
import com.kirkk.bill.*;

public class Customer implements DiscountCalculator {
   private List bills;

   public BigDecimal getDiscountAmount() {
      if (bills.size() > 5) {
         return new BigDecimal(0.1);
      } else {
         return new BigDecimal(0.03);
      }
   }

   public List getBills() {
      return this.bills;
   }
```

```
      public void createBill(BigDecimal chargeAmount) {
         Bill bill = new Bill(this, chargeAmount);
         if (bills == null) {
            bills = new ArrayList();
         }
         bills.add(bill);
      }
}
```

Listing 4.4 The DiscountCalculator Interface

```
package com.kirkk.bill;

import java.math.BigDecimal;

public interface DiscountCalculator {
   public BigDecimal getDiscountAmount();
}
```

4.4.2 CREEPING CYCLES

We don't intentionally create cyclic dependencies between modules. Instead, they tend to creep into our design. They commonly surface when cyclic or acyclic relationships at one level cause cycles at another. For instance, if `Customer` and `DiscountCalculator` are placed in a `customer.jar` module and `Bill` is placed in a `billing.jar` module, a cyclic dependency between the `customer.jar` and `billing.jar` modules exists even though the bidirectional relationships between classes has been broken. Figure 4.4 shows the cyclic dependencies between modules.

To break the cycle, we must move `DiscountCalculator` to its own module or the billing module. Figure 4.5 illustrates that moving the `DiscountCalculator` to the `billing.jar` module has broken the cyclic dependency between the modules. Obviously, this is a trivial example. For larger software systems with potentially thousands of classes and numerous modules to manage, the challenge is much greater. Remember this:

> In fact, if you don't consider the physical design of your system, then your logical design, no matter how beautiful, may not provide you the benefits you believe it does.

logical and physical design, 3

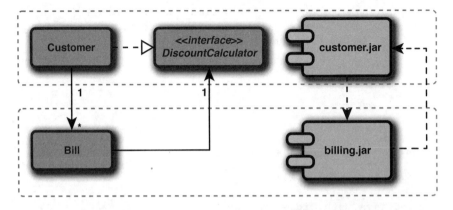

Figure 4.4 Cyclic dependencies between modules

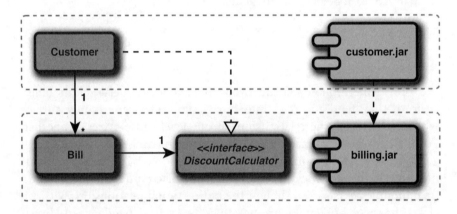

Figure 4.5 Acyclic dependencies between modules

The example perfectly supports this statement and represents an instance where a quality class design may not result in quality architecture. This is where the patterns in this book and first-class support for modularity on the Java platform will serve as a valuable aid.

4.4.3 MANAGING CYCLES

Fortunately, there are many ways (some easier than others) to manage dependencies and eliminate cycles. Test-driven development (TDD) is a great way to manage class cycles assuming we strive to test classes in isolation. JDepend allows you to manage package cycles, either by writing package constraint tests or by including JDepend static analysis within your Ant build script. Cycles between modules can be managed using a Levelize Build, where individual modules are built, including only neces- *Levelize Build, 253* sary modules in the build class path. Additional patterns are useful in managing and massaging module dependencies.

JarAnalyzer can also be included in your build script, generating a component diagram illustrating the relationship between JAR files or generating a dependency report similar to that of JDepend. Maven and Ivy also provide ways to help manage dependencies. Of course, looming on the horizon is OSGi, which offers runtime support for modularity and enforces module dependencies.

4.4.4 Are Cycles Always Bad?

Generally speaking, cycles are always bad! However, some cycles are worse *design* than others. Cycles among classes are tolerable, assuming they don't cause *encapsulation, 37* cycles among the packages or modules containing them (for example, the classes must be in the same module, essentially encapsulating the design). Cycles among packages may also be tolerable, assuming they don't cause cycles among the modules files containing them (again, packages are in the same module). Most important is that we are aware of the relationships existing between the modules. Module relationships must never be cyclic.

In the Real World

On a project, we were integrating with a vendor product. The vendor product would help us fulfill the needs of the business processing by applying industry-standard medical coding that helped us comply with federal mandates. The relationship with the vendor was volatile, and negotiation with an alternative vendor was underway.

Unfortunately, our project deadline didn't align well with the vendor *Separate* contract. We knew we'd have a production release about three months before *Abstractions, 237* the vendor decision would be made. In light of this, we encapsulated all vendor code into a single module and separated the interface classes to a separate module by applying the Separate Abstractions pattern. When the decision was finally made to establish a relationship with the new vendor, making the switch was less painful. We created a new module that integrated with the new vendor and implemented the interfaces. The ripple effect throughout the system was minimal, and we were able to easily test the integration independently. We'll see this example play out in front of us when we walk through the reference implementation in Chapter 6.

4.5 JOINTS, MODULES, AND **SOLID**

SOLID
principles, 319

It's imperative to manage dependencies between our modules. The SOLID (Martin 2000) principles of object-oriented design help minimize class coupling and increase class cohesion, making software easier to maintain and extend. The appendix provides an overview of the SOLID principles. Yet there is also a cost to applying the principles. The additional layers of abstraction increase the complexity of the system. Blindly applying the principles to all classes within a system can actually decrease our ability to maintain and extend the software because of the resulting increase in complexity. Remember this paradox: With flexibility comes complexity. This begs the question, "Where is the most appropriate place to apply the SOLID principles?"

Every system has joints, which is the point where two modules connect. These joints within the system require the greatest flexibility and resiliency. The reason for this is driven by change. Change that is encapsulated within a single module poses less threat and risk than change that ripples across many modules. This is trivial, and it's why changing the private methods of a class are easier than changing the public methods. Likewise, change confined to a single module is easier than change that spans modules. That's logical. So if we're able to create well-designed modules, it makes our life a bit easier. We want to use the SOLID design principles, and other proven design patterns, to design more modular software.

These joints, or module boundaries, within a system represent the ideal opportunity to leverage the SOLID principles. Using the SOLID principles to minimize coupling between modules offers the greatest opportunity and reward. For example, it's not realistic to design an entire system open for extension but closed to modification (the Open Closed Principle [OCP]). But, we can use OCP at the module boundaries (or joints) to create modules with enough design flexibility to confine change to a single module. Using the SOLID principles when designing the relationships between modules provides a low barrier point of entry for using these principles to create better designs. For instance, it's much easier to refactor if we know the refactoring is confined to a single module. With a rich suite of unit tests, we can prove it has no impact on the outside world. But, if we have to refactor the classes and the refactoring spans the joints of the system, well . . . that's an architectural refactoring. It gets difficult and messy.

This is a major reason why frameworks such as OSGi and the patterns in this book are so important—they make it just a little bit easier to design really big software systems that we can understand, maintain, and extend. If we apply the SOLID principles in conjunction with the module patterns, we have guidance on how to best design large software systems. As interest in designing more modular software continues to increase, and especially as OSGi continues to gain momentum, the module design patterns will grow in importance in helping us manage complexity. New patterns will also likely emerge.

4.6 MANAGING COMPLEXITY

Many of the benefits of modularity can be gleaned from the definition of a software module. Deployable! Manageable! Reusable! Composable! Indeed, they are substantial benefits. But, the greatest benefit of modularity is that it helps us tame the complexity of a software system as it evolves. By taming complexity, it's much easier to understand the impact of change within large software systems. Because 90 percent of the total cost of a system involves making change to an existing system, this is a substantial benefit. Modularity is the work we do to help manage the complexity of a system as it evolves. It's time for an example that illustrates this benefit.

4.6.1 ILLUSTRATING THE BENEFIT

Figure 4.6 illustrates the benefit of modularity. The top-left quadrant shows a sample system with a relatively complex class structure. When change occurs within a single class, shown circled in the bottom-left quadrant, understanding the impact of change is difficult. It appears possible that it can propagate to any class dependent on the circled class. Assessing the impact of change requires that we analyze the complete class structure. The ripple effect appears significant, and change instills fear.

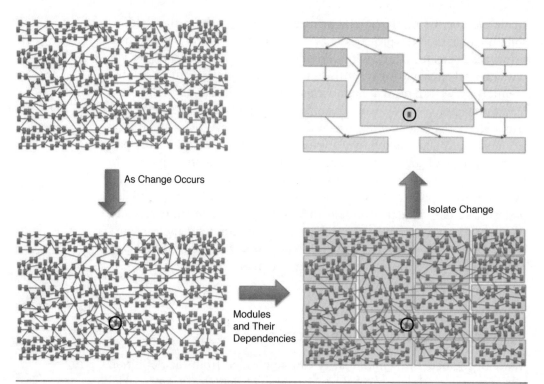

Figure 4.6 Modules make understanding change easier.

But, if the system is modular with classes allocated to their appropriate modules, as shown in the bottom-right quadrant, then understanding the impact of change can be isolated to a discrete set of modules. This makes it much easier to identify which modules contain classes that might also change, as shown in the top-right quadrant. Change is isolated to classes within modules that are dependent on the module containing the class that is changing.

This is a simple example, but it serves as evidence of the need for modular architecture. Modularity makes understanding the system easier. It makes maintaining the system easier. And it makes reusing system modules much more likely. As systems grow in size and complexity, it's imperative that we design more modular software.

Of course, the object-oriented paradigm promised similar benefits, but experience has shown that objects are too fine-grained. Even a system of moderate size might be composed of thousands of classes, making it virtually impossible for any single person to fully understand the entire system. Does this undermine the benefits of the object-oriented paradigm? Certainly not. But, more is needed to help manage the complexity of large enterprise software systems.

Modules are more coarse-grained units than objects and allow us to encapsulate complex design decisions. A module might contain many classes, but the design decisions surrounding the relationships between classes can be encapsulated within a module. Cohesive modules encapsulate behavior and expose it only through well-defined interfaces. Because modules are cohesive, change is isolated to the implementation details of a module. Module behavior that is exposed through interfaces ensures new modules containing alternative implementations can be developed without modifying existing modules. The result is a reduction in complexity that helps ease the maintenance effort. In general, a well-designed modular system is simply easier to understand.

Of course, modularity doesn't guarantee these benefits any more than using object orientation guarantees the benefits of the object-oriented paradigm. It still requires that we design our modules correctly. We'll explore these ideas further in Chapter 5.

4.7 Benefits of Modularity

Almost all discussions on modularity mention reuse as a prime advantage. But, there are other advantages, of course. There is a reduction in complexity that helps ease the maintenance effort, as we've just discussed. Cohesive modules encapsulate behavior and expose it only through well-defined interfaces. Because modules are cohesive, change is isolated to the implementation details of a module, as discussed in Chapter 3. Figure 4.7 illustrates the benefits of modularity.

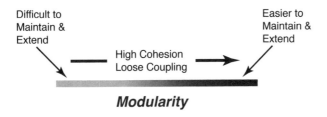

Figure 4.7 Benefits of modularity

Because behavior is exposed through interfaces, new modules containing alternative implementations can be developed without modifying existing modules. There are also other benefits to modularity that extend beyond design to runtime. These include the ability to hot-deploy new modules without restarting an application and deploy multiple versions of a module. But from the design perspective, modularity helps increase reuse, ease maintenance, and increase extensibility.

4.8 CONCLUSION

Software complexity is our worst enemy. Complexity inhibits our ability to gracefully adapt software systems in response to changing demands. And change is good, because it means our software systems are gaining acceptance. Modularity helps tame this complexity, but only if the software modules we create are of high quality. It's as simple to create a mess using modules as it is with objects and services. This chapter illustrated the benefit of modularity. Subsequent chapters discuss how we can realize this benefit.

4.9 REFERENCES

Parnas, David. 1972. "On the Criteria to Be Used in Decomposing Systems into Modules." Communications of the ACM.

Lehman, M. M. 1980. "On Understanding Laws, Evolution, and Conservation in the Large-Program Life Cycle." *Journal of Systems and Software* 1.

Koskinen, Jussi. 2010. "Software Maintenance Costs." Department of Computer Science and Information Systems, University of Jyväskylä.

Fowler, Martin. 2009. *Technical Debt.* http://martinfowler.com/bliki/TechnicalDebt.html

Martin, Robert C. 2000. "Design Principles and Design Patterns." www.objectmentor.com/resources/articles/Principles_and_Patterns.pdf

REALIZING 5 REUSE

Reuse is software development's unattainable panacea. The ability to compose systems from reusable elements has long been our Achilles' heel. We want reuse so badly, yet our failures are spectacular. Almost all major technology trends of the past 20 years, and probably before, tout reuse as the saving grace. Vendors have sold billions of dollars in software through the broken promise of increased reusability.

What happened? Reuse was supposed to save software development. In the early 1990s, object orientation promised to save it. It hasn't. In the late 1990s, component-based development promised to save software development. It didn't either, and the movement died. In the early 2000s, service-oriented architecture (SOA) promised to save it. SOA didn't, although development teams are still trying. Why is reuse so difficult?

Foremost, reuse is achieved by designing flexible software entities that can be tailored based on need. In other words, we reuse an entity by configuring it to a specific context. But, as we've seen, flexibility breeds complexity. This leads us to the use/reuse paradox.

flexibility versus complexity, 34

5.1 THE USE/REUSE PARADOX

The problem stems from this rather simple statement, which is depicted in Figure 5.1:

Maximizing reuse complicates use.[1]

In general, the more reusable we choose to make a software module, the more difficult that same software module is to use. In the extreme, an infinitely reusable module is infinitely difficult to use. The driving force behind this was discussed in Chapter 3, Section 3.3.1. Developing a module that's reusable demands that module be flexible, and with the increase in flexibility comes a corresponding increase in complexity. Likewise, increasing the ease with which a module can be used, managed, and deployed often decreases a module's reusability. Dealing with the tension between reuse and use is a complex issue, and often we fail. Largely, the problem has to do with dependencies.

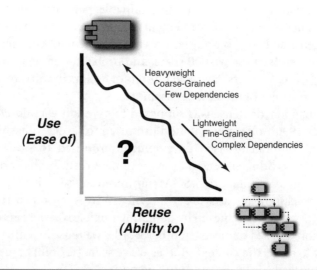

Figure 5.1 The use/reuse paradox

---

1. On page 45 in *Component Software, Beyond Object-Oriented Programming* (Addison-Wesley 2002), Clemens Szyperski states, "Maximizing reuse minimized use." This is a variation of his statement.

5.2 THE REUSE DISCLAIMER

We've done a decent job in achieving reuse at certain levels, and we're much further along the reuse curve than we were 20 years ago. Today, we have a plethora of frameworks to choose from that aid development: Web frameworks, ORM frameworks, and security frameworks, to name a few. But, most of these frameworks are horizontal, not vertical. That is, they address problems related to infrastructure and plumbing code, not business problems. And I want to focus explicitly on vertical reuse, because that's the unattainable panacea we've struggled with for so long. That's the broken promise. Why have we struggled to create reusable business software?

5.2.1 GRANULARITY

Granularity is the extent to which a system is broken down into parts. Coarse-grained modules tend to be richer in behavior than fine-grained modules. Because coarse-grained modules do more, they tend to be larger than fine-grained modules. To maximize reuse, we try composing coarse-grained modules from fine-grained modules. Of course, this results in a lot of dependencies between the fine-grained modules, making the fine-grained modules more difficult to use. In general, we can say the following:

> Coarse-grained modules are easier to use, but fine-grained modules are more reusable.

It's time for an example. Let's say we're creating a module that processes health insurance claims. Let's keep the business process relatively simple to maintain our sanity. There are four steps in the process: 1) The system is fed the claim information; 2) the system checks to make sure it's not a duplicate submission; 3) the system reprices the claim based on HMO and PPO agreements; 4) the system remits payment. A coarse-grained module would perform all four steps.

In doing this, we've made it easy to use because we need to invoke only one operation to complete the entire process. Additionally, if any part of the process changes, we have only a single module that needs to be built and redeployed. But, it's also more difficult to independently reuse only a portion of this process, such as the remit payment code. The logical solution is to create four fine-grained modules (one for each step in the process) and one coarse-grained module composed of the four others that pulls everything together. The fine-grained modules make things more reusable but are also more difficult to use since we have to do more to pull them all together to perform a unit of work. Additionally, managing the deployment of four separate modules is more complex than deploying a single module. In this situation, the coarse-grained module is an example

Module Facade, 212

of applying the Module Facade pattern. This example is explored in more detail in Chapter 6, Section 6.2.5.

5.2.2 WEIGHT

Weight is the extent to which a module depends on its environment. A heavyweight module depends on its operating environment, while a light-weight module avoids these dependencies. When creating a module that runs in multiple environments, we're forced to move the environment-specific dependencies (i.e., context dependencies) from code to configuration. This makes the module more reusable, but it's also more difficult to use because the module must be configured for each environment. The

Independent Deployment, 178

Independent Deployment and Container Independent patterns discuss module weight in more detail.

Container Independence, 170

Designing and configuring a lightweight module is more difficult than simply dropping in a module programmed to operate in that specific environment. In general, we can say the following:

> Lightweight modules are more reusable, but heavyweight modules are easier to use.

Let's elaborate using the previous example, where the solution was to create one coarse-grained module composed of four fine-grained modules. If each of these modules needs to run within only a single application in a single operating environment, we can encapsulate all of this environmental code into each module, making each heavyweight. But, if we want to reuse these modules across applications and operating environments, then we have to move this code outside of the module and ensure it can be configured for each environment in which we want it to operate.

5.3 REUSE OR USE

The challenge we run into when attempting to create a highly reusable module is to manage the tension between reusability and usability. In the example, breaking out the coarse-grained modules into fine-grained modules makes it more difficult to use each of the resulting fine-grained modules. It's also likely that fine-grained modules have more module dependencies than coarse-grained modules. This is sensible, since multiple fine-grained modules would be needed to accomplish the same amount of work as a coarse-grained module. Likewise, creating a lightweight module makes using the module more difficult since the module must be configured each time the module is used.

Granularity and weight are important considerations in module design. Coarse-grained, heavyweight modules may be easier to use, but fine-grained, lightweight modules are more reusable. The key is to strike a balance.

5.4 MODULAR TENSION

Let's explore the tension between use and reuse through an example. Assume we define an interface to decouple client classes from all classes implementing the interface. In doing this, it's easy to create new implementations of the interface without impacting other areas of the system. The principle surrounding this idea is the Open Closed Principle (Martin 2000): *Systems should be open for extension but closed to modification.* For more information on OCP, see the appendix. Logical design makes extending the system easier, but it's also only half the equation. The other half is how we choose to modularize the system.

SOLID principles, 319

Let's assume the interface we've created has three different implementations and that each implementation class has underlying dependencies on other classes. We're faced with a contentious issue. On one hand, grouping all the classes into a single module guarantees that change is isolated to only that module (meaning that it's easier to use and maintain). If anything changes, we'll have only one module to worry about. Yet, this decision results in a coarse-grained and heavyweight module (meaning that it's harder to reuse), and a desire to reuse a subset of that module's behavior leaves us with one of two choices: Duplicate code or refactor the module into multiple lighter-weight and finer-grained modules. In general, logical design impacts extensibility, while physical design impacts reusability and usability.

logical versus physical design, 3

As we refactor a coarse-grained and heavyweight module to something finer-grained and lighter weight, we're faced with a set of trade-offs.

In addition to increased reusability, our understanding of the system architecture increases! We have the ability to visualize the module structure and identify the impact of change at a higher level of abstraction beyond just classes. Grouping all classes into a single module may isolate change to only a single module, but understanding the impact of change is more difficult. With modules, we can assess the impact of change among not only classes but modules, as well.

Unfortunately, if modules become too lightweight and fine-grained, we're faced with the dilemma of an explosion in module and context dependencies. Modules depend on other modules and require extensive configuration to deal with context dependencies! Overall, as the number of dependencies increase, modules become more complex and difficult to use, leading us to the corollary we just presented:

> Maximizing reuse complicates use.

Creating lighter-weight and finer-grained modules increases reuse but also increases module and context dependencies, while creating fatter modules decreases dependencies but also decreases reuse. Modules that are too lightweight provide minimal value and may require other modules to be useful. Modules that are too heavyweight are difficult to reuse because they do more than what the client needs. Of course, there are other challenges beyond reuse, such as the ability to understand and maintain the system.

Coarse-grained and heavyweight modules may do a good job of encapsulating change to a single module, but understanding the impact of change is more difficult. Conversely, fine-grained and lightweight modules make it easier to understand the impact of change, but even a small change can ripple across many modules. The key is to balance this tension, especially when developing large software systems where these challenges are even more pronounced.

5.5 MODULAR DESIGN

Large software systems are inherently more complex to develop and maintain than smaller systems. In addition to increasing reuse, breaking a large system into modules makes the system easier to understand. By understanding the behaviors contained within a module and the dependencies that exist between modules, it's easier to identify and assess the ramification of change.

For instance, software modules with few incoming dependencies are easier to change than software modules with many incoming dependencies. Likewise, software modules with few outgoing dependencies are much easier to reuse than software modules with many outgoing dependencies. This tension surrounding module weight and granularity is an important factor to consider when designing software modules. *dependencies, 48*

Today, frameworks like OSGi aid in designing modular software systems. Although these frameworks can enforce runtime modularity, they cannot guarantee that we've modularized the system correctly. Correct modularization of any software system is contextual and temporal. It depends on the project, and the natural shifts that occur throughout the project impact modularity. As shown in Figure 5.2, the modularity patterns help address the design paradigm surrounding modularity and provide balance in dealing with the tension between use and reuse.

5.6 CONCLUSION

Modularity patterns provide guidance and wisdom in helping design modular software. They explain ways that we can minimize dependencies

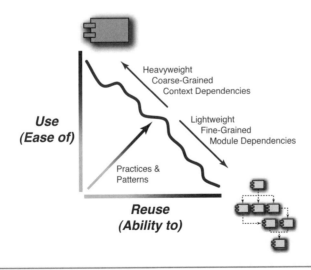

Figure 5.2 Modularity patterns

while maximizing reuse potential. They help balance module weight and granularity to make a system easier to understand, maintain, and extend. For those who have attempted to design modular software, it's common for modularity to drive the class design decisions.

Manage Relationships pattern, 116

The chapters in Part II present a list of modularity patterns that I've used on past projects. These patterns also build atop proven object-oriented design concepts. Some of the patterns, such as Manage Relationships, may be intuitively obvious, while others are less so. Certainly, other patterns exist that are not listed, and I hope that, as you discover your own patterns, you'll share them with others. I also hope that technology-specific idioms emerge that show how these patterns can be applied using specific module frameworks and technologies, such as OSGi. Before we deeply delve into patterns, we'll first walk through a sample system to illustrate the wonders of modularity.

5.7 REFERENCE

Martin, Robert C. 2000. *Design Principles and Design Patterns.* www.objectmentor.com/resources/articles/Principles_and_ Patterns.pdf

MODULARITY AND SOA

6

At this point, it's doubtful that any of us will confuse modularity with service-oriented architecture. The two appear to be distinctly different beasts. Yet, they are similar in nature, and each offers tremendous benefit to organizations. At one level, the principles behind service design apply equally to module design. Like we try to create services that are loosely coupled and highly cohesive, we also try to design modules with similar benefits.

Yet, module design and service design are incredibly complementary in other ways. Chapter 1 defined a module and illustrated how modules are excellent candidates for intraprocess reuse, while service reuse crosses process boundaries. Chapter 3 discussed modularity in a broader architectural context, illustrating how it helps us achieve the goal of architecture. Before we progress onto the pattern discussion, it's important to discuss modularity in the context of other architectural principles and illustrate how modularity helps us realize many of the benefits we've discussed thus far.

goal of architecture, 33

6.1 ALL THE WAY DOWN, REVISITED

In Chapter 3, we talked about how important it is that we "architect all the way down." It helps increase transparency and understanding between

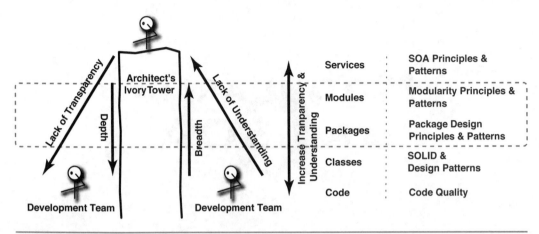

Figure 6.1 Social architecture all the way down[1]

developers and architects by emphasizing a lot of the middle ground that few development teams ever seem to emphasize. Figure 6.1 illustrates the point. Look at the huge gap that exists if we don't focus on what's highlighted in the dotted gray box.[1]

architecture all the
way down, 30

This figure illustrates the social aspect of software architecture. Yet, there are other significant advantages to architecture all the way down that we haven't explored yet, such as structural flexibility.

6.1.1 STRUCTURAL FLEXIBILITY—DIFFERENT ENTITIES, DIFFERENT PURPOSE

Another benefit of module design in filling that middle ground is that modules can offer different benefits than classes and services. Figure 6.2 illustrates some of the capabilities of different types of entities.

For example, classes are pretty easily reused within an application, but because classes aren't a unit of deployment, it's difficult to use them across applications. Of course, interapplication reuse is a sweet spot of services, because their method of invocation is through some distributed protocol (SOAP, HTTP, and even RMI/IIOP). Because services are invoked remotely, we typically like to make them coarser-grained because of the

---

1. This diagram is an adaptation of the diagram found at www.rendell.org/jam/upload/2009/1/tower-12054835.jpg.

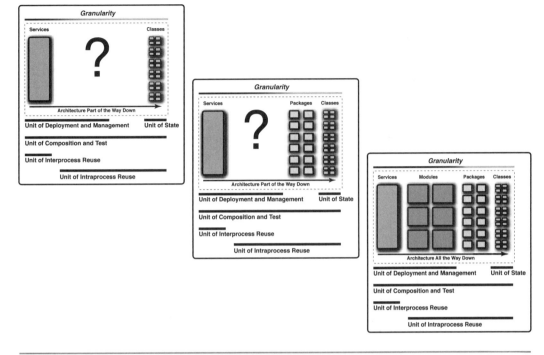

Figure 6.2 Structural architecture all the way down

performance implications of distributed requests. This begs the question: If a service is too coarse-grained to reuse (meaning that it does more than what we want), how do I reuse some desirable behavior across applications? Well, without modules, the only other choice is the class. Because a class can't be reused across processes, we do one of either two things: expose it as a service or copy the class (code). Neither option is ideal.

Modules represent the other option. They are a finer-level unit of granularity than services but are also a unit of deployment. Because each of these different types of entities are units of composition, we have tremendous flexibility in how we assemble applications. Possibly more important, though, is our increased ability to accommodate the architectural shifts that naturally occur as requirements evolve, because one of the most difficult aspects of architecture is designing entities at the right level of granularity.

6.2 GRANULARITY—ARCHITECTURE'S NEMESIS

reuse and granularity, 63
Granularity is the extent to which a system is broken down into its behavioral entities. Coarse-grained entities tend to be richer in behavior than fine-grained entities. Because coarse-grained entities do more, they tend to be larger than fine-grained entities and are easier to use. In general, a fine-grained entity is more reusable than a coarse-grained entity because it does a little bit less. If it does less, then it's more likely to apply across a wider variety of usage scenarios. We spent some time discussing this tension in Chapter 5. Now, I hope this more clearly illustrates the concept of "architecture all the way down."

Unfortunately, although there are many patterns, principles, and idioms that offer really good guidance surrounding many aspects of architecture and design, there isn't a lot of guidance surrounding granularity. Let's start with a really simple example that illustrates the challenge.

6.2.1 A REALLY SIMPLE EXAMPLE

Consider the following **save** method on the **Person** class, as shown in Listing 6.1.

Listing 6.1 The Person Class

```
public class Person {
private String firstName;
private String lastName;
private String ssNumber;
   public void save() {
      ValidationErrors errors = this.validate();
         if (errors != null) {
            //handle the errors somehow
         } else {
             //save to the database.
         }
   }
   private ValidationErrors validate() {
      //perform validation
   }
}
```

As Listing 6.1 shows, the **save** method invokes the validate method before saving the information to the database. Generally speaking, this makes saving the information easier and possibly safer, because whatever invokes `save` doesn't have to worry about validating. And this seems to be a good thing.

Yet, what happens when a new consumer of this method wants to save the information but apply a slightly different set of rules than the current validation method provides? Here's where the existing `save` method is simply too coarse-grained. It does a little bit too much. We've made it easier to use but also less reusable.

At this point, there are many variations I could go with to improve the design. One would be to make the validate method public and have clients invoke the validate method before invoking save. Then, if validate didn't do what it was supposed to, clients could always opt out of invoking the validate method and apply their own validation before invoking save. That is certainly less safe, though, because validation is now optional.

Yet another alternative might be what's shown in Listing 6.2.

Listing 6.2 Modified Person Class

```
public class Person {
    private String firstName;
    private String lastName;
    private String ssNumber;
    public void save(Validator validator) {
        ValidationErrors errors = validator.validate();
        if (errors != null) {
            //handle the errors somehow
        } else {
            //save to the database.
        }
    }
}
```

This seems to offer the best of both worlds. I now require a `Validator` to be passed into the `save` method upon invocation. Assuming the `Validator` is an interface, I can allow clients to pass in their `Validator` of choice. Of course, I could easily pass in a NOP validator, as well.

There are many options, and each has its own set of trade-offs. I'd like to avoid extensive debate surrounding which approach to save and validation is best and instead focus on the main point, which is that achieving the right level of granularity for an entity can be challenging. It requires more than just looking at the problem from a code-level viewpoint and demands that we possess contextual information that helps us answer the question, "What's the right level of granularity?"

6.2.2 BRING IT UP A LEVEL

granularity, 63 The example in Section 6.2.1 illustrates the challenges of granularity at the method and class levels. But the same challenges exist when developing packages, modules, and services, as we'll see by example shortly. But what I really want to know is this:

How do I determine the appropriate level of granularity?

This is the million-dollar question. Granularity is a significant inhibitor to creating reusable software that's easy to use. Again, if something does too much (meaning it's coarse-grained), it's less reusable. If something does too little (meaning it's fine-grained), it's more difficult to reuse.

The bottom-right portion of Figure 6.2 illustrates one dimension of granularity. Services are more coarse-grained than modules, which are more coarse-grained than packages, which in turn are slightly more coarse-grained than classes. This is the same view of modularity we used to defined a module in Chapter 1. This begins to help answer the question, "What's the right level of granularity?"

If I'm concerned that a service I create is simply too coarse-grained and fails to maximize its reuse potential, I can break the behaviors of the service into modules that are a bit finer-grained and more reusable. Then I can compose the services from the modules and reuse the modules across services. The result is different entities at different levels of granularity that lends tremendous flexibility to how I compose, use, and reuse software entities.

This provides some guidance on the level of granularity at which different types of software entities should be defined. However, it still doesn't offer enough guidance to determine the right level of granularity for the save method in Section 6.2.1.

6.2.3 ANOTHER DIMENSION

Another relevant dimension ties in nicely (in a rather subtle way) with the first dimension that's illustrated in the bottom right of Figure 6.1. It has to do with the way we traditionally layer our software. Figure 6.3 illustrates

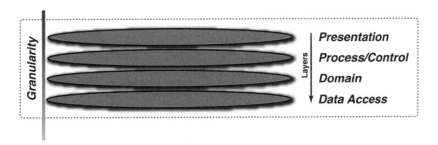

Figure 6.3 Architectural layers

the typical architectural layers commonly found in many systems. Generally, as we move down the layered hierarchy, entities become finer-grained.

Although this isn't absolute and it depends on your architectural principles and style, entities in higher-level layers tend to be more coarse-grained than entities in lower-level layers because they are an amalgamation of their own behavior and the behavior of entities in the lower-level layers.

Armed with this information, we can determine the right level of granularity for the `save` method as long as we understand in which layer the code containing the `save` method lives. If it's in the data access layer and we place architectural constraints on business rules living in the data access layer, then we shouldn't have any validation code that lives in the data access layer. If the `save` method lives in a class in the domain layer, however, it may be suitable for the `save` method to contain validation code in the domain layer and invoke another method in the data access layer that actually performs the save operation.

6.2.4 The Complete Picture

At this point, we can make the following general statements:

- Entities in higher-level layers are more coarse-grained than entities in lower-level layers.
- Services are coarser than modules, which are coarser than packages, which are coarser than classes.

If we combine these two ideas into a single thought and overlay the bottom right portion of Figure 6.2 with Figure 6.3, we can begin to visualize the level of granularity for different types of software entities. Figure 6.4

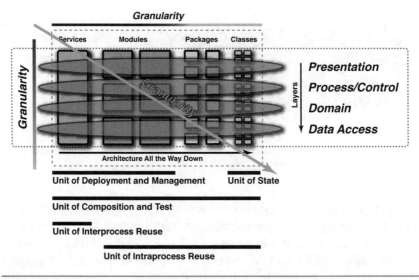

Figure 6.4 Granularity and architecture all the way down

illustrates how entities become finer-grained as we move from both left to right and top to bottom.

Certainly, this doesn't offer hard guidance. Realistically, few architecture and design principles and patterns are universally applicable. In fact, I'm not certain you'd ever create a "presentation service." But certainly, you might create a data service that is composed of multiple data access modules. And you might have separate data services that reuse a data access module. And you might have a business service that uses a data service and is also composed of multiple domain modules. But you definitely do not want a data access module that invokes a business service or a business service that references a presentation module.

This general guidance can serve as useful information to help answer the question, "How do I determine the appropriate level of granularity for a software entity?" It can also serve as guidance when establishing architectural principles and constraints that help determine where software entities with specific behaviors should reside. That's because, without some scheme that will help determine the appropriate level of granularity, it's hopeless to imagine that we'll be able to design reusable software entities that are also easy to use.

6.2.5 A SERVICE EXAMPLE

Let's revisit the simple example we began discussing in Chapter 5, Section 5.2.1. Say that I have a business function called Pay Bill for which I develop a Web service that can be invoked by many different consumers. That service happens to be relatively coarse-grained and performs all the steps involved in paying the bill. These happen to include the following:

- **Audit bill**: Apply a discount to the bill based on payee.
- **Check for duplicate**: Ensure the bill hasn't already been paid.
- **Remit payment**: Cut the check.
- **Reconcile payment**: Reconcile with accounts payable financials.

This seems reasonable. We have a nice little service that we can reuse any time we want to pay a bill. Unfortunately, the real world often gets in the way of our idealistic solutions. In fact, two problems will eventually surface, and modularity benefits both scenarios. Let's start by looking at the first scenario:

> What should I do when a different scenario arises that demands I follow a slightly modified Pay Bill workflow?

As part of the remit step, I have a new payee that demands electronic payment. This is pretty easy, actually. I simply modify the service to support electronic payments and then configure the service to context for that specific payee. So, how does modularity help here?

If the service is composed of modules, it's going to be much easier for me to understand the structure of the service, assess the impact of what it's going to cost to change the service, and then introduce a new module (or modify the existing module) to provide the new capability. Without modules, I'm simply wading through the code trying to figure out all of these things. Now, here's the second scenario:

> What should I do when I want to reuse just one step of the Pay Bill function?

Let's say another new requirement emerges. Whereas traditionally bills were entered by data entry personnel, we now have to support electronic receipt of bills. We also know that bills received electronically are often duplicates. It's just one of those business things, you know? If we don't pay the bill on the day it's received, the billing party sends us the bill again, asking for payment. So, we need to check for duplicates before we save the bill to the database and prepare it for processing. What do we do?

granularity, 63

We could take the same approach as before and modify the Pay Bill service so that the duplicate check could be invoked separately from the higher-level Pay Bill function. But that's a compromised design solution. Why? We are exposing behavior of the Pay Bill service that shouldn't be exposed. The application programming interface (API) is coarse-grained in some areas and fine-grained in others.

architecture all the way down, 30

Maybe exposing the finer-grained capabilities of the Pay Bill function isn't a severe compromise, but it is a compromise nonetheless. And we are forced to compromise because of architectural inflexibility. We don't have architecture all the way down and are therefore left with limited choice as to how we support the new requirement. We can either modify the service to reuse what we know is already encapsulated within the service or copy the code to create something new. But those are the two options we have, and neither may be ideal.

As we continue to hack the system in this manner, with a multitude of other similar changes, the design will rot. Eventually, our Pay Bill service is transformed into a utility that performs all general-purpose bill func-

Lehman's Law, 46

tions. Its API is a mix of coarse-grained and fine-grained operations. It's become the monolith that we're trying to avoid. Lehman's Law in action!

Our decision to modify the Pay Bill service to expose the duplicate check was driven by one thing: ease. It was our easiest option. Really, it was our only option. But it isn't the best option.

If we architect all the way down, we have another option. A Pay Bill service composed of modules that audit the bill, check for duplicates, remit payment, and reconcile the payment means we can choose the desirable solution over the easiest short-term choice. We can avoid the long-term compromises that degrade architectural integrity.

As shown in Figure 6.5, we see the service composed of modules. If we have a check for duplicates module, we can simply reuse that module in the new service or application that's going to process electronic bills. Or we might expose the capabilities of the check for duplicates module as a separate service. We have multiple reuse entry points, as well as different levels of granularity through which our software entities can be managed, deployed, built, and much more.

My point isn't to debate the original design or the decisions made to reuse the check for duplicates functionality in another service or

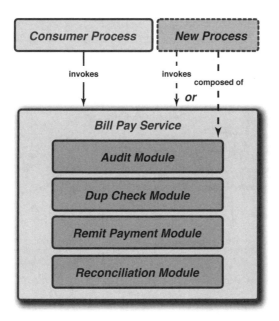

Figure 6.5 Service composed of modules

application. Certainly, debating architectural and design decisions is a favorite pastime of all developers. We can support new requirements as they emerge in a variety of ways. Some are better than others, and all are contextual.

6.3 AN ALTERNATE VIEW

When designing software systems, teams often have a tendency to over-emphasize service design and the aesthetics of the user experience (UX). Although designing the UX and services using SOA principles are incredibly important, neglecting to pay careful attention in designing the service implementation can result in software that is difficult to change. As I enjoy saying to tease my SOA friends, within each service awaits a rotting design.

Modularity shines in helping to design flexible service implementations. Figure 6.6 illustrates this concept.

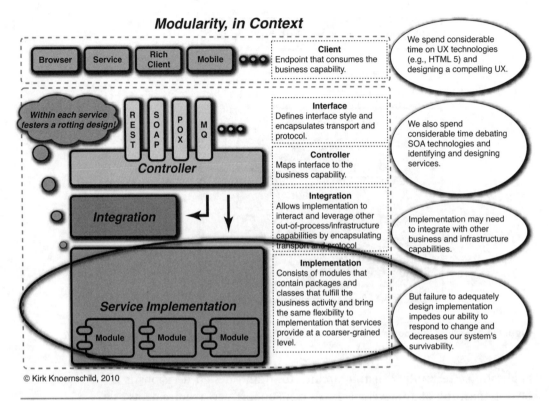

Figure 6.6 Designing service implementations

When designing services, teams often pay careful attention to designing the service interface and devote time to understanding and adopting the appropriate interface style, such as REST, POX, SOAP, or messaging. A great benefit of SOA is that individual services can be autonomously reused and evolve independent of other services. Unfortunately, if careful attention isn't given to how the service implementation is structured, the service loses its ability to evolve and survive.

6.4 CONCLUSION

The notion of architecture all the way down gives us options, and these options help maintain architectural integrity. They increase our options when making decisions and allow our system to accommodate unforeseen architectural shifts. I can modify an existing application or service to give me what I need. Or I can reuse an existing module that's already available for me. Or I can compose a new service from an existing set of modules. Or I can break apart existing modules to create new modules that result in new services. And I can do a lot of this refactoring without significant impact on the existing code. We see this idea in action in the next chapter, as well as throughout Part II.

REFERENCE IMPLEMENTATION

Thus far, we've spent the majority of Part I making the case for modularity. Before we delve too deeply into the patterns, let's witness firsthand the benefits of a modular architecture. Here, we'll provide a glimpse into how we can apply several of the patterns to create a software system with a highly modular architecture. We'll start by examining a sample system and exploring its initial architecture, including some code. Through a series of refactorings, we'll apply several techniques that increase the architectural resiliency of the system. Through these series of relatively small changes, we'll see the system undergo an astonishing transformation from a huge monolith to one of several collaborating modules. Plan on examining numerous snippets of code throughout this chapter.

7.1 WHY NO OSGI?

The following example doesn't use OSGi. You would think that if I'm going to modularize my system, I'd want to use a proven module framework, such as OSGi. There are a couple of reasons I chose not to do so.

OSGi, 273

Although OSGi is a module system, it does not help you design more modular software. In other words, it doesn't help us with the design paradigm. Among other things, designing modular software requires that we understand the weight and granularity of individual modules and use the right techniques to manage the coupling between modules. In other

design paradigm, 23

weight and granularity, 63

dependencies, 48

words, designing good software is our job. Tools and technologies may help, but they make no guarantee.

Many of us aren't able to leverage OSGi today because the platforms and languages we use don't support it. I want to use the same tools and techniques that we can leverage in the enterprise right now. Additionally, once OSGi or another module system is available, it's quite easy to extend the system to leverage it. The example at the end of Chapter 3 provided a glimpse of how we can take advantage of OSGi if we have a modular architecture already in place. Several of the examples later in this book[1] also demonstrate how designing a modular architecture using the patterns in this book serves as a migration path toward leveraging OSGi when it's available.

In this book, I didn't want to shroud the examples in technology. Instead, I focus purely on modular design. In fact, even if I had used OSGi in this example, you'd see that the module structure remains the same. Instead, OSGi allows us to take advantage of the runtime benefits of modularity, such as hot deployments.

In general, this chapter focuses on the design paradigm, not the tools and technologies. So, instead of answering, "How do I use OSGi?" this chapter focuses on "How do I develop a system with a modular architecture?"

7.2 BACKGROUND ON THIS EXERCISE: BUILDING THE SYSTEM

SOLID principles, 319

Interestingly, I've found that when designing modular software, it's tough to identify the modules early in the life cycle. Instead, shifts typically occur, and as things unfold, the modules become more apparent as development progresses. With a SOLID object-oriented design, it'll make it much easier to move things around and create new modules. So to start, although the system is small, I favor coarser-grained and heavier-weight modules.

As specific needs emerge, we'll break larger modules out into a bunch of finer-grained and lighter-weight modules that address specific

---

1. Part III of this book builds upon several of the pattern examples and demonstrates how applying the modularity patterns provides a nice migration path toward taking advantage of OSGi. To explore this migration path, first review the Colocate Exceptions pattern sample code and then begin exploring the migration to OSGi by looking at Chapter 15, which builds upon the sample code used in Colocate Exceptions.

functional and nonfunctional needs. Remember that the material in the first six chapters describes the essence of my motivation here. If you skipped right to the code and haven't read any of the previous material, I encourage you to check it out now. (Of course, you can choose to wait and see what I'm talking about, because we'll experience this phenomenon as we move through this chapter's exercise. I hope that will peak your curiosity and you'll review the material in the previous chapters.)

Here's a simple, high-level description of the system we'll develop. It's the bill payment system cited in previous chapters' discussions:

> We've been asked to develop a system to handle payment of bills. Prior to paying the bill, the system should apply a discount to the bill in an amount that has been negotiated with the payee (we call this the process of auditing the bill). Applying this discount is a fairly complex process, and a third-party vendor has been commissioned that will apply this discount. Additionally, we must integrate with a legacy financials system that must be fed payment information for reconciliation.

We'll flesh out additional details as development progresses.

7.3 VERSION I

The initial version for this system uses Struts as the Web framework and packages everything into a single WAR file. The initial class diagram is shown in Figure 7.1. It's not a complete class diagram, but it shows the main set of classes. I've simplified the system for this example.

As you can see, some `Action` and `ActionForm` classes leverage Struts. There are also a couple of Java Server Pages (JSPs) that you don't see here. A `Customer` has a list of `Bill` instances, and each `Bill` has a reference to an `AuditFacade` class and a `Payment` class. The `Audit-Facade` integrates with the third-party vendor software that applies the discount, and the `Payment` class integrates with a legacy financial system. Note the bidirectional relationship between `Bill` and the `Audit-Facade` and `Payment` classes; this is a sure sign of a problem that will haunt us later. But, we'll fix it.

For the sake of simplicity, I hard-coded the database into the data access layer, which is represented by the `Loader` interfaces. This way, you can experiment with the system without running any scripts to create the database. If you are compelled to do so, feel free to add a real database

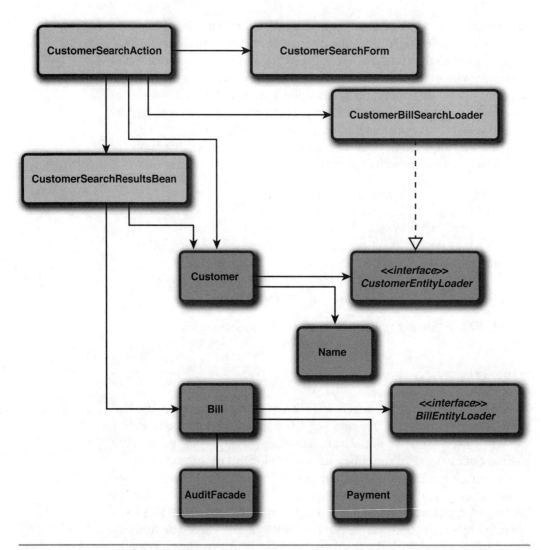

Figure 7.1 Initial version class diagram

backend. It wouldn't be difficult, but it's not what I want to focus on. Although we'll show some code snippets as the example progresses, I set up a Google Code Repository that shows each step in the evolution.[2]

_____

2. The repository can be found at http://code.google.com/p/kcode/source/browse/#svn/trunk/ billpayevolution/billpay, and each of the subprojects represents a single step in the example.

7.4 FIRST REFACTORING

Packaging everything into a single WAR file for deployment certainly isn't modular. In most systems we develop, we try to design layers that encapsulate specific behaviors and isolate certain types of change. Typical layers include a UI layer, a business or domain object layer, and a data access layer. In this system, we have these three layers. The Struts `Action` and `Form` classes, along with the JSP, represent part of the UI layer. The UI layer is represented by the upper-portion classes in Figure 7.1. The `Customer`, `Bill`, `Name`, `AuditFacade`, and `Payment` form the business object layer, and the `Loader` classes form the data access layer. These classes are shown in the lower portion of Figure 7.1. Now, here's a key statement that you need to take with you:

Physical Layers pattern, 162

> If I truly have a layered system, then I should be able to break out each layer into a separate module where modules in the upper layers depend on modules in lower layers, but not vice versa.

If you try this for one of your systems, it's likely you'll find it's not so easy. Most development teams feel they have a layered architecture, but in reality, they don't because somewhere deep within the bowels of the system lies an import or reference to a class in a higher-level layer that we aren't aware of.

In fact, if I really do have a layered system, then I shouldn't have to change anything other than my build script to break the layers into separate JAR files. If I do have to change more than a build script, then I didn't have a layered system to begin with, and I should perform some architectural refactoring to clean things up. Anyway, the end result is relatively simple to understand. No code changes. Only a build script change so that certain classes are allocated to specific modules. Figure 7.2 shows the structure. This refactoring was an example of applying the Physical Layers pattern.

Listing 7.1 illustrates a portion of the initial build script where all of the classes were bundled into the WAR file. Listing 7.2 shows the changes we've made to the build script to create modules for the various layers. Here, we show only the business object layer. We created a new build target where we create the module and then added a new line to the `dist` target where that module is now included in the WAR file.

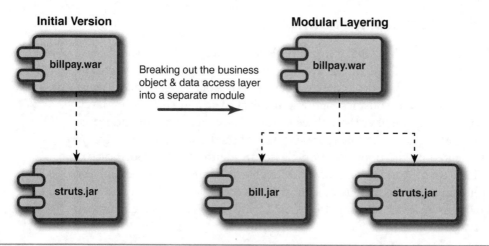

Figure 7.2 Applying the Physical Layers pattern

Listing 7.1 Initial Build Script

```
<target name="compile" depends="init">
   <javac srcdir="${javasrc}:${testsrc}" destdir="${build}">
     <classpath refid="project.class.path"/>
     </javac>
</target>

<target name="bundle" depends="dist">
   <mkdir dir="${deploy}"/>
   <war destfile="${deploy}/billpay.war"
    webxml="WEB-INF/web.xml">
      <fileset dir="jsp"/>
      <webinf dir="WEB-INF">
         <exclude name="web.xml"/>
         <exclude name="lib/servlet-api.jar"/>
      </webinf>

        <classes dir="${build}"/>
   </war>
</target>
```

Listing 7.2 Build Script with Physical Layers

```
<target name="compile" depends="init">
   <javac srcdir="${javasrc}:${testsrc}" destdir="${build}">
     <classpath refid="project.class.path"/>
```

```
    </javac>
</target>

<target name="dist" depends="compile">
    <mkdir dir="${bindist}"/>
    <jar jarfile="${bindist}/bill.jar" basedir="${build}"
      excludes="com/extensiblejava/bill/test/**,
      com/extensiblejava/ui/**"/>
</target>

<target name="bundle" depends="dist">
    <mkdir dir="${deploy}"/>
    <war destfile="${deploy}/billpay.war"
      webxml="WEB-INF/web.xml">
        <fileset dir="jsp"/>
        <webinf dir="WEB-INF">
            <exclude name="web.xml"/>
            <exclude name="lib/servlet-api.jar"/>
        </webinf>
        <lib dir="${bindist}" excludes="test.jar"/>
        <classes dir="${build}"
          includes="com/extensiblejava/ui/**"/>
    </war>
</target>
```

7.4.1 WRAPPING UP AND GETTING READY FOR THE NEXT REFACTORING

This first refactoring was simple, but it has significant implications. Foremost, it proves that my class-level architecture was decent. I was able to break the system out into modules for the various layers without changing a bunch of code. Really, that's the reason why it was so simple—because the logical design was decent. Had there been violations in the layered structure, it would have been significantly more difficult pulling off this refactoring because I would have been forced to remove the undesired dependencies.

Yet, as we'll see, the existing design may meet the needs of today, but it's going to have to evolve as change emerges. In the second refactoring, we look at what we need to do to integrate with another auditing system and how modularity can help us do this. As we progress, the amazing transformation of a system lacking modularity to a highly modularized version will unfold. In the next few steps, we apply two refactorings using

Abstract Modules pattern, 222

Acyclic Relationships pattern, 146

two different modularity patterns: Abstract Modules and Acyclic Relationships. First, we separate the bill and audit functionality into separate modules so we can independently manage (develop, deploy, and so on) them. Second, we remove the cyclic dependency between these two modules.

7.5 SECOND REFACTORING

In the class diagram shown in Figure 7.1, the `Bill` class has a bidirectional relationship to the `AuditFacade` class. This design has two fundamental flaws. The `Bill` is tightly coupled to the concrete `AuditFacade` class, and the relationship is bidirectional. Bad all around! This can be seen in Listing 7.3, illustrating the `Bill` class's `audit` method.

Listing 7.3 Audit Method of the Bill Class

```
public void audit() {
    AuditFacade auditor = new AuditFacade();
    this.billData.setAuditedAmount(auditor.audit(this));
    this.persist();
}
```

Notice that the `audit` method actually creates the `AuditFacade`, calls the `audit` method, and passes a reference to `Bill`. Ugly. Let's clean this up a little bit. Although there are obvious technology reasons why we need to clean this up, there is also a motivating business force.

> The system needs to go live with the current vendor's auditing system, but the business has indicated that they aren't renewing the contract with the vendor and are in ongoing negotiation with another vendor. The contract expires in six months, but we deliver the initial version of the system in three months.

So, three months after deployment, we know we need to swap out auditing systems.

Abstract Modules pattern, 222

We will apply the Abstract Modules pattern, which states that we should *depend upon the abstract elements of a module*. We'll start by refactoring the `AuditFacade` class to an interface and create a separate `Audit-Facade1` implementation. This solves the first half of our problem, which is the tight coupling between the `Bill` and `AuditFacade` implementation. The result is the class diagram shown in Figure 7.3.

Of course, the `Bill` can no longer create the `AuditFacade` implementation. Doing so would compromise the work we've done because `Bill` would still be coupled to `AuditFacade1`. To deal with this challenge, the `AuditFacade` interface is now passed into the Bill's `audit` method, allowing us to swap out `AuditFacade` implementations. Listing 7.4 shows the modified `audit` method.

Listing 7.4 The New Audit Method Accepting the AuditFacade Interface

```
public void audit(AuditFacade auditor) {
    this.billData.setAuditedAmount(auditor.audit(this));
    this.persist();
}
```

If we take this flexible class structure and continue to deploy in the single `bill.jar` module, we have the flexibility to swap out `AuditFacade` implementations at the class level, but we're still required to package everything up into a single bundle and deploy it as a single module. So, what we really must do is separate the audit functionality into a module separate from the bill. Separating the `AuditFacade` interface and `AuditFacade1` implementation into separate modules results in the diagram illustrated in Figure 7.4. Here's where the bidirectional relationship

cyclic dependencies, 50

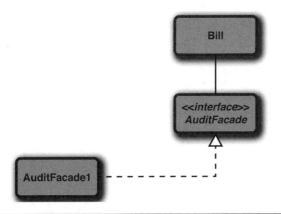

Figure 7.3 Refactoring AuditFacade to an interface

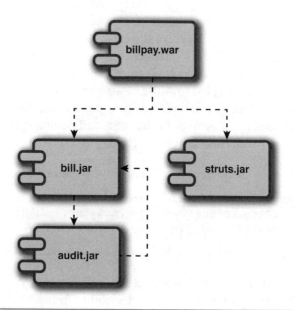

Figure 7.4 Abstract modules

between `Bill`, the `AuditFacade` interface, and the `AuditFacade1` implementation rears its ugly head. We have a cyclic dependency between our `bill.jar` and `audit.jar` modules, which is especially bad. We need to fix this issue.

This change will also be reflected in the build file that packages up these modules, as shown in Listing 7.5, where we can see the `audit.jar` module created.

Listing 7.5 The Build Script Creating the Audit.jar Module

```
<target name="dist" depends="compile">
   <mkdir dir="${bindist}"/>
   <jar jarfile="${bindist}/audit.jar" basedir="${build}"
includes="com/extensiblejava/audit/**"/>
   <jar jarfile="${bindist}/bill.jar" basedir="${build}"
   excludes="com/extensiblejava/bill/test/**,
   com/extensiblejava/ui/**"/>
</target>
```

7.6 THIRD REFACTORING

Because cyclic dependencies are so bad, we need to remove the cyclic dependency between the `bill.jar` and `audit.jar` modules. To do this, we'll apply the Acyclic Relationships pattern, which states that *module relationships must be acyclic*. We'll introduce an additional abstraction, called `Auditable`, that our `Bill` class implements. Upon applying this little trick, we can see that we have now removed the bidirectional relationship between `Bill` and the `AuditFacade` interface, as shown in Figure 7.5.

Acyclic Relationships pattern, 146

Whereas previously the `AuditFacade` accepted a `Bill` to the audit method, it now accepts an `Auditable` type. The new `AuditFacade` interface can be seen in the code snippet shown in Listing 7.6.

Listing 7.6 AuditFacade Interface

```
package com.extensiblejava.audit;
import java.math.*;
public interface AuditFacade {
    public BigDecimal audit(Auditable auditable);
}
```

The `Bill` will pass itself to the `AuditFacade` interface as an `Auditable` type. The key element at this point is how we allocate these classes to their respective modules. Here's a simple rule to abide by when determining how to allocate classes and interfaces to modules:

> Interfaces should be closer to the classes that use them and further away from the classes that implement them.

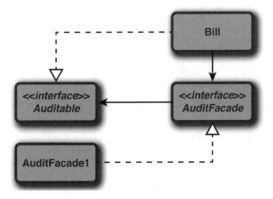

Figure 7.5 Acyclic relationships between classes

*Extensibility
Patterns, 249*   The Extensibility patterns discuss this idea in more detail, and we'll leverage this concept later to address another problem that has surfaced. But, by applying this rule now, it's clear that `Auditable` should be bundled with the `AuditFacade` interface, not in the same module as the `Bill` class. Although we haven't discussed the new `financial.jar` module, we applied a similar refactoring to the `Payment` class by implementing a `Payable` interface and breaking it out into a separate module. Allocation of classes to modules is done at build time, so after modifying our build script, we have the module structure shown in Figure 7.6.

As you no doubt noticed, we broke our rule and bundled the `Audit-Facade1` implementation close to the interface it implements, which is the other problem that has surfaced. The problem, however, is that if we apply our rule in this situation, we'd bundle the `AuditFacade` interface and `Bill` class in the same bundle, which won't work because it would result in the cyclic dependency between the `bill.jar` and `audit.jar` modules that we've worked so hard to remove.

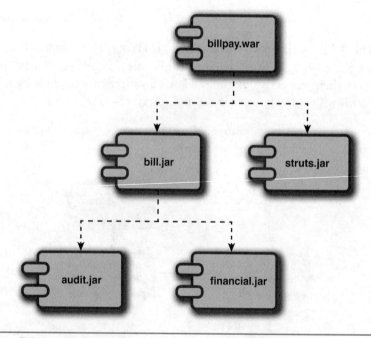

Figure 7.6 Acyclic relationships

7.6.1 WRAPPING UP AND GETTING READY FOR THE FOURTH REFACTORING

Since our last recap in Section 7.4.1, we've applied two separate refactorings. The first was to separate the bill and audit functionality into separate modules. The second was to remove the cyclic dependency between the bill and audit modules. This offers us decent flexibility. We can introduce a new `AuditFacade` implementation, knowing that we'd need to rebuild only the `audit.jar` module. We can test the `audit.jar` module independent of any other module because it doesn't have any outgoing dependencies. And if we wanted, we could deploy the audit functionality separately (in other words, we can reuse it elsewhere). So, overall we've made some decent progress.

reuse, 61

Test Module pattern, 263

However, some problems remain. If we really want the ability to swap out audit systems, bundling the `AuditFacade` interface and `Audit-Facade1` implementation into the same module doesn't give us the flexibility we need. Although we can easily create a new `AuditFacade` implementation and allocate it to the `audit.jar` module, this requires us to redeploy `audit.jar` unnecessarily. In the next refactoring, we explore how we can change the module structure to allow a new `AuditFacade` implementation while also allowing the existing `AuditFacade1` implementation to be removed from the system and while allowing a new module to be deployed. To recap, thus far we've applied the following patterns:

- Physical Layers
- Abstract Modules
- Acyclic Relationships

Although we haven't specifically mentioned it, we could also easily apply the following patterns:

- Levelize Modules
- Levelize Build

7.7 FOURTH REFACTORING

At this point, if we want to deploy a new `AuditFacade` implementation, we have two options: We can bundle it in the existing `audit.jar` module or deploy it in a new module. The second approach offers us some flexibility because we wouldn't need to modify any classes in the existing `audit.jar` module. Unfortunately, we cannot remove the existing `AuditFacade` implementation because it's bundled in the same module as the `AuditFacade` interface. Obviously, if we deploy a new `AuditFacade` implementation, we need the interface. Additionally, if both of the implementations of `AuditFacade` live in the same module, we can't rip one out (that is, uninstall) when we add (that is, install) the other. In other words, because they are in the same module, they must be managed together.

Separate Abstractions pattern, 237

To solve this tricky challenge, we apply the Separate Abstractions pattern, which states that we should *separate abstractions from the classes that realize them*. We actually applied this pattern when allocating the `Auditable` interface to the `audit.jar` module, but we didn't apply it to the `AuditFacade1` class. Now, we'll apply it to the `AuditFacade1` and new `AuditFacade2` implementations. But first, we must answer this question:

> Where do we put the `AuditFacade` interface so that new implementations of the interface can be managed separately from the interface and other implementations?

The answer can be found by looking at the module structure shown in Figure 7.7. Note that I included the `financial.jar` module in this diagram, which was introduced in a previous step when we introduced the `Payable` interface. We'll use this soon, but let's ignore it for now.

We separate the `AuditFacade` interface into its own module: `auditspec.jar`. The `AuditFacade1` and `AuditFacade2` implementations are also placed in their own modules. Aside from moving a few things around, no real coding changes are necessary beyond the new `AuditFacade2` implementation we created. Note that we also separated each implementation into different packages to avoid splitting packages across modules. After adding this new class, we modified the build script to allocate the classes to the appropriate modules.

7.7.1 A NOTE ON THE BENEFIT OF OSGi

OSGi, 273

At this point, we have increased the architectural flexibility of our system. The `AuditFacade` implementation classes are allocated to separate modules, allowing us to manage the two independently. From a maintenance perspective, we can work on each of the implementations

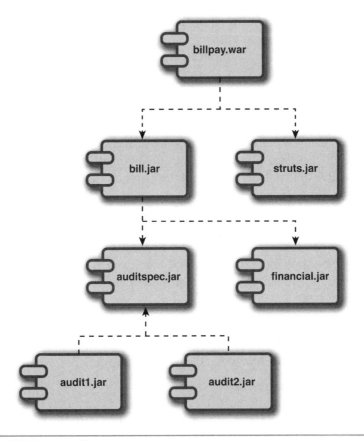

Figure 7.7 Separate Abstractions

separately, resting assured that changes to one implementation won't negatively impact changes to the other. We can also test each independently and reuse each independent of the other.

This change also increases the resiliency of the `bill.jar` module because it's no longer tightly coupled to any `AuditFacade` implementation. We can test the `bill.jar` module using only the `auditspec.jar` module by creating a mock implementation of `AuditFacade` for testing purposes. While the `bill.jar` module is still dependent on the `financial.jar` module, we're going to solve that problem in the next refactoring. In general, we have completely eliminated the dependencies between the `bill.jar` module and the `AuditFacade` implementations in the `audit1.jar` and `audit2.jar` modules. Remember, at the beginning of Section 7.6, these modules containing the bill and audit behavior had a cyclic relationship.

OSGi, 273

Although this example doesn't leverage OSGi, it is important to point out the benefit that OSGi can provide. Because we don't have a runtime module system, we still need to deploy these modules within a WAR file. Changing any of the modules still requires that we redeploy the entire WAR, even though it's possible to only rebuild the modules that have changed. The presence of OSGi, however, brings the same degree of flexibility to the runtime that we have at development time. With OSGi, we would be able to install and uninstall the `audit1.jar` and `audit2.jar` modules without redeploying the entire system.

design encapsulation, 37

Additionally, we are unable to fully encapsulate the implementations details within any specific module. Classes still have access to all other classes and can reach inside a module to gain access to the classes to provide implementation details. With OSGi, we can ensure implementations details remain hidden and expose only the behaviors we want through OSGi μServices.

7.7.2 WRAPPING UP AND GETTING READY FOR THE NEXT REFACTORING

We made some progress since the initial version of the system, which lacked a modular architecture. By breaking the system into modules, we ease the maintenance effort and increase overall system flexibility. In the next refactoring, we turn our attention to the `financial.jar` module that focuses on payment. Recall that, in the third refactoring in Section 7.6, we separated the `Payment` class into a separate module and decoupled `Bill` and `Payment` through the `Payable` interface. Soon, we will focus on the `financial.jar` module and try to decouple `bill.jar` from `financial.jar` so the two are completely independent. I think you'll really like this one. But first, some additional housekeeping.

7.8 FIFTH REFACTORING

Before we decouple the `bill.jar` module from the `financial.jar` module, we must talk about exceptions. In general, we need to answer this question:

Where do exceptions belong?

Let's introduce an `AuditException` that is thrown if an error is encountered. The Colocate Exceptions pattern says that *exceptions should be close to the classes (or interfaces) that throw them.* Because the `Audit-Facade` interface throws the exception, as shown in Listing 7.7, we should put the `AuditException` in the same module as the `AuditFacade` interface, which is the `auditspec.jar` module. Note that if we put the exception anywhere else, we'd create an unwanted dependency between modules.

Colocate Exceptions pattern, 246

Listing 7.7 AuditFacade Method That Throws an AuditException

```
package com.extensiblejava.audit;

import java.math.*;
public interface AuditFacade {
    public BigDecimal audit(Auditable auditable)
        throws AuditException;
}
```

7.9 SIXTH REFACTORING

The previous refactoring was relatively simple. This next refactoring is interesting. Here's the motivating force behind this step:

> A new requirement has emerged, and we need to use the `bill.jar` module in another system. In this other system, we don't need the `financial.jar` module to make the payment. We just want to use the `bill.jar` functionality. So, what do we do?

First, recall the initial version of the class structure (refer to Figure 7.1). Although we didn't spend much time discussing it, in Section 7.6, we introduced a `Payable` interface and created the `financial.jar` module. We finished the fourth refactoring, which is shown in Figure 7.7. The goal now is to eliminate the dependency between the `bill.jar` and `financial.jar` modules so that we can deploy the `bill.jar` module without the `financial.jar` module. We'll apply a little trick called *escalation*. Essentially, we will escalate the dependency to a higher-level module. First, let's look at the new class structure that will allow us to remove the module dependency.

escalation, 147

As shown in Figure 7.8, we see the new class structure that's going to allow us to decouple the `bill.jar` and `financial.jar` modules. Things are starting to get a bit tricky here, so before we allocate these classes to their respective modules, let's walk through the steps to illustrate how these classes will collaborate to give us what we need.

We start by passing a `BillPayAdapter` instance to the `Bill` as a `BillPayer` type. The `BillPayAdapter` is going to manage the relationship between `Bill` and `Payment`. When the `pay` method on `Bill` is called, it will turn around and invoke a `generateDraft` method on `BillPayAdapter`. The `BillPayAdapter` invokes a `generateDraft` method on `Payment`, passing itself in as a `Payable`. This allows the `Payment` to call back on the `Payable` and invoke the appropriate method (either `getAmount` or `getAuditedAmount`) on `BillPayAdapter`. The `BillPayAdapter` can now query the `Bill` to obtain the audited amount and pass it back to the `Payment`. Once the `Payment` has this amount, it can make the payment.

This is a fairly complex collaboration, but it ensures that we can decouple the `bill.jar` module from the `financial.jar` module. The

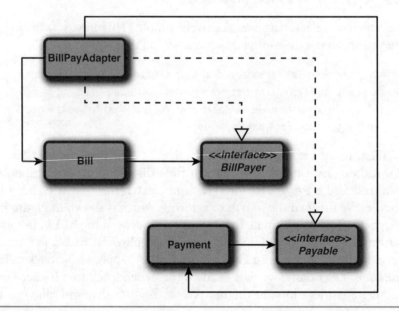

Figure 7.8 Independent deployment

code for the new `BillPayerAdapter` class, which mediates the relationship between `Bill` and `Payment`, is shown in Listing 7.8.

Listing 7.8 The BillPayerAdapter Class

```
public class BillPayerAdapter implements BillPayer,
    Payable {
    private Bill bill;
    public BillPayerAdapter(Bill bill) {
        this.bill = bill;
    }

    public BigDecimal generateDraft(Bill bill) {
        Payment payer = new Payment();
        return payer.generateDraft(this);
    }

    public BigDecimal getAmount() {
        return this.bill.getAmount();
    }

    public BigDecimal getAuditedAmount() {
        return this.bill.getAuditedAmount();
    }
}
```

Now, it's time to allocate these classes to the appropriate modules. The key decision here is where we place the `BillPayerAdapter` class. Because this controls the `Bill` and `Payment` interaction, we can't put it in either of those two modules. In fact, we will create a new module that contains the `BillPayAdapter`. Let's call it `billpay.jar`, and it will depend on both the `bill.jar` and `financial.jar` modules, as shown in Figure 7.9. This refactoring is an example of the Independent Deployment pattern, which states that *modules should be independently deployable units*. That's exactly what we've done. *Independent Deployment pattern, 176*

For the most part, our system is complete. But, we have one nasty problem that we haven't yet solved: We have two different `AuditFacade` implementations, but the current system hard-codes creation of `AuditFacade1` within the `AuditAction` class. All this flexibility compromised by a single line of code. Unnerving how that happens! We really do have to architect all the way down. Let's fix this problem.

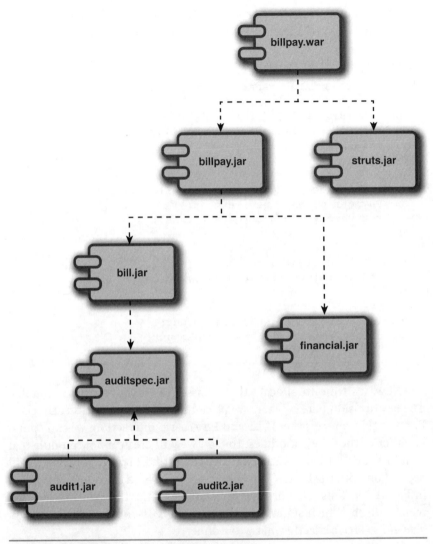

Figure 7.9 Independently deployable modules

7.10 SEVENTH REFACTORING

Implementation Factory pattern, 229 The problem of creating instances is common, so the solution is relatively easy. There are many different ways to do this, but we take the easiest route (and not the most flexible, mind you) by creating an

`AuditFacadeFactory` class. This refactoring is an example of the Implementation Factory pattern, which states that we should *use factories to create a modules implementation classes*. Now, instead of the `Audit-Action` creating the `AuditFacade` implementation, it invokes the factory and is returned an instance, as shown in Listing 7.9. An alternative, and possibly a better solution, would have been to inject the appropriate `AuditFacade` implementation into the `AuditFacade` using a dependency injection framework, such as Spring.

Listing 7.9 The AuditFacade Invoking the AuditFacadeFactory Class

```
try {
    bill.audit(AuditFacadeFactory.getAuditFacade(bill));
    request.setAttribute("bill",bill);
    return mapping.fineForward("success");
} catch (AuditException e) {
    throw new ServletException(e);
}
```

7.11 THE POSTMORTEM

We made considerable progress. Amazing, really. We went from having a single monolithic application to a fully modularized architecture with considerable flexibility. But, we haven't yet talked about many of the interesting takeaways. Many positive side effects have resulted that aren't immediately obvious. In this section, we really look at the impact of modularity.

Through this series of refactorings, we made considerable progress in modularizing the application using a few of the modularity patterns. In fact, the modularity patterns we applied throughout this example include the following:

- Physical Layers
- Abstract Modules
- Acyclic Relationships
- Separate Abstractions
- Colocate Exceptions
- Independent Deployment
- Implementation Factory

Base patterns, 115
We also followed the lessons taught by the base patterns: Manage Relationships, Module Reuse, and Cohesive Modules. Additional patterns that could also be useful in this sample include the following:

- Levelize Build to enforce the module dependency structure
- Published Interface to establish a published API for the Audit functionality
- Test Module to test each module in isolation

Figure 7.10 illustrates the progress we've made. We started with everything bundled into a single WAR file and wound up with a highly modularized system that satisfied the evolutionary requirements. Aside from the many advantages we spoke about in each section, I want to take a moment to explore a few other thoughts.

7.11.1 A NOTE ON MODULE TESTING

If you've explored the system by getting the code from the Google code repository,[3] you'll notice that there are a corresponding set of test modules for each module that we've created. These can be found in the bin directory after building the final version of the system. Like we do with unit testing, I tried to create a test component for each module in the system. Unfortunately, there's a flaw in the `billtest.jar` module. Possibly the interested reader will explore a remedy.

Test Module pattern, 263
Similar to unit testing, where we create mocks and stubs to avoid undesirable dependencies, an ideal test module shouldn't pull in other modules that contain implementation classes. Instead, we should create mocks or stubs to avoid this situation. In other words, *a test module should be dependent only on the same set of modules as the module it's testing*. The Test Module pattern discusses this further.

Unfortunately, the `billtest.jar` module breaks this rule by using the `AuditFacade` implementations to perform the tests. That means the `billtest.jar` module is also dependent on the `audit1.jar` and `audit2.jar` modules, but the `bill.jar` module is not. So, `billtest.jar` is really a module integration test, not a module unit test. It could easily be fixed by creating a mock `AuditFacade` implementation that lived in the `billtest.jar` module.

---

3. The Google Code Repository can be found at http://code.google.com/p/kcode/source/browse/#svn/trunk/billpayevolution/billpay

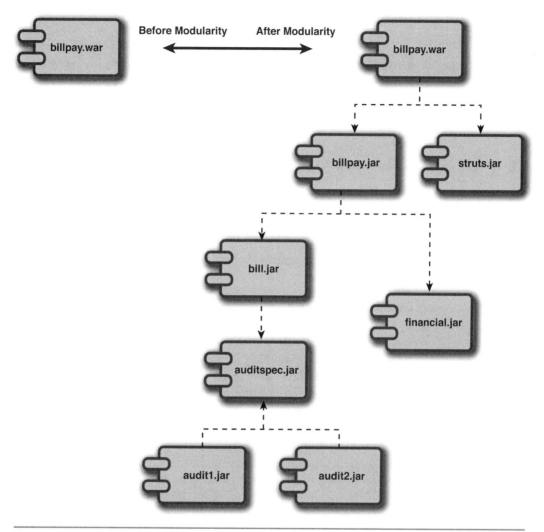

Figure 7.10 Modular architecture

This begs another question:

How do we keep track of module relationships so that we recognize when something bad like this happens?

Even for small systems, without a module system like OSGi, it can be incredibly challenging.

7.11.2 A NOTE ON MANAGING MODULE DEPENDENCIES

module dependencies, 48

Modularizing a system on a platform that supports modularity is challenging. Modularizing a system on a platform that doesn't support modularity is even more challenging. One of the greatest challenges is in managing module dependencies. Tracking the dependencies between modules is quite difficult.

This is where module systems like OSGi help tremendously by enforcing the module dependencies. In Java today, and most platforms used in the enterprise today, there is no module system available, so there is nothing to help enforce modularity. The first unwanted dependency that creeps into our system compromises architectural integrity. This is where a tool like JarAnalyzer[4] can be helpful. By incorporating JarAnalyzer into the build script, we're able to more easily manage the dependencies between modules.

JarAnalyzer has two output formats. The first is a GraphViz[5] compliant dot file that can be easily converted to an image showing module relationships. The image shown in Figure 7.11, which includes the test modules, clearly illustrates the problem with the `billtest.jar` module.

As can be seen, the `bill.jar` module has only a single outgoing dependency on the `auditspec.jar` module. So, the module that tests the `bill.jar` module should not be dependent on any other modules, either. However, if you look at the `billtest.jar` module, you'll see that it depends upon the `audit1.jar` and `audit2.jar` modules. So, instead of using a mock or stub to test the `bill.jar` module, I got lazy and used the various `AuditFacade` implementations. Look at a few of the other modules, and you'll discover that none include additional dependencies beyond the dependencies already present within the modules they test.

The second output format for JarAnalyzer is an HTML file that provides some key design quality metrics, as well as listing the dependencies among modules. Essentially, it's a textual view of the same information provided by the visual diagram. I've included the Summary header of the JarAnalyzer report for the system, which is shown in Figure 7.12. Numerous other code samples throughout this book leverage JarAnalyzer in the build script.

---

4. JarAnalyzer is a utility I wrote to visualize the dependencies between JAR files. It can be found at http://code.google.com/p/jaranalyzer/.

5. GraphViz is a visualization tool that allows you to represent structural information as graphs.

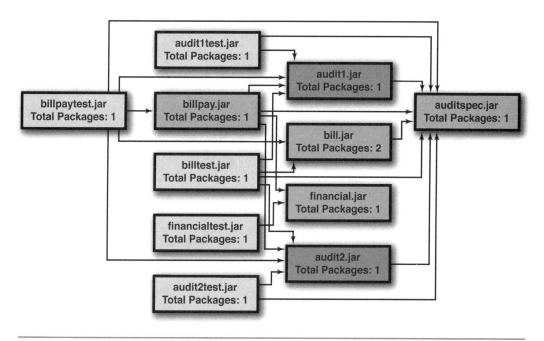

Figure 7.11 JarAnalyzer visual output

Summary

[summary] [jars] [cycles] [explanations]

Jar Name	Total Classes	Abstract Classes	Packages	Level	Abstractness	Efferent	Afferent	Instability	Distance
audit1.jar	1	0	1		0.00	1	4	0.20	0.80
audit1test.jar	3	0	1		0.00	2	0	1.00	0.00
audit2.jar	1	0	1		0.00	1	4	0.20	0.80
audit2test.jar	3	0	1		0.00	2	0	1.00	0.00
auditspec.jar	3	2	1		0.67	0	8	0.00	0.33
bill.jar	12	4	2		0.33	1	3	0.25	0.42
billpay.jar	2	0	1		0.00	5	1	0.83	0.17
billpaytest.jar	6	0	1		0.00	5	0	1.00	0.00
billtest.jar	9	0	1		0.00	4	0	1.00	0.00
financial.jar	2	1	1		0.50	0	2	0.00	0.50
financialtest.jar	3	0	1		0.00	1	0	1.00	0.00

Figure 7.12 JarAnalyzer HTML output

Look at the `auditspec.jar` module. Note that it has eight incoming dependencies (afferent coupling) and zero outgoing dependencies (efferent coupling). Its abstractness is 0.67, and its instability is 0.00. This is a good sign. Why? Its instability is low, implying it's highly resistant to change. It possesses this resistance to change because of the large number of incoming dependencies. Any change to this module may have serious implications (the ripple effect of change). But because it's abstract, it's less likely to change than a module with a lot implementation classes. The distance for the module is 0.33 (ideal is 0.00), so we're not far from where we ideally want to be.

Note

If you're wondering about all these metrics, look at the Martin Metrics. In general, without a utility like JarAnalyzer (or a module framework like OSGi), it would have been incredibly difficult to manage the modules composing this system.

7.11.3 A NOTE ON MODULE REUSE

SOLID
Principles, 319

The *Release Reuse Equivalency Principles* states that the unit of reuse is the unit of release (Martin 2000). Modules are a unit of release and therefore are a unit of reuse. Naturally, the devil is in the details, and we're going to discuss a few of these details here.

reuse versus
use, 62

Chapter 5 described the tension between reuse and use. That tension is evidently at play here. Earlier versions of the system had coarser-grained modules that were easier to use but more difficult to reuse. As we progressed, we broke these coarser-grained modules out into finer-grained modules, increasing their reusability but decreasing their ease of use. A perfect example of this is the `bill.jar` module. In the final version, it was reusable, because it was dependent only on the `auditspec.jar` module. However, this came at the price of usability.

Let's elaborate. In the sixth refactoring in Section 7.9, we decoupled the `bill.jar` and `financial.jar` modules so the two could be deployed independently (that is, increase reuse). But the runtime structure still has some dependencies. To reuse `bill.jar`, we need a `BillPayer` type. While an alternative `BillPayer` implementation could be created, the existing implementation is the `BillPayAdapter` in the `mediator.jar` module, which also has a relationship to the `financial.jar` module. This means using the `bill.jar` module without the `mediator .jar` and `financial.jar` modules would require a new consuming module to implement the `BillPayer` interface.

What do we do if we want to break this runtime coupling? We need to move the pay method on the bill up to the `BillPayAdapter` class and get rid of the `BillPayer` interface. Now the `Bill` class has no dependency on the `BillPayer` interface, but it also can't make payments. Every action has an equal and opposite reaction, eh?

7.11.4 A NOTE ON THE BUILD

The build was a key element in helping enforce modularity.[6] Even a framework such as OSGi is going to manage module relationships only at runtime. We talked about the design paradigm in Chapter 2, and it's why we need really good tools that help us design more modular software. It's our responsibility to craft the modules, and the build is one way to help put in place a system of checks and balances that helps enforce modularity before discovering at runtime that one module has a relationship to another. As part of the third refactoring in Section 7.6, we could have easily refactored our build script to a Levelize Build. If you look at the code in the Google code repository, you'll notice how the build changes after we applied the Acyclic Relationships pattern.

This means that as we build each module, we include only the required modules in the build classpath. We speak more about this when discussing the Levelize Build pattern. To elaborate on this a bit, we build the modules with fewer outgoing dependencies first, followed by those that are dependent on the modules previously built. For example, when we build the `auditspec.jar` module, we include nothing else in the build classpath because the `auditspec.jar` module doesn't require anything. When we build the `audit1.jar` module, we'll include only the `auditspec .jar` module in its build classpath. This pattern recurs throughout the remainder of the build scripts. Introducing a module dependency that violates the dependency structure enforced by the build results in a failed build.

Levelize Build pattern, 253

---

6. JarAnalyzer helped me manage module relationships. The Build enforced the module relationships.

7.11.5 A Note on Object Orientation

The way we managed, massaged, and modified module relationships was through object-oriented techniques, especially using the SOLID principles and various design patterns. By introducing interfaces and abstractions and allocating them to their respective modules, we were able to significantly change the module structure of the system. While we used object orientation to do this, that is not a prerequisite. We could just as easily have used other techniques, such as aspects (AOP). The key is that we are managing the dependencies between modules. We made modular design a conscious design activity.

7.12 Conclusion

In this chapter, we saw an involved tutorial that illustrated the benefits of modularity. The example also showed how we might use many of the modularity patterns, which are detailed in Part II.

7.13 Reference

Martin, Robert C. 2000. *Design Principles and Design Patterns*. www.objectmentor.com/resources/articles/Principles_and_ Patterns.pdf

THE PATTERNS II

In this part, we present the Patterns of Modular Architecture (POMA). Here's a synopsis of each category of patterns.

CHAPTER 8: BASE PATTERNS

The base patterns are the fundamental elements upon which many of the other patterns exist. They establish the conscientious thought process that go into designing systems with a modular architecture. They focus on modules as the unit of reuse, dependency management, and cohesion. Each is an important element of well-designed modular software systems. The base patterns include the following:

- **Manage Relationships**: Design module relationships.
- **Module Reuse**: Emphasize reusability at the module level.
- **Cohesive Modules**: Module behavior should serve a singular purpose.

CHAPTER 9: DEPENDENCY PATTERNS

I find it fascinating that development teams spend so much time designing class relationships but so little time creating a supporting physical structure. Here, you'll find some guidance that will help you create a physical structure that emphasizes low coupling between modules. You'll also find some discussion exploring how module design impacts deployment. The dependency patterns include the following:

- **Acyclic Relationships**: Module relationships must be acyclic.
- **Levelize Modules**: Module relationships should be levelized.
- **Physical Layers**: Module relationships should not violate the conceptual layers.
- **Container Independence**: Modules should be independent of the runtime container.
- **Independent Deployment**: Modules should be independently deployable units.

CHAPTER 10: USABILITY PATTERNS

Although coupling is an important measurement, cohesion is equally important. It's easy to create and manage module dependencies if I throw all of my classes in a couple of JAR files. But in doing so, I've introduced a maintenance nightmare. In this chapter, we'll see patterns that help ensure our modules are cohesive units. It's interesting that you'll find some contention between the dependency patterns and usability patterns. I'm going to talk about this contention, what you can do to manage it, and when you want to do it. The usability patterns include the following:

- **Published Interface**: Make a module's published interface well known.
- **External Configuration**: Modules should be externally configurable.
- **Default Implementation**: Provide modules with a default implementation.
- **Module Facade**: Create a facade serving as a coarse-grained entry point to another fine-grained module's underlying implementation.

CHAPTER 11: EXTENSIBILITY PATTERNS

A goal in designing software systems is the ability to extend the system without modifying the existing codebase. Abstraction plays a central role in accomplishing this goal, but simply adding new functionality to an existing system is only part of the battle. We also want to be able to deploy those new additions without redeploying the entire application. The extensibility patterns focus on helping us achieve this goal. The extensibility patterns include the following:

- **Abstract Module**: Depend upon the abstract elements of a module.
- **Implementation Factory**: Use factories to create a module's implementation classes.
- **Separate Abstractions**: Place abstractions and the classes that implement them in separate modules.

CHAPTER 12: UTILITY PATTERNS

The utility patterns aid modular development. Unlike the other patterns, they don't emphasize reuse, extensibility, or usability. Instead, they discuss ways that modularity can be enforced and that help address quality-related issues. The utility patterns include the following:

- **Colocate Exceptions**: Exceptions should be close to the class or interface that throws them.
- **Levelize Build**: Execute the build in accordance with module levelization.
- **Test Module**: Each module should have a corresponding test module.

BASE PATTERNS

The base patterns are the fundamental elements upon which many of the other patterns exist. They establish the conscientious thought process that goes into designing systems with a modular architecture. They focus on modules as the unit of reuse, dependency management, and cohesion. They are important elements of well-designed modular software systems. The base patterns include the following:

- **Manage Relationships**: Design module relationships.
- **Module Reuse**: Emphasize reusability at the module level.
- **Cohesive Modules**: Module behavior should serve a singular purpose.

MANAGE RELATIONSHIPS

STATEMENT

Design module relationships.

DESCRIPTION

A relationship between two modules exists when a class within one module imports at least a single class within another module. In other words:

If changing the contents of a module, M2, may impact the contents of another module, M1, we can say that M1 has a Physical Dependency on M2 (Knoernschild, 2001).

Figure 8.1 shows a diagram and the accompanying code that illustrates the different types of module dependencies.

module dependencies, 48

In general, a module has incoming dependencies, outgoing dependencies, or a combination of each. Incoming dependencies are present when a module has other modules dependent on the classes it contains. Outgoing dependencies are present when a module is dependent on classes in one or more other modules. As shown in Figure 8.1, the `client.jar` module has only outgoing dependencies, the `subsystem.jar` module has only incoming dependencies, and the `service.jar` module on the right portion of the diagram has both.

A module's dependencies can also be direct or indirect. Indirect dependencies are also known as *transitive dependencies*. Direct dependencies, where a client module depends directly on a service module, are most straightforward. The left portion of Figure 8.1 illustrates a direct dependency.

Indirect, or transitive, dependencies involve at least three modules, where a service module is also a client module that is dependent on some other module. The module diagram shown at the right side of Figure 8.1 illustrates an indirect dependency, where the service module is a client module of the subsystem module and a service module to the client module. Here, the client module has an indirect relationship to the subsystem module, and if something changes in the subsystem module, it may ripple through the other two modules.

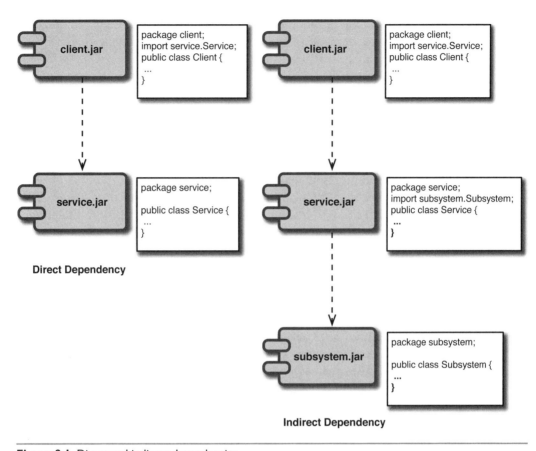

Figure 8.1 Direct and indirect dependencies

IMPLEMENTATION VARIATIONS

When designing module relationships, there are many important implementation details to consider. Different forces affect modules depending on the types of dependencies they possess.

Dependencies

Modules with excessive incoming and outgoing dependencies are the most difficult to manage because they are widely used by other modules, as well as use a large number of modules themselves. It's ideal if modules are either depended upon or depend upon other modules, though this

module dependencies, 48

isn't realistic for all modules. Modules with both incoming and outgoing dependencies demand the most flexibility. The dependency patterns will help you manage this flexibility.

A module with a large number of incoming dependencies should be stable,[1] implying that it is less likely to change. Modules with a lot of incoming dependencies are reused more, and changing them requires more ceremony. They must be tested thoroughly and pushed out to all applications that use them. Changing modules with many incoming dependencies is primarily a maintenance and deployment issue. The best way to ensure a module's stability is by making it an Abstract Module.

Abstract Modules pattern, 222

Modules with a lot of outgoing dependencies can be changed easily but not tested easily. It's difficult to independently verify modules with many outgoing dependencies, since they cannot be tested in isolation. Your goal should be to minimize outgoing dependencies, and where outgoing dependencies are necessary, the outgoing dependency should be on Abstract Modules. By minimizing a module's outgoing dependencies, you increase the testability of the module since you can mock out the dependent abstractions.

Separate Abstractions pattern, 237

Use caution any time you import a new class where a module's relationship doesn't already exist between the modules because the coupling of the modules increases. A new module dependency is an important design decision and should be part of your conscientious thought process when designing modules. Do you really want to create the new dependency, or is the decoupling of modules important enough to warrant additional design flexibility? This additional flexibility can often be achieved by using interfaces to enable classes to communicate with other classes in nondependent modules. In fact, this is one example of how patterns emerge within your system, and Separate Abstractions shows how interfaces can be used to avoid module coupling.

reuse versus use, 62

Each time you define a new outgoing dependency on another module, you are expanding the knowledge of a module. While you may be increasing the behavioral richness of the module, you may also be limiting its reusability across a wider array of contexts. In other words, the module may be easier to use but more difficult to reuse.

Abstract Modules pattern, 222

It's highly likely that some modules will have incoming and outgoing dependencies. The goal is to manage these module relationships as

---

1. Stability is a metric that indicates how difficult it is to change a module. Modules with many incoming dependencies are stable and difficult to change.

effectively as possible because modules with incoming and outgoing dependencies present testing, maintenance, and deployment challenges. Cyclic relationships should be avoided at all costs. Abstract Modules and Separate Abstractions can help you manage module dependencies.

Separate Abstractions Pattern, 237

Packaging and Build

With Java, a service module must be included in the build classpath of the client module. Failing to do so will result in a compile error. If the client module references a class in the service module at runtime, then the service module must also be included in the runtime classpath. There are some situations in Java where the required build and runtime dependencies may differ. A client module may reference a class in a service module at compile time, but if the code isn't executed at runtime, the `Class-Loader` won't require the service module at runtime. It's a rather dangerous practice to ignore runtime dependencies that are required build-time dependencies because a `ClassNotFoundException` might arise if a class is referenced in a module not found on the runtime classpath.

Levelize Build pattern, 253

A Test Module can be created for each module that allows you to test a module in isolation, helping to ensure the module's correctness. Including the Test Module as part of an automated build process will allow you to verify the functionality of the module immediately after compilation to help you identify any potential runtime issues.

Test Module pattern, 263

Java does not enforce that a fully qualified class be included in a single module. In fact, there are some situations where this is violated. For instance, the `javax.servlet.http.HttpServletRequest` class can be found in both the `j2ee.jar` and `servlet-api.jar` JAR files. You should exercise caution before placing the same fully qualified class in two different modules. First, if you are compiling with one JAR file and deploying with another, you run the risk of inconsistent versions. Your application may compile with the correct version, but experience runtime problems if the deployed JAR file contains classes from a different version. Second, only one version of a class can be deployed if the two different versions are loaded by the same `ClassLoader`. If you deploy multiple versions of a class, you'll risk a `ClassCastException` at runtime if the same `ClassLoader` attempts to load both classes. This can be an especially tricky problem to debug. So, while it's possible to bundle a class in multiple modules, I'd recommend against the practice.

In addition to deploying the same class in multiple modules, you also want to avoid splitting packages[2] across modules. With split packages, the same fully qualified package name spans modules, but the classes in the modules are different. Split packages are also difficult to manage and can result in runtime issues with some module systems, such as OSGi.

A good way to manage and enforce module dependencies is to use a Levelize Build. If you're performing a Levelize Build, indirect dependencies need not be included in a module's build-time classpath, but they should still be included in the runtime classpath. Tooling can also help manage relationships between modules. Today, many IDEs help avoid cyclic relationships. Tools such as JarAnalyzer can help identify module relationships in an automated fashion.

CONSEQUENCES

Excessive dependencies make modules difficult to maintain, reuse, and test. Modules with a lot of incoming dependencies are more difficult to change because they are used by multiple client modules. Because of this, it's imperative that they undergo more thorough and rigid testing, and steps should be taken to minimize changes to these modules. Modules with a lot of outgoing dependencies are easier to change because they are used by fewer modules. Unfortunately, these modules are more difficult to test in isolation because of their dependencies on other modules.

There are significant advantages to designing module relationships. They allow you to view the system from a perspective that is much different from what can be seen by browsing the class structure. A medium-sized application might consist of thousands of classes but may be composed of only a few dozen modules. Browsing these module relationships allows you to more easily see how the system is structured. It's an especially helpful way to see how changes might impact other areas of the system. Knowing the module dependencies enables you to identify those classes that may be affected by changing a class in a dependent module.

JarAnalyzer example, 106 Understanding the relationships between modules makes it easier to isolate the impact of change to a specific set of modules, which is not something easily done at the class level. In Figure 8.1, changes to the `client.jar` module clearly indicate that the impact of change is isolated only to the `client.jar` module. Likewise, changes to the `service.jar` module indicate the impact

---

2. Split packages occur when the fully qualified package name appears in multiple bundles. Split packages are undesirable.

of change could spread to other classes within the `service.jar` module as well as classes within the `client.jar` module. Without designing and understanding module relationships, it's difficult to understand the impact of change.

understanding module relationships, 58

Defining module relationships also serves as a system of checks and balances against a system's logical structure. When layering a system, it's important that each layer has a clearly defined set of responsibilities. Layering modules guarantees consistent responsibilities within each layer. This is the purpose of physical layers. Only importing those classes from dependent modules ensures you're well aware of the ramification of change. These relationships enforce architecture, and new relationships created between two previously independent modules should be given serious consideration.

Physical Layers pattern, 162

Note

I've actually written several batch applications in Java. Typically, these batch applications are not projects of their own but part of a larger project that also has a Web interface. For instance, a batch application might receive an incoming data feed and save the data to a database. It may perform some validation and flag some records in error. The Web interface may provide users with the ability to correct those errors, perform the same validation, and persist the cleansed data back to the database for downstream processing.

To avoid duplication in the batch and Web application, it's important to reuse the code that performs the validation and saves the information to the database. Because the batch application will likely run in a separate JVM, and usually outside the context of a Java EE container, the core modules used by both the batch and Web applications must be separated into files independent of either application. Knowing the module's relationships makes this much easier.

reuse across applications, 77

Neglecting to define module dependencies has a tremendous impact on reuse. While you will reuse behavior at the class level, the inability to deploy self-contained units will often deflate your hopes of reusing your logic across applications. Planning the deployment strategy is a critical step in establishing a robust infrastructure. It's a frustrating experience to find that what you thought was a reusable software module is actually dependent on code that you don't want to deploy with a given application. Defining your Physical Layers and Cohesive Modules allows you to realize your reuse goals much more easily.

Cohesive Modules pattern, 139

SAMPLE

JarAnalyzer example, 106 Tight coupling between modules is a bad idea. Fortunately, there are techniques we can apply to manage these relationships. In fact, it's possible to take an existing module relationship, and with a bit of work, we can invert or eliminate the relationship altogether. These techniques in this sample are leveraged by a lot of the modularity patterns. Each example includes a build script and a simple test case. To invoke the build target that runs JarAnalyzer, you'll need GraphViz installed. To invoke the build scripts without invoking JarAnalyzer, you can simply type the following:

```
ant compile
```

Keep in mind that each variation of the system that we'll discuss in this sample has the exact same behavior!

Figure 8.2 illustrates two modules, a `customer.jar` module and a `billing.jar` module. Obviously, the `customer.jar` module depends on the `billing.jar` module, implying that `billing.jar` is required by `customer.jar` at both build and runtime. But what if we wanted to use the `customer.jar` module without the `billing.jar` module? With some trickery, I can actually invert the relationship between the `customer.jar` and `billing.jar` modules.

Inverting Relationships

I start by refactoring the `Bill` class to an interface. Then, to avoid split packages, I move the `Bill` interface into the same module as the `Customer`

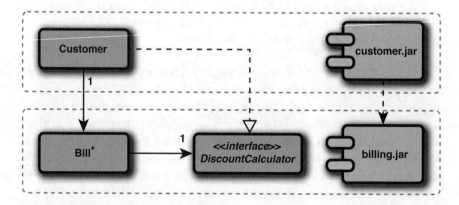

Figure 8.2 Acyclic module relationships

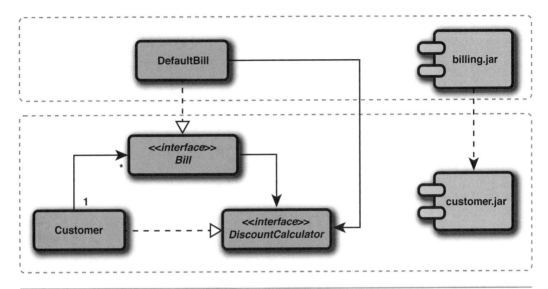

Figure 8.3 Inverting module relationships

class. Figure 8.3 shows the new class diagram, along with the inverted module relationships shown at right.

Eliminating Relationships

Inverting the relationships allows us to deploy the `customer.jar` module independent of the `billing.jar` module. But I'd like to explore another option based on another important need: the ability to test and deploy modules independently. Before inverting the relationships, I am able to test and deploy the `billing.jar` module independently. After inverting the relationships, I can test and deploy the `customer.jar` module independently. But what if I want to test or deploy both modules independently? To do this, I need to completely eliminate the relationship altogether.

Test Module pattern, 263

As it turns out, because I have a pretty flexible class structure after I inverted the relationships, I can do this by simply bundling the two interfaces, `Bill` and `DiscountCalculator`, into a separate module. No other coding changes are required. I start by moving them to a new module. Then, I modify the build script to bundle these two interfaces into a separate `base.jar` module, and we have successfully eliminated the relationship between the `bill.jar` and `cust.jar` modules. This is illustrated in Figure 8.4.

Separate Abstractions pattern, 237

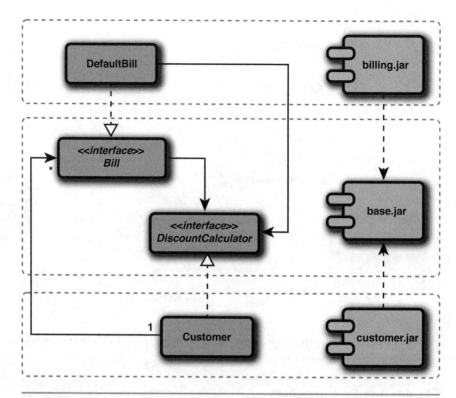

Figure 8.4 Eliminating relationships between modules

WRAPPING UP

joints, 56 Identifying the modules is the first step in designing modular software systems. Shortly following, however, is managing the relationships between those modules. It's these relationships between modules that I refer to as the joints of the system, and it's these areas of the system that demand the most nurturing to ensure a flexible system design. If care isn't given to managing the relationships between modules, separating the system into a set of modules isn't going to provide significant advantages.

MODULE REUSE

STATEMENT

Emphasize reusability at the module level.

DESCRIPTION

One of the oft-cited benefits of object-oriented development is reuse. *reuse, 61*
Mostly, we failed miserably in achieving any degree of reuse that is directly
attributable to objects. The heart of the problem is identifiable.

The object paradigm introduced many new ideas to the development *object*
community, but none was so revolutionary as polymorphism and inheri- *orientation, 23*
tance. Giving developers these two powerful language constructs created
a new way of thinking about, and designing, software applications. Given
that the advantage of object-oriented development was higher degrees of
reuse, there was a natural tendency to believe that it was these two new constructs that would enable, and virtually guarantee, reuse. However, these
two powerful constructs have little to do with facilitating reuse directly.

In the last few years, we've actually found that implementation inheritance often hinders reusability more so than facilitating reuse by locking a
developer into a rigid design with little ability to meet the changing needs
of most complex software systems. In fact, structured programming techniques, which have been around for more than 30 years, can be used to
achieve reasonable degrees of reuse. I've witnessed many situations where
legacy COBOL code that was well-written could easily be reused.

We need to break away from the thinking that objects help us create *reuse versus*
more reusable software. Instead, objects help us create more extensible *use, 62*
software, which is an enabler of reuse. Using inheritance and polymorphism allows us to create designs that are more flexible. It's this flexibility,
and the ability to plug different implementations into a class referencing
an abstraction, that allows us to create generic software that can be configured to meet our needs. The ability to slightly modify the behavior of a
chunk of code typically results in more reusable code. As a guideline, the
less something does, the more reusable it will be. The trick, of course, is
to make something general and configurable enough so that it's reusable
in a variety of contexts, while also making it do enough so that it's useful.
Given that extensibility and configurability are indirect enablers of reuse,
it's much more common to reuse a set of collaborating classes over an
individual class.

Herein lays one of the greatest challenges with achieving reusability using object-oriented development. The class, a combination of attributes and behaviors, which is commonly the focal point of most object-oriented designers, is not an adequate reuse construct. Reuse is a matter of scale, and attempting reuse at the class level is too small scale to realistically expect that high degrees of reuse can be achieved.

logical and physical design, 3   Of course, other factors contribute to our inability to achieve higher degrees of reuse. Many highly touted design techniques, such as the Unified Modeling Language (UML) and patterns, tend to draw our attention toward class design. Attempts to use the design techniques to create robust designs before coding only exacerbates the problem, and for large systems with many classes and many developers, the problem grows even worse. Instead of attempting to reuse at the class level, we should turn our attention to using object-oriented concepts to design more flexible class relationships.

Of course, most of us have experienced some degree of success with class-level reuse, especially within an application. Utility classes are common in most applications and are generally reusable. But, even these utility classes can be difficult to reuse across applications. To reuse within an application, all classes can be bundled together. But to reuse across applications, classes need to be bundled separately into cohesive modules. If dependencies between the modules are not managed carefully, reuse will not follow. Failure to modularize your code correctly is one of the leading causes for the most common form of reuse: copy and paste.

SOLID principles, 319   To effectively achieve higher degrees of reuse, we need a higher-level unit of modularity around which code can be organized, bundled, and deployed. This higher-level unit of modularity is the module, or in Java, the JAR file. The Reuse Release Equivalence Principles states this more succinctly:

The unit of reuse is the unit of release.

Instead of emphasizing reuse at the class level, we should emphasize reuse at the module level. Then, using object-oriented design concepts, we create flexible class designs that are extensible, configurable, and exhibit low degrees of coupling. We bundle these classes into cohesive and independently deployable modules that can then be reused. A flexible class design allows you to refactor modules by moving classes to different modules based on need.

The most compelling evidence suggesting that we should emphasize reuse at the module level is through examination of the open source community and many of its frameworks. The most widely adopted and successful open source products are JAR files that can be easily incorporated into your application. The most flexible of these offerings provide hooks into the framework that allow you to customize it to your need. But all emphasize the module as the unit of reuse.

IMPLEMENTATION VARIATIONS

There are several important items to consider when designing modules for reuse.

Horizontal and Vertical Behavior

Horizontal modules span business domains and do not contain functionality that is specific to your domain. It's much easier to develop horizontal modules for reuse because their usage pattern is consistent and well-known. Most open source software, such as Struts, Hibernate, and Spring, fall into this category. Vertical modules, on the other hand, are specific to a business domain. They offer behavior rich with functionality specific to your organization. Many of the modules developed for business software fall into this category.

Horizontal modules are much easier to develop than vertical modules. The challenge with vertical modules is that you are forced to predict the requirements of future usage scenarios, which is an impossible task. For instance, Hibernate, a widely used persistence framework, allows you to bridge the object and relational worlds regardless of which backend relational database you are using. Attempting to develop an `Employee` class that is reused across the enterprise is virtually impossible since different applications within your organization will require different behaviors of the Employee.

Since vertical modules are so much more difficult to reuse, it's important to create these modules with the least amount of functionality that is common to all applications that will use it. Therefore, you have to be very cautious in adding any degree of rich behavior. A good starting point is a module that serves as a facade for a backend datasource and returns raw business objects with little functionality. These business objects, while offering little functionality, contain the data and other methods that allow the object to be configured to its context.

There are two main impediments you'll encounter when trying to reuse modules. First, the module doesn't offer the right level of functionality that you need, and you cannot customize the modules to fit your context. This is typically a problem when the module has not been created at the correct level of granularity. The module does more than what you want. When developing modules, it's important to offer only the functionality that you know is appropriate. If you question whether the module should do something extra, you should either avoid putting the behavior in the module or offer the ability to configure the module so that the behavior can be turned off. Second, you may find that a module has too many heavyweight dependencies on something else, thus preventing you from reusing it because you do not want those heavyweight dependencies. If you separate abstractions and provide external configuration, you're likely able to remove some of the undesirable dependencies and allow the module to be more easily configured to context.

Services

Services differ from modules in that services typically span distribution boundaries, whereas modules are invoked in-process. For years, industry luminaries have predicted that services will revolutionize software reuse. I'm not convinced that this is true. Services alone will not provide the revolutionary boost to software architecture that's necessary. It will be just as easy to create heavyweight and unusable services as it is to create heavyweight and unusable modules. Chapter 3 discussed the concept of architecture all the way down. Applications with a truly great architecture require a solid design from the class structure, to the module structure, and finally up to the service level. If you create a robust suite of modules that are loosely coupled and wired together at runtime, these modules can be used to compose your services.

Module Management

Module management can be difficult. A large number of modules with multiple versions of each make it difficult for others to ensure they are using the correct version of a module. A repository in your version control software is a great place to store the binaries of your modules. An application's build process can be configured to pull the correct version of the module from the repository during each build.

Module frameworks provide runtime support for managing different versions of a module. For instance, with OSGi, each Java package can be assigned a version. You can deploy multiple versions of the same packages in separate modules, and other dependent modules can specify which version they require. There is no other way to effectively achieve this without a module framework that supports versioning.

CONSEQUENCES

Emphasizing reuse at the module level offers a much greater probability that you'll succeed in your reuse efforts. However, the dream of assembling complete applications from prebuilt modules is still difficult to achieve. Organizational change will always dictate that software be customized, and it's unlikely that organizations within an industry will highly standardize their business processes since this standardization can eliminate a company's competitive advantage. As the business processes change, so too must the modules that support them. All software systems are in a constant state of evolution. However, a suite of robust modules will help an organization deliver software more quickly. The ability to assemble these modules, add to them, and build custom software on top of them will help an organization achieve and sustain their competitive advantage.

software evolution, 46

Maximizing the reuse of a module usually means creating smaller modules that do less. This can make module management a difficult task. Contrarily, larger modules that do more will be easier to manage but may not be as reusable. It can be very difficult to balance these two competing agendas. I have found that early in the development life cycle, while the software is still in a dynamic state, larger modules tend to be easier to manage. As distinct areas of reuse are identified, these larger modules can be broken out into smaller, more reusable modules. Attempting to define smaller fine-grained modules earlier in the life cycle is difficult since you are forced to guess the functionality of a module. This is usually a lost cause.

reuse versus use, 62

SAMPLE

An insurance company receives policy applications that are scanned into a system. The scanned copy of the image is stored in an enterprise document management system. Optical Character Recognition (OCR) software extracts data from the scanned image and stores the data to an operational application database. Before storing the data to the database, the data must pass through a series of business rule validations, and the policy is flagged with a status based upon the outcome of the business rules.

A separate Web application is used by the underwriting department to review the policy information, cleanse any data incorrectly interpreted by the OCR software, and ultimately allow the underwriter to assess the insurability of the customer. Any changes to the policy information must pass through the same set of business rule validations. However, if any of the validation rules fail, instead of setting a flag on the policy, the underwriter is prompted to correct the information.

In this scenario, we have two independent systems that must share some common validation rules. One approach is to develop a distributed service that is deployed once and invoked by each of the applications. In lieu of incurring the performance hit of a distributed call, we'll opt to develop a module that helps us validate the policy information. To do this, however, we must ensure that the module does not have any application dependencies. Of course, we'd have to do the same for a service, but more on that a bit later.

The OCR software sends the data feed in XML format. Our initial pass at validating the information leads us to creating a `Policy` class, as shown in Listing 8.1. The constructor of the `Policy` class accepts the XML string and parses it out to build the `Policy` object. The validate method can then be called to ensure the data is correct before calling the save method to store the data to the application database.

Listing 8.1 The Policy Class

```
package com.extensiblejava.policy;

import java.util.*;
import java.io.*;
import javax.xml.parsers.*;
import org.xml.sax.helpers.*;
import org.xml.sax.*;

public class Policy {

    private String firstName;
    private String lastName;
    private String tobaccoUser;
```

```
private Date dateOfBirth;
private String maritalStatus;

public Policy(String xmlString) {
   try {
      SAXParserFactory factory = SAXParserFactory.
         newInstance();
      SAXParser parser = factory.newSAXParser();
      InputSource source = new InputSource(
         new StringBufferInputStream(xmlString));
      parser.parse(source,
                  new PolicyDefaultHandler(this));
   } catch (Exception e) {
      e.printStackTrace();
   }
}
void setFirstName(String firstName) {
   this.firstName = firstName;
}
void setLastName(String lastName) {
   this.lastName = lastName;
}
void setTobaccoUser(String tobaccoUser) {
   this.tobaccoUser = tobaccoUser;
}
void setDateOfBirth(Date dateOfBirth) {
   this.dateOfBirth = dateOfBirth;
}
void setMaritalStatus(String maritalStatus) {
   this.maritalStatus = maritalStatus;
}
public String getFirstName() {
   return this.firstName;
}
public Date getDateOfBirth() {
   return this.dateOfBirth;
}
public String getLastName() {
   return this.lastName;
}
public String getMaritalStatus() {
   return this.maritalStatus;
}
public String getTobaccoUser() {
   return this.tobaccoUser;
}
```

```
      public void validate() {
         //validate the data.
      }
      public void save() {
         //save the data.
      }
}
```

The `PolicyDefaultHandler`, in the same module as `Policy`, sets the individual attributes on the `Policy` instance as the XML string is parsed. Listing 8.2 shows the `PolicyDefaultHandler`.

Listing 8.2 The PolicyDefaultHandler Class

```
package com.extensiblejava.policy;

import java.util.*;
import org.xml.sax.helpers.*;
import org.xml.sax.*;

class PolicyDefaultHandler extends DefaultHandler {
   private Policy policy;
   private String attribute;
   public PolicyDefaultHandler(Policy policy) {
      this.policy = policy;
   }
   public void characters(char[] ch, int start,
                           int length) {
      String element = new String(ch, start, length);
      this.setPolicyAttribute(element);
   }
   public void startElement(String uri,
                            String localName,
                            String qName,
                            Attributes attributes) {
      this.attribute = qName;
   }
   private void setPolicyAttribute(String value) {
      if (this.attribute.equals("firstname")) {
         policy.setFirstName(value);
      } else if (this.attribute.equals("lastname")) {
         policy.setLastName(value);
      } else if (this.attribute.equals("dateofbirth")) {
         Calendar cal = Calendar.getInstance();
```

```
            Integer month = new Integer(value.substring(0,2));
            Integer day = new Integer(value.substring(3,5));
            Integer year = new Integer(value.substring(6,10));
            cal.set(year.intValue(), month.intValue() - 1,
                    day.intValue());
            policy.setDateOfBirth(cal.getTime());
        } else if (this.attribute.equals("tobaccouser")) {
            policy.setTobaccoUser(value);
        } else if (this.attribute.equals("maritalstatus")) {
            policy.setMaritalStatus(value);
        }
    }
}
```

The result is a valid `Policy` instance that can now be validated and saved to the database. The previous approach works well for the OCR and scanning application. However, `Policy` is tightly coupled to the XML and cannot be used in our underwriting application. For the validation rules and persistence behavior on our `Policy` class to be reusable in another application, we must not only decouple our `Policy` class from this XML String but also ensure that the `Policy` class can be deployed independent of the XML behavior. In this situation, because the `Policy` class is so heavily dependent on the XML parsing functionality, the `Policy` behavior we want to reuse cannot be deployed separately. Instead, a single `policy.jar` module is our only deployable unit, as shown in Figure 8.5.

To fix this problem, we must physically separate the process of constructing the `Policy` instance from the format of the data used to construct `Policy`. To achieve this separation, the `Policy` class has been refactored to accept an abstract `PolicyBuilder` to its static `build-Policy` method. Listing 8.3 shows the refactored `Policy` class.

Figure 8.5 The Policy module

Listing 8.3 Refactored Policy Class

```java
package com.extensiblejava.policy;

import java.util.*;
public class Policy {
    private String firstName;
    private String lastName;
    private String tobaccoUser;
    private Date dateOfBirth;
    private String maritalStatus;
    public static Policy buildPolicy(
                        PolicyBuilder policyBuilder) {
        return policyBuilder.build();
    }
    public Policy(String firstName, String lastName,
                String tobaccoUser, Date dateOfBirth,
                String maritalStatus) {
        this.firstName = firstName;
        this.lastName= lastName;
        this.tobaccoUser = tobaccoUser;
        this.dateOfBirth = dateOfBirth;
        this.maritalStatus = maritalStatus;
    }
    public String getFirstName() {
        return this.firstName;
    }
    public Date getDateOfBirth() {
        return this.dateOfBirth;
    }
    public String getLastName() {
        return this.lastName;
    }
    public String getMaritalStatus() {
        return this.maritalStatus;
    }
    public String getTobaccoUser() {
        return this.tobaccoUser;
    }
    public void validate() {
        //validate the data.
    }
    public void save() {
        //save the data.
    }
}
```

The `Policy` class has now been decoupled from the construction of the `Policy` object using XML as the input source. The `PolicyBuilder` interface defines the build method that the implementing class must provide to construct the `Policy` instance. Listing 8-4 shows the `PolicyBuilder`.

Listing 8.4 PolicyBuilder Class

```
package com.extensiblejava.policy;
public interface PolicyBuilder {
   public Policy build();
}
```

We now define a `PolicyXMLBuilder` implementation, which we'll put in a separate module that will build the `Policy` instance. Listing 8.5 shows the `PolicyXMLBuilder` class.

Listing 8.5 PolicyXMLBuilder Class

```
package com.extensiblejava.builder.xml;

import java.util.*;
import java.io.*;
import javax.xml.parsers.*;
import org.xml.sax.helpers.*;
import org.xml.sax.*;
import com.extensiblejava.policy.*;
public class PolicyXMLBuilder implements PolicyBuilder {
   private String xmlString;
   private String firstName;
   private String lastName;
   private String tobaccoUser;
   private Date dateOfBirth;
   private String maritalStatus;
   public PolicyXMLBuilder(String xmlString) {
      this.xmlString = xmlString;
   }
   public Policy build() {
      try {
         SAXParserFactory factory =
            SAXParserFactory.newInstance();
         SAXParser parser = factory.newSAXParser();
         InputSource source = new InputSource(
            new StringBufferInputStream(xmlString));
```

```
            parser.parse(source,
                        new PolicyDefaultHandler(this));
        } catch (Exception e) {
            e.printStackTrace();
        }
        return new Policy(this.firstName, this.lastName,
            this.tobaccoUser, this.dateOfBirth,
            this.maritalStatus);
    }
    void setFirstName(String firstName) {
        this.firstName = firstName;
    }
    void setLastName(String lastName) {
        this.lastName = lastName;
    }
    void setTobaccoUser(String tobaccoUser) {
        this.tobaccoUser = tobaccoUser;
    }
    void setDateOfBirth(Date dateOfBirth) {
        this.dateOfBirth = dateOfBirth;
    }
    void setMaritalStatus(String maritalStatus) {
        this.maritalStatus = maritalStatus;
    }
}
```

Finally, a simple integration test proves correctness, as shown in Listing 8.6.

Listing 8.6 PolicyXMLTest Class

```
package com.extensiblejava.policy.test;

import junit.framework.*;
import junit.textui.*;
import com.extensiblejava.policy.*;
import com.extensiblejava.builder.xml.*;
import java.util.*;
import java.io.*;
public class PolicyXMLTest extends TestCase {
    public static void main(String[] args) {
        String[] testCaseName = {
                PolicyXMLTest.class.getName() };
        junit.textui.TestRunner.main(testCaseName);
    }
    protected void setUp() {}
```

```
public void testPolicy() throws Exception {
   String policyXML =
      ""+"Jane"+"Doe"+"M"+"01/10/1967"+"N"+"";
   Policy policy = Policy.buildPolicy(
      new PolicyXMLBuilder(policyXML));
   assertEquals("Jane", policy.getFirstName());
   assertEquals("Doe", policy.getLastName());
   assertEquals("M", policy.getMaritalStatus());
   assertEquals("N", policy.getTobaccoUser());
   Calendar cal = Calendar.getInstance();
   cal.setTime(policy.getDateOfBirth());
   assertEquals(10, cal.get(Calendar.DAY_OF_MONTH));
   assertEquals(1967, cal.get(Calendar.YEAR));
   assertEquals(1, cal.get(Calendar.MONTH) + 1);
   }
}
```

Because the construction of the `Policy` class has now been separated into a separate module, we have the ability to deploy the `Policy` behavior independent of the XML construction process. Figure 8.6 shows the new module structure.

Because the functionality to validate and save policy information has been separated from the XML construction process, the `policy.jar`

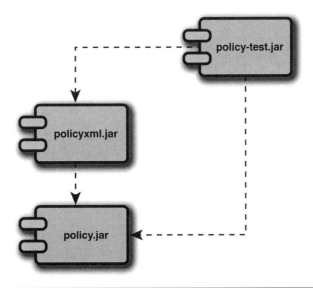

Figure 8.6 Policy module

module can now be deployed independent of the `policyxml.jar` module. Defining a new implementation of `PolicyBuilder` in the underwriting application should allow us to construct the `Policy` instance from the data retrieved from the application database.

This resulting structure offers some significant advantages. Through the example, we already illustrated how the policy functionality can be reused across applications. In the future, if we decide to deploy the policy functionality as a service invoked via a distributed protocol, such as EJB or JMS, the modular approach we've taken will help facilitate that endeavor.

WRAPPING UP

module definition, 17 The Reuse Release Equivalence Principle implies that software is reused at the same unit of functionality at which it is deployed. By definition, modules are the only software entity that match this set of criteria, and designing good software modules presents development teams another option for how they choose to reuse software entities.

COHESIVE MODULES

STATEMENT

Module behavior should serve a singular purpose.

DESCRIPTION

Cohesion is a measure of how closely related and focused the various responsibilities of a module are. In the worst-case scenario, little emphasis is placed on the allocation of classes to modules. Instead, behavior is allocated randomly, and the likelihood that modules suffer from lack of cohesion is high. In the best-case scenario, modules exhibit high degrees of functional cohesion, and the entities composing the module each work in conjunction to fulfill module behavior.

In general, cohesion is a qualitative measurement that is difficult to measure objectively. Instead, we typically refer to a software module as possessing either high cohesion or low cohesion. Modules with higher degrees of cohesion are preferred.

IMPLEMENTATION VARIATIONS

Two key elements affect module cohesion:

- The rate at which the behavior among the classes within a module change
- The likelihood that the classes within a module are reused together

  Based on these statements, it's easy to draw the following conclusion:

- Classes that change at different rates belong in separate modules.
- Classes that change at the same rate belong in the same module.
- Classes not reused together belong in separate modules.
- Classes reused together belong in the same module.

Unfortunately, this simple logic is flawed because it doesn't consider the intricate relation between the rate of change, reuse, and the natural shifts that occur throughout the development life cycle. It's possible, even likely, that classes change at different rates but are reused together or that classes change at the same rate but are rarely reused together. Indeed,

architectural shifts, 36

there is a tension between rate of change and reuse, and we must consider the following combinations:

- Classes within a module that change at the same rate and are reused together
- Classes within a module that change at a different rate and are reused together
- Classes within a module that change at the same rate and are not reused together
- Classes within a module that change at a different rate and are not reused together

The first and fourth scenarios are the easiest to accommodate. When classes change at the same rate and are reused together, it's logical that they belong in the same module. Likewise, classes that change at different rates and are not reused together belong in separate modules. The final two scenarios, which tend to be most common, are also the most challenging.

Fortunately, the natural shifts that occur throughout the development life cycle provide insight to dealing with the second and third scenarios and encourage us to emphasize one of these aspects more than the other. Early in the development life cycle, when the system is volatile and change is rampant, packaging the classes based on rate of change should supersede packaging based on reuse. As the system stabilizes, we should focus on packaging the classes based on reuse since the rate of change is much less.

CONSEQUENCES

understanding module relationships, 58

Some key difficulties arise when modules suffer from low cohesion, including the inability to understand the software system and difficulty maintaining the software system. Reusing modules that lack cohesion is also difficult. Module consumers rarely need all of the random behaviors provided by modules lacking cohesion, and the random behaviors often increase dependencies on other modules. In general, modules that lack cohesion degrade the overall quality of a software system's architecture.

granularity, 63

Early in the development life cycle, when change is rampant, we are encouraged to package classes into more coarse-grained modules. This is logical. Because change is rampant and widespread, packaging into coarse-grained modules means less module management as change occurs. We don't have to worry as much about managing dependencies between modules. Unfortunately, this can lead to dire consequences if not dealt with on an ongoing basis. Failure to refactor the modules as the system requirements stabilize results in a software system composed of all coarse-grained modules.

Coarse-grained modules make the modules easier to use, but the increased ease of use comes at the price of reusability. It's vital to recognize that shifts will occur throughout development. As the rate of change lessens, it's imperative to turn our attention toward the cohesive properties of the modules that affect reuse.

SAMPLE

Figure 8.7 illustrates the initial version of our system, where `Bill` instances are routed to an appropriate place so they can be handled (in other words, rejected or paid). Unfortunately, the `bill.jar` module lacks cohesion, since the `Bill` and `Router` types are each bundled and deployed in that module. The lack of cohesion affects reuse, because we cannot reuse `Bill` without the `Router` or reuse the `Router` to handle other types of entities that might require routing.

Listing 8.7 shows the code for the `Bill` class. As shown, a `Router` is passed to the `Bill` constructor, which is used when the `Bill.route()` method is called. The `Router` is an abstract class with an abstract `route` method on it. The `TypeARouter` shown in Figure 8.7 extends the `Router` and provides an implementation for the `route` method.

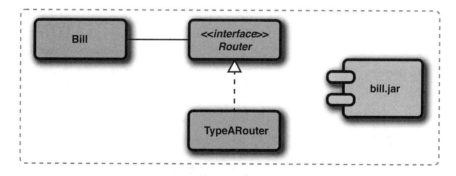

Figure 8.7 Module lacking cohesion

Listing 8.7 The Bill Class

```java
package com.extensiblejava.bill;

import java.math.*;
import com.extensiblejava.route.*;

public class Bill {
    private String type;
    private String location;
    private BigDecimal amount;
    private Router router;

    public Bill(String type, String location,
                BigDecimal amount, Router router) {
        this.type = type;
        this.location = location;
        this.amount = amount;
        this.router = router;
    }
    public String getType() {return this.type;}
    public String getLocation() {return this.location;}
    public BigDecimal getAmount() {return this.amount;}
    public String route() {
       return this.router.route(this);
    }
}
```

To increase cohesion of the `bill.jar` module, routing functionality can be moved to its own module, as shown in Figure 8.8.

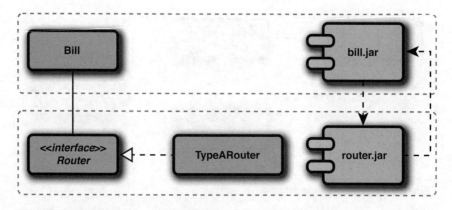

Figure 8.8 Cohesive bill and route modules

The only change required to bundle the functionality separately was to modify the build script. Previously, the build bundled all classes into a single module. The modified script, shown in Listing 8.8, illustrates how the functionality is allocated to the separate bundles.

Listing 8.8 Modified Build Script

```
<target name="dist" depends="compile">
   <jar jarfile="${dist}/bill.jar" basedir="${bin}"
     includes="com/extensiblejava/bill/**"/>
   <jar jarfile="${dist}/route.jar" basedir="${bin}"
     includes="com/extensiblejava/route/**"/>
   <jar jarfile="${dist}/bill-test.jar" basedir="${bin}"
     includes="com/extensiblejava/test/**"/>
   <junit printsummary="yes" haltonfailure="yes">
     <classpath>
        <pathelement path="${dist}/route.jar"/>
        <pathelement path="${dist}/bill.jar"/>
        <pathelement path="${dist}/bill-test.jar"/>
        <pathelement path="${lib}/junit.jar"/>
     </classpath>
     <test name="com.extensiblejava.test.RouterTest"
       outfile="junitresults">
        <formatter type="plain"/>
     </test>
   </junit>
</target>
```

Unfortunately, there is still a glaring problem with the module structure illustrated in Figure 8.8. A cyclic dependency exists between the `bill.jar` and `route.jar` modules. Applying the Acyclic Relationships pattern will help eliminate the cyclic dependency. When applying the Acyclic Relationships pattern to break the cycle between the `bill.jar` and `route.jar` modules, we also applied the Separate Abstractions pattern. Otherwise, the cycle would have persisted. Upon doing so, the final module structure would resemble what's illustrated in Figure 8.9. Note the addition of the `Routable` interface, which is implemented by `Bill`. It's the `Routable` interface, and its placement in the `route.jar` module eliminates the cycle. For more information on the Acyclic Relationships and Separate Abstractions patterns, refer to the pattern discussion.

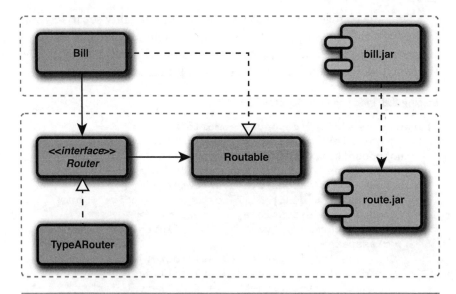

Figure 8.9 Cohesive modules with acyclic relationships

WRAPPING UP

Highly cohesive modules are easier to understand, maintain, and reuse. In many cases, however, it can be difficult to create cohesive modules early in the development life cycle, when the team may not have a clear understanding of system behavior. As this insight is gained, the development team should structure the system to ensure modules are cohesive.

DEPENDENCY PATTERNS

9

The dependency patterns help manage the relationships between modules, something that few development teams seriously consider. In fact, I've found it personally fascinating that development teams spend so much time designing class relationships but yet spend so little time creating a supporting physical structure. Here, you'll find some guidance that will help you create a module structure that emphasizes low coupling between modules. You'll also find some discussion exploring how module design impacts deployment. The dependency patterns include the following:

- **Acyclic Relationships**: Module relationships must be acyclic.
- **Levelize Modules**: Module relationships should be levelized.
- **Physical Layers**: Module relationships should not violate the conceptual layers.
- **Container Independence**: Modules should be independent of the runtime container.
- **Independent Deployment**: Modules should be independently deployable units.

ACYCLIC RELATIONSHIPS

STATEMENT

Module relationships must be acyclic.

DESCRIPTION

cyclic
dependencies, 50

When you define a relationship between two system modules, their coupling increases. Some degree of coupling is necessary simply because modules need to work together with each other to accomplish some task. But, certain types of coupling should be avoided. The right part of Figure 9.1 illustrates a cyclic, or bidirectional, relationship between two modules. That is, each module has a dependency on the other, and the accompanying code to the right of this module diagram shows the import statement in the classes within each of the respective modules. A more desirable approach is the left side of Figure 9.1, where an acyclic or unidirectional relationship exists between the two modules.

To determine whether a cyclic relationship exists between any set of modules, you can always apply the following rule:

> If beginning with a module A, you can follow the dependency relationships between the set of modules that A is directly or indirectly dependent upon and you find any dependency on module A within that set, then a cyclic dependency exists between your module structure.

Although Figure 9.1 illustrates an obvious cyclic relationship, not all violations of this pattern are as apparent. In more complex situations, indirect cyclic relationships might exist between three or more modules. Because most medium to large applications consist of dozens of modules, it's imperative that you are judicious when evaluating the module structure for cyclic dependencies.

IMPLEMENTATION VARIATIONS

There are a few ways to resolve cycles in the dependency relationships among your modules, regardless of whether you're attempting to break a direct or indirect cyclic dependency:[1]

---

1. Escalation, Demotion, and Callback are three techniques discussed in John Lakos book, *Large-Scale C++ Software Design*.

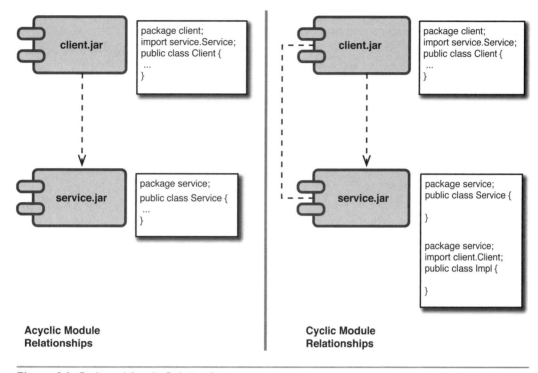

Figure 9.1 Cyclic and Acyclic Relationships

- **Escalation** is the process of moving the cause of the cyclic dependency to a managing module at a higher level.
- **Demotion** is the process of moving the cause of the cyclic dependency to a lower-level module.
- **Callback** is where the module defines an abstraction that is injected into the dependent module, resulting in an implementation that resembles the Observer pattern. Using callbacks, it is possible to completely remove the dependency.

Examples of each of these three techniques are illustrated in the section "Sample."

CONSEQUENCES

Ensuring modules do not have any cyclic dependencies is vital. Never allow cyclic dependencies to creep into an application because of the significant impact these dependencies have on maintainability and reusability. The coupling caused by a cyclic dependency has severe implications.

Whenever a dependency exists between two modules, the impact of change is increased. If the two modules have a cyclic dependency, the ripple effect of change is dramatically increased. Changing one module may cause changes to all dependent modules, which in turn can cause a rather dramatic ripple effect throughout the application, and potentially across, applications. Because of this, modules with a cyclic dependency come with the same maintenance and reuse attributes of a single module. One can never be reused, built, deployed, or maintained without the other module.

Any set of modules with a direct or indirect cyclic relationship will inevitably be less reusable. To use the contents of one module, you also require the behavior of all modules it is dependent upon. Finally, cyclic relationships inhibit testability since modules involved in a cyclic dependency cannot be testing independently.

Levelize Build
pattern, 253

Levelize Modules
pattern, 157

Test Module
pattern, 263

Breaking the dependency cycles in your module structure allows you to leverage a number of other patterns. You can levelize your modules. Any cycles in the dependency structure prevents you from levelizing your application. Levelization allows you to perform a levelized build and enforce your module relationships. Levelization also facilitates testing by allowing you to create a Test Module that can verify your modules in isolation.

SAMPLE

Recall from Chapter 4, Section 4.4, the cyclic relationship between our `Customer` and `Bill` classes, which were each allocated to their respective modules, a `customer.jar` and `billing.jar`, respectively. Figure 9.2 shows the initial structure. Note the cyclic relationship between the two classes, which causes a cyclic relationship between the two modules.

Listing 9.1 shows the code for the `Bill` class. Note how the `Bill` class accepts a `Customer` instance in its constructor so that the `Bill.pay()` method can use the `Customer` class to calculate the discount.

Listing 9.1 Bill Class

```
package com.kirkk.bill;

import com.kirkk.cust.*;
```

```
import java.math.BigDecimal;

public class Bill {

   private BigDecimal chargeAmount;
   private Customer customer;

   public Bill(Customer customer,
              BigDecimal chargeAmount) {
      this.customer = customer;
      this.chargeAmount = chargeAmount;
   }
   public BigDecimal getChargeAmount() {
      return this.chargeAmount;
   }

   public BigDecimal pay() {
      BigDecimal discount = new BigDecimal(1).
         subtract(this.customer.
         getDiscountAmount()).
         setScale(2, BigDecimal.ROUND_HALF_UP);
      BigDecimal paidAmount =
         this.chargeAmount.multiply(discount).setScale(2);
      //make the payment...
      return paidAmount;
   }
}
```

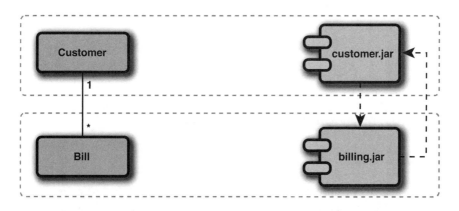

Figure 9.2 Cyclic relationship between modules

Listing 9.2 shows the code for the Customer class. Note that the Customer class has a list of Bill instances, and when the Customer .createBill(BigDecimal chargeAmount) method is called, a new Bill instance is created and added to the list. The Customer .getDiscountAmount() method is called by Bill in Listing 9.1 to calculate the customer discount, which is the reason for the cyclic relationship between Customer and Bill.

Listing 9.2 Customer Class

```
package com.kirkk.cust;

import java.util.*;
import java.math.BigDecimal;
import com.kirkk.bill.*;

public class Customer {
   private List bills;

   public BigDecimal getDiscountAmount() {
      if (bills.size() > 5) {
         return new BigDecimal(0.1);
      } else {
         return new BigDecimal(0.03);
      }
   }

   public List getBills() {
      return this.bills;
   }

   public void createBill(BigDecimal chargeAmount) {
      Bill bill = new Bill(this, chargeAmount);
      if (bills == null) {
         bills = new ArrayList();
      }
      bills.add(bill);
   }
}
```

Our goal is to break the cyclic dependency between customer.jar and billing.jar, and we're going to look at three different ways to do this.

Escalation

The first technique we apply is called *escalation*. With escalation, we break a cyclic dependency by escalating the cause of the dependency to a higher-level module. Before we do that, we need to more fully understand why a cyclic dependency exists:

> A Customer has a list of Bill instances. When the pay method on Bill is invoked, the Bill needs to determine whether a discount should be applied. The discount is a product of the Customer the bill belongs to, not necessarily the Bill. Therefore, the Bill class calls a method on Customer to determine the appropriate discount amount. Think of it this way—the Customer represents a payee, and we negotiate a discount with each Payee. The calculation of this discounted amount is encapsulated within the Customer.

The cause of the dependency centers around the discount calculation and payment of a bill. To break this dependency, we want to escalate the cause of the dependency up to a higher-level class: the **Payment-Mediator**. Figure 9.3 shows the new structure. The mediator now

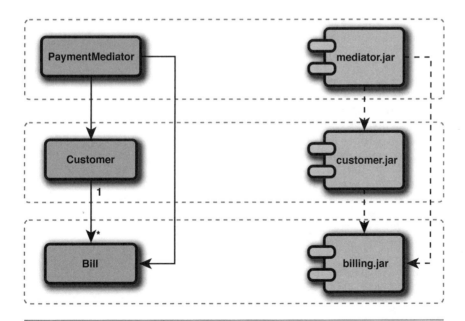

Figure 9.3 Breaking the cycle by using escalation

encapsulates calculation of the discount and passes that to the `Bill` class. Once the cycle is broken, I can modify the build script to bundle the mediator into its own module. If you dig more deeply into the class structure, you'll wonder why I didn't just pass the discount amount from `Customer` into `Bill`. Don't worry about that. This example is slightly contrived because escalation isn't the best way to solve this type of problem. The key takeaway is that we've escalated the dependency up to the `mediator.jar` bundle, breaking the cyclic dependency.

Listing 9.3 shows the code for the `PaymentMediator` class. Note the `PaymentMediator.pay(Bill bill)` and `PaymentMediator` `.getDiscount()` methods; these methods now coordinate interaction between the `Bill` and `Customer` instances, and the cyclic dependency between the modules is broken.

Listing 9.3 PaymentMediator Class

```
package com.kirkk.mediator;
import java.math.*;
import java.util.*;
import com.kirkk.cust.*;
import com.kirkk.bill.*;

public class PaymentMediator {
   private Customer customer;

   public PaymentMediator(Customer customer) {
      this.customer = customer;
   }
   public BigDecimal pay(Bill bill) {
      BigDecimal discount = new
         BigDecimal(1).
         subtract(this.getDiscountAmount()).
         setScale(2, BigDecimal.ROUND_HALF_UP);
      BigDecimal paidAmount =
         bill.getChargeAmount().multiply(discount).
         setScale(2);
      //make the payment...
      return paidAmount;
   }
   private BigDecimal getDiscountAmount() {
      if (this.customer.getBills().size() > 5) {
         return new BigDecimal(0.1);
      } else {
```

```
        return new BigDecimal(0.03);
    }
  }
}
```

Demotion

Another way to resolve a cyclic dependency is to use *demotion*. With demotion, we push the cause of the dependency to a lower-level module. Demotion is exactly the opposite of escalation. We do this by introducing a `DiscountCalculator` class that will be passed into the `Bill` class. The `Customer` class will serve as the factory for the `DiscountCalculator`, since the `Customer` knows the discount that must be applied. Figure 9.4 shows the new structure.

Listing 9.4 shows the code for the `DiscountCalculator` class. When the `Customer` class creates the `DiscountCalculator`, it will pass in the number of bills. When the `Bill.pay()` method is called, it invokes the `DiscountCalculator.getDiscountAmount()` to determine the discount amount.

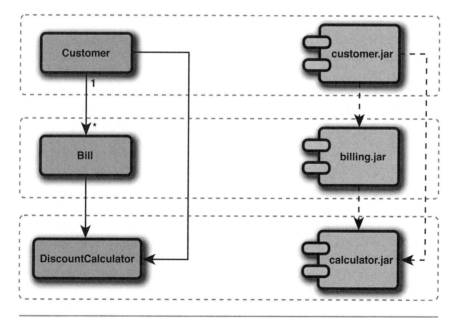

Figure 9.4 Breaking the cycle by using demotion

Listing 9.4 DiscountCalculator Class

```
package com.kirkk.calc;

import java.math.*;
import java.util.*;

public class DiscountCalculator {
    private Integer numBills;

    public DiscountCalculator(Integer numBills) {
        this.numBills = numBills;
    }

    public BigDecimal getDiscountAmount() {
        if (numBills.intValue() > 5) {
            return new BigDecimal(0.1);
        } else {
            return new BigDecimal(0.03);
        }
    }
}
```

reuse versus use, 62

Already, you can see how this is a more natural solution than escalation for this particular type of cyclic dependency problem. What's the key difference between escalation and demotion? With escalation, the logic that manages the collaboration is escalated to a higher-level entity, which can hinder usability. In this situation, reusing `billing.jar` and `customer.jar` will require another piece of code to manage the collaboration if you don't want to reuse the `PaymentMediator`. The result are modules that are more reusable but less usable. While demotion is a more natural solution in this situation, it also means that to deploy `billing.jar` or `customer.jar`, I must also deploy the `calculator .jar` module. Because you don't need to worry about writing the collaboration code, the result is a more usable solution but may sacrifice reuse. The solution chosen is always going to be contextual, and the ideal solution is likely to shift throughout the development life cycle.

Callback

Using a Callback is similar to the Observer pattern. With this approach, we'll refactor the `DiscountCalculator` class to an interface and then modify the `Customer` class to implement this interface. Figure 9.5 shows

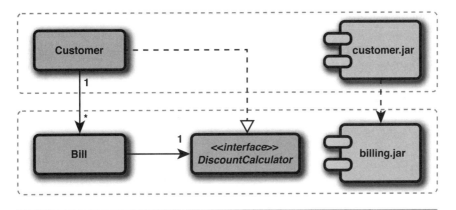

Figure 9.5 Breaking the cycle by using a Callback

this new class structure. In fact, we've already seen this example. In Section 4.4.2, we broke the cyclic dependency between `Customer` and `Bill` using a Callback.

As it happens in this specific situation, using a Callback represents a combination of demotion and our initial solution. We'll go back to passing the `Customer` into the `Bill`, but will pass it in as a `DiscountCalculator` type. Whereas in the Demotion example we bundled the `DiscountCalculator` in a separate module, we'll now just include it in our `billing.jar` module. Note that putting the `DiscountCalculator` in the `customer.jar` module would introduce the cyclic dependency we're trying to get rid of. The `DiscountCalculator` interface is quite simple, as shown in Listing 9.5.

Listing 9.5 DiscountCalculator Interface

```
package com.kirkk.bill;
import java.math.BigDecimal;
public interface DiscountCalculator {
    public BigDecimal getDiscountAmount();
}
```

WRAPPING UP

Cyclic relationships are the worst form of dependency between modules. The increased coupling that accompanies cyclic relationships hampers understanding, inhibits reuse, and increases the overall complexity of the software system. If modules have cyclic relationships, they essentially function as a single module. Either the relationships should be broken or the development team might as well combine them into a single module. If there is an absolute surrounding module design, it is that cyclic relationships between modules should be avoided at all costs.

LEVELIZE MODULES

STATEMENT

Module relationships should be levelized.

DESCRIPTION

Levelizing modules[2] demands that module relationships be acyclic. Any cycles in module relationships prevent levelization. There is a close relationship between levelized modules and Physical Layers, though the two are not the same. Physical Layers aims to create one or more modules that are functionally equivalent to the typical layers composing an application. Levelized modules are more fine-grained than physical layers. Although a typical software system may have only three or four layers, within each layer there might be multiple levels.

Physical Layers pattern, 162

To levelize modules, follow these guidelines:

- External modules are assigned level 0.
- Modules dependent only on level 0 modules are assigned level 1.
- Modules dependent on level 1 are assigned level 2.
- Modules dependent on level n are assigned level $n + 1$.

Figure 9.6 shows levelized modules. Even though the `topclient.jar` module depends on `client.jar`, a level 1 module, `topclient.jar` also depends on the `midlevel.jar` module, which is a level 2 module. Because of this, the `topclient.jar` module is a level 3 module. More generally, if a module is dependent on an $n - 1$ level module, the module is an n level module, even if it's also dependent on modules lower in the level hierarchy.

IMPLEMENTATION VARIATIONS

Levels and layers, what's the difference? Layers have much more to do with responsibility, whereas levels have much more to do with understanding the system structure, especially the dependencies. Levels are more granular than layers. Within a single layer, there might be multiple levels, but multiple layers can never exist at a single level.

---

2. Levelization is a term introduced in John Lakos's *Large-Scale C++ Software Design* (1996).

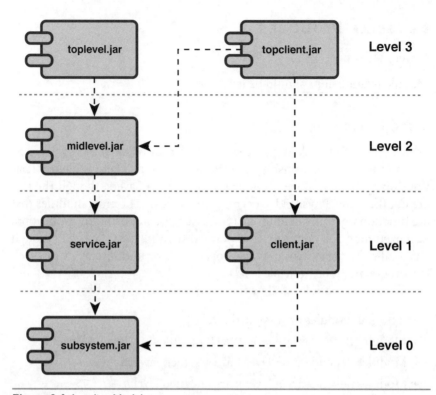

Figure 9.6 Levelize Modules

Acyclic Relationships
pattern, 146

The Levelize Modules pattern sits squarely between Physical Layers and Acyclic Relationships. Levelize Modules demands that the module structure be acyclic. If it weren't, the cycle would make it impossible to clearly identify the levels. And just discussed, levels tend to be more granular than layers.

weight and
granularity, 63

Coarse-grained modules at lower levels of the system have a significant impact on the ability to easily reuse these modules. In general, lower-level modules should have fewer outgoing dependencies and more incoming dependencies. In other words, modules in lower-level layers should be lower-level modules, and these modules should be finer grained and lighter weight than higher-level modules. Likewise, modules in higher-level layers will likely be higher-level modules, though it's perfectly acceptable for a level 1 module to exist in a higher-level layer. For instance, a UI Utility module may have no outgoing dependencies and therefore be a level 1 module but exist in the UI layer because of its behavior.

An especially important piece of criteria to consider when levelizing modules is whether you'll allow module relationships to span levels. With strict levelization, modules can reference other modules only in the level directly beneath it. With relaxed levelization, modules can reference other modules in any level beneath it. The decision to enforce a strict levelization scheme over allowing a relaxed scheme will have a significant architectural impact. In theory, a strict scheme might seem better, but in practice a relaxed scheme is easier. A mixture of the two is likely most pragmatic, and it must be a conscious decision each time you decide to allow a module to reference another modules more than one layer beneath it.

CONSEQUENCES

Levelization can provide insight to the complexity of dependencies. For instance, a level 5 module found in the data access layer indicates a rather complex set of dependencies for a module that is likely heavily used throughout the system. Excessive dependencies in lower-level modules have the greatest capacity to increase overall cost of maintaining a system. A good candidate for refactoring, perhaps!

Levelize Modules also offer the opportunity to perform a levelized build. If a team cannot easily identify the levels within the system, the only opportunity to perform a levelized build exists across the physical layers, which may not offer the flexibility necessary. For very large and complex systems, a levelized build might be necessary to keep build time fast, which is especially important for teams practicing continuous integration.

Levelize Build pattern, 253

Levelization also helps improve module testability. Test Modules can be used to create a test module for each module, and the levelization will provide guidance on the module test strategy. Lower-level modules are inherently easier to test than higher-level modules because they lack the complex dependency structure. For instance, modules in the UI layer can be perceived as more difficult to test independently because we have to create mocks and stubs for all of their dependencies. But a level 1 module in the UI layer indicates no outgoing dependencies and therefore provides insight to how easy the module will be to bring under test.

Test Module pattern, 263

Levelization improves ability to understand the system structure. The team has the ability to extract and understand the module relationships in a large software system, allowing us to efficiently and accurately verify throughout the development life cycle that these dependencies are

understanding module relationships, 58

consistent with our overall architectural vision. Levelization also provides insight to how reusable modules are. For example, reusing a level 3 module comes with the implicit knowledge that one or more level 2 and one or more level 1 modules must also be included in the application.

reuse versus use, 62   Levelization can serve as the foundation for an enterprise reuse strategy. Look at it this way: If modules are levelized, lower-level modules are inherently easier to reuse because they have no outgoing dependencies. Because they have no outgoing dependencies, we can build these modules independent of the rest of the system. This separate build means that the module can evolve independently. Development of the module can exist outside the context of the application, in parallel with other modules. Each time the module is built, it can be included as part of the application.

SAMPLE

As mentioned, levelizing modules is slightly different than physical layers. Figure 9.7 illustrates this difference. As shown, the levels don't necessarily coincide with layers. At least, a single layer isn't necessarily confined to contain a specific set of levels. The `billpayutils.jar` module is in the control layer based on the set of responsibilities it provides. However, it lacks dependence on any level 3 or level 4 modules in the domain layer. Even though the `billpayutils.jar` module is in the control layer and it's a level 2 module, its only dependency is on the level 1 `dbutils.jar` module.

Because the modules are levelized, we now have the opportunity to perform a levelized build, and we can more clearly understand build order. The level 1 `dbutils.jar` module must be built first. Once finished, possibly as part of a completely separate build, the `billdata.jar` and `findata.jar` modules can be built. Yet so, too, can the `billpayutils.jar` module, even though it's in the Control Layer. Unless we understand module levelization, the opportunity to maximize the efficiency of the build may be lost.

WRAPPING UP

Levelize Modules sit squarely between Acyclic Relationships and Physical Layers. If the module structure is acyclic, then module relationships can be levelized. Levelization helps you understand the dependency structure of the application, and its benefits include build optimization, reuse, ease of testing, and a clear understanding of system structure.

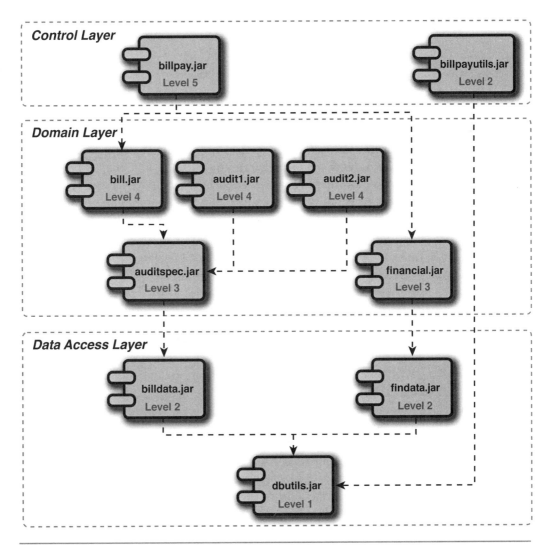

Figure 9.7 Levelize Modules and Physical Layers

PHYSICAL LAYERS

STATEMENT

Module relationships should not violate the conceptual layers.

DESCRIPTION

When designing a software system of moderate to high complexity, it's common for developers to separate the presentation, business logic, and data access into distinct layers. Each layer should be responsible for a functional aspect of the application. The most common layering scheme is a three-layer approach consisting of presentation, business logic, and data access. The presentation layer is responsible for structuring and rendering the user interface. A business logic, or domain, layer is responsible for containing the business objects, and a data access layer is responsible for encapsulating access to the persistent data store and external systems. Typically, you'll apply certain patterns to each layer, such as MVC in the presentation layer and DAO in the data access layer, contributing to a well-defined set of functionality within each layer. Such logical separation of functionality can help ease maintenance of the application.

example of different types of reuse, 70

Acyclic Relationships pattern, 146

Functionally separating your application into logical layers is not enough, though. One of the oft-cited advantages of separating the application into various layers is to allow you to reuse the functionality exposed by lower layers. For instance, if you're developing a Web application, you may find a need to reuse the business logic within another Web application, or possibly even a batch style application. To achieve this, you cannot logically divide your layers based only on behavior, but you can also physically separate the layers structurally. Figure 9.8 shows the allowable structural relationships between the physical layers. Note that it's important that Acyclic Relationships exist between the modules.

IMPLEMENTATION VARIATIONS

Acyclic Relationships pattern, 146

To effectively divide your application into Physical Layers, your modules must exhibit Acyclic Relationships. Because you cannot reuse any module without all dependent modules, cycles in the relationships between the modules in the physical layers prevents you from achieving the structural separation you want. This holds true regardless of how well you've logically separated the behavioral aspects of your application.

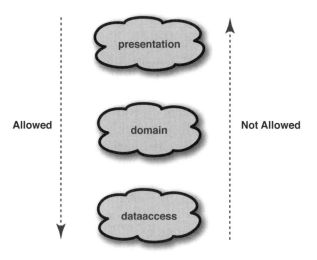

Figure 9.8 Allowable relationship between physical layers

An important consideration when defining your physical structure is whether you'll use a strict or relaxed layering scheme. With a strict layering scheme, upper-level layers communicate only with the layer directly beneath them. With a relaxed scheme, upper-level layers can use directly any layer underneath them. A strict layering scheme brings greater clarity to the structure of the application but can also result in inefficiencies since code may need to be duplicated or pass through methods used for upper-level layers to leverage the desired behavior.

Strict and Relaxed Levelization, 159

Don't try to exactly define your physical structure based upon what you think you might want to reuse. This predictive form of reuse typically doesn't work very well, and you'll wind up with a bunch of modules where not one can be used independent of others. Instead, start with fewer modules, carefully managing the relationships between them, and break apart the modules as you find you need reuse. It's okay to start with a single module that represents each layer. As the application grows, maintain the physical layers and break apart the coarse-grained modules representing each layer to multiple finer-grained modules that compose each layer. Levelizing modules can help maintain an understanding of system structure. Don't be afraid to refactor to more flexible module relationships when you find the need.

Levelize Modules pattern, 157

CONSEQUENCES

Physical Layers
pattern, 162

Test Module
pattern, 263

Separating your physical layers helps ease some kinds of maintenance. For instance, changes to the presentation layout are isolated to a single level. Behavioral changes to your business logic are also isolated. However, some types of changes are difficult to isolate. Adding new columns to a database table that must be displayed on the user interface is typically going to require changes across all of the layers. But the value in separating your Physical Layers is still useful because managing these changes is much easier. Test Module can be used to independently test the changes made in a specific layer, allowing you to ensure that your modification functions as expected before changing the other levels.

If you are lucky enough to have isolated change to a single layer, instead of deploying the entire application, you have the option of deploying only the physical module that has changed. This type of deploy can be especially useful if there are multiple applications that use the module that has changed. Instead of deploying each application in its entirety, you can deploy only the module that has changed.

Levelize Build
pattern, 253

other tools for
modular design, 106

It's much easier to enforce physical separation than it is logical separation. You may have a wonderful initial class structure that appears to be functionally separated. But how do you enforce and maintain this logical separation as the system grows? If even a single violation of your logical layers creeps into your structure, the entire logical layer structure is compromised. While tools such as JDepend can help enforce logical separation, it's still cumbersome to enforce. On the other hand, the separation between physical layers can be strictly enforced by performing a levelized build.

reuse versus
use, 62

In general, logical separation of classes into layers helps ease maintenance. But, physical separation helps you increase reusability, because a module is a deployable entity that can be reused.

SAMPLE

It's common when developing business applications to separate your application into three layers. The presentation layer is responsible for structuring and rendering the user interface. A business logic, or domain, layer is responsible for containing the business objects, and a data access layer is responsible for encapsulating access to the persistent data store and external systems.

The business objects in the business logic layer are typically constructed using a combination of key values and data provided by the user interface in conjunction with data retrieved from a persistent datastore. In Web applications, presentation frameworks, such as Struts, help shield the developer from working with various HTTP request objects and instead pass the data from a page using an **ActionForm**, which is a POJO. It would seem, therefore, that there could be little harm in using the **ActionForm** to help build the business object.

Consider an enterprise billing application that allows users to pay bills through a Web interface. A bill can enter the system via two mechanisms. Smaller customers typically send their bills through standard mail, and the user keys the data off the bill into a Web interface and saves the information to a database. Large customers send their bills electronically by using a standard electronic data interchange (EDI) format. The EDI feed is processed by a batch application that runs nightly and saves the bills to the database. Regardless of the input mechanism, all bills must pass through the same set of validation rules before being saved. Certainly, we want to avoid replicating the domain logic and persistence mechanism across the Web and batch applications.

From the Web world, the **Bill** instance is typically created using a **billid** that is passed from a JSP page via an **ActionForm**. Initially, it may seem feasible to simply pass the **ActionForm** to the **Bill** instance and allow the **Bill** to use the key value to initialize itself. Knowing that I'm likely going to need flexibility in how I load the data for **Bill** instances, I create a **BillEntityLoader** interface that is passed to the **Bill** class when a **Bill** instance is requested. Listing 9.6 shows this **Bill** class.

Listing 9.6 Bill Class

```
package com.extensiblejava.bill;
import com.extensiblejava.audit.*;
import com.extensiblejava.financial.*;
import java.math.*;
import com.extensiblejava.bill.data.*;
public class Bill {
   private BillDataBean billData;
   public static Bill loadBill(BillEntityLoader loader) {
      return loader.loadBill();
   }
   public Bill(BillDataBean billData) {
      this.billData = billData;
   }
```

```
      public String getBillId() {
         return this.billData.getBillId().toString();
      }
      public String getName() {
         return this.billData.getName();
      }
      public BigDecimal getAmount() {
         return this.billData.getAmount();
      }
      public BigDecimal getPaidAmount() {
         return this.billData.getPaidAmount();
      }
      public void pay() {
         if (this.billData.getPaidAmount() == null) {
            Payment payer = new Payment();
            this.billData.setPaidAmount(
               payer.generateDraft(this));
            this.persist();
         }
      }
      private void persist() {
         BillDb.update(billData);
      }
}
```

The `BillEntityLoader` accepts the `BillDetailForm`, which extends the Struts `ActionForm`, so that it can use the `billId` to retrieve the appropriate information for the `Bill` being created. While not shown, we'll assume the appropriate Struts action class is instantiating the `DefaultBillEntityLoader` and passing it to the `loadBill` method. The `DefaultBillEntityLoader` loads the `BillData-Bean` from the database, as shown in Listing 9.7.

Listing 9.7 DefaultBillEntityLoader

```
package com.extensiblejava.bill;
import com.extensiblejava.bill.data.*;
import com.extensiblejava.ui.BillDetailForm;
public class DefaultBillEntityLoader implements
   BillEntityLoader {
   private BillDetailForm billForm;
   public DefaultBillEntityLoader(BillDetailForm billForm) {
      this.billForm = billForm;
   }
```

```
    public Bill loadBill() {
        BillDataBean billBean = BillDb.getBill(new
Integer(this.billForm.getBillId()));
        return new Bill(billBean);
    }
}
```

At first glance, this structure seems sensible. The `Bill` class depends upon an abstract `BillEntityLoader` and is therefore effectively decoupled from any concrete implementations. Therefore, the `Bill` class can use different implementations of `BillEntityLoader`, and the design seems flexible. However, as shown in Figure 9.9, the `DefaultBillEntityLoader` being passed to the `Bill` is dependent on the `BillDetailForm`, which extends the Struts `ActionForm` class. This relationship results in a cyclic dependency with the `ui.jar` module and effectively couples the `bill.jar` module to both the `ui.jar` and `struts.jar` modules.

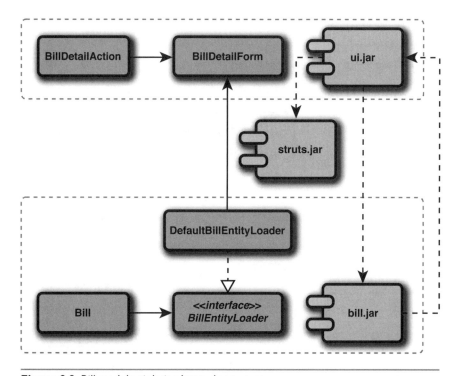

Figure 9.9 Bill module violating layered structure

Although we have a flexible class design that is nicely layered, our module structure is not layered and ultimately prohibits us from reusing the `bill.jar` module without these other modules.

In this situation, the remedy is simple. Because our `Bill` is coupled to the `BillEntityLoader` interface, and not the concrete implementation of the `DefaultBillEntityLoader`, we can `SeparateAbstractions` and refactor by escalating the `DefaultBillEntityLoader` to the `ui.jar` module. Upon doing so, the `bill.jar` is now completely independent of Struts, as illustrated in Figure 9.10.

It's worth mentioning that, in this example, we could have gotten away with leaving the `DefaultBillEntityLoader` in the `bill.jar` module. Since the `BillDetailForm` extends only the `ActionForm`, which is a POJO, it won't attempt to use any Struts-specific functionality that is tied to a J2EE container. Therefore, our batch application would have likely worked fine since the default `ClassLoader` for our batch application would likely have never come across a situation where it tried to load

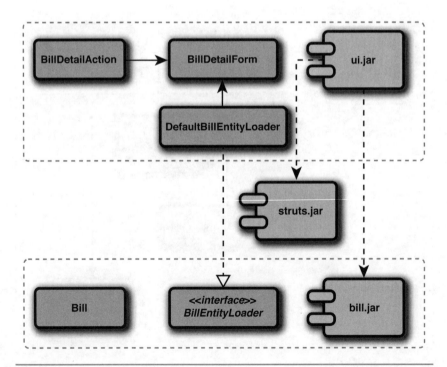

Figure 9.10 Correct layered structure

a class specific to the container, such as `HttpServletRequest`. However, it's confusing to require deploying the `struts.jar` module with our batch application; it has a bad smell and increases the risk of strange errors at runtime. We talked about this exact scenario when discussing Manage Relationships.

WRAPPING UP

Layering your application is a common architectural pattern. When layering an application, it's important to separate behavior as discrete and granular modules, but it's also important to separate the layers structurally. A flexible class design that adheres to a layered structure can be compromised if our module structure isn't layered as well. Unfortunately, it can be incredibly difficult to identify violations in the layered module structure. One way to help enforce the structure is through a levelized build. Tools can also help.

Levelize Build pattern, 253

CONTAINER INDEPENDENCE

STATEMENT

Modules should be independent of the runtime container.

DESCRIPTION

weight and granularity, 63

EJB, 24

Modules with excessive runtime container dependencies are heavyweight modules that cannot execute outside the confines of the runtime container. A good example of a heavyweight technology is Enterprise JavaBeans (EJB), and the meteoric rise in popularity of lighter-weight frameworks, such as Spring, are the direct result of the shortcomings of heavyweight technologies. While lightweight modules are not container dependent, they are still able to leverage the infrastructure capabilities (e.g., security, transactions) of the container. Lightweight modules with no container dependencies have two significant advantages.

Test Module pattern, 263

- **They are portable across runtime environments**: For instance, a lightweight module can be deployed in a Java EE environment, but it can also run directly atop the JVM. Or, a module might be designed to work in a runtime supporting OSGi, but it can also function if an OSGi framework isn't available.

- **They are testable**: Because they lack environmental dependencies, they can be tested in isolation, outside the confines of the environment to which they'll ultimately be deployed.

Additionally, it's easy to argue that lighter-weight modules are also easier to maintain, since their contents aren't polluted with excessive dependencies on infrastructure capabilities. Developing lightweight modules demands that container dependencies be abstracted away. Figure 9.11 illustrates how the `client.jar` module is made independent of the `runtime.jar` module through the use of the `abstraction.jar` module, which encapsulates the container dependencies and coordinates the interaction of `client.jar` module in the runtime environment. As a result, the `Client` class will have no dependencies on the `runtime.jar` or the `abstraction.jar` modules' APIs.

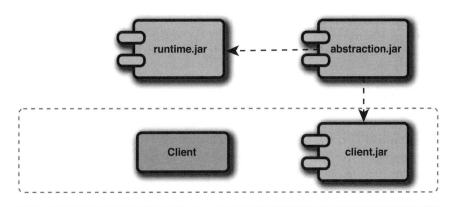

Figure 9.11 Container Independence

IMPLEMENTATION VARIATIONS

External Configuration can be used to configure a module so that it operates correctly in a specific runtime environment. In these situations, External Configuration is a pattern that is used to achieve Container Independence since the configuration dependencies are moved to an external configuration file. A superseding framework then manages module configuration. However, there are subtle differences between External Configuration and Container Independence. External Configuration is used to configure a module so that it can be used across contexts. Container Independence is leveraged to ensure a module is portable across containers.

External Configuration pattern, 200

For instance, configuring a module with a user ID and password combination so that it can be used to access different database instances is an example of External Configuration, not Container Independence. Although it's poor practice, hard-coding the user ID and password combination wouldn't create dependencies on any runtime container, though obviously would limit the context in which the module could be reused.

In many cases, developers don't need to roll their own code to abstract away the container dependencies. Instead, a framework such as Spring is used. The most common mechanism to achieve Container Independence is through dependency injection, where a module's dependencies are injected at runtime. Many dependency injection frameworks also provide important infrastructure capabilities that help ensure the module remains container independent. For instance, in the following example

OSGi, 271

that uses Spring DM, the framework provides dependency injection capabilities but also provides critical functionality surrounding OSGi service management.

CONSEQUENCES

Container Independence ensures that a module is portable across runtime environment because the infrastructure behavior is separate from module behavior. The Spring framework is an example of a framework that helps you create lightweight modules. Because the infrastructure code is encapsulated by the framework, there is less likelihood that errors will arise related to infrastructure. In general, application code is easier to write, maintain, and port across runtime environments, and the amount of infrastructure code a developer needs to write is much less.

Test Module pattern, 263

Container Independence also increases the ease of testing a module because there are no container dependencies to contend with. A Test Module can verify module behavior without also testing the infrastructure code.

While Container Independence provides significant benefits that enable testing and increases portability across a variety of different runtime environments, it can also result in complex infrastructure code that is challenging to write and manage. When a dependency injection framework is used, XML configuration files tend to proliferate. Fortunately, the trade-off is often worth the benefit.

SAMPLE

Let's consider two simple modules: a `client.jar` and a `service.jar`, as illustrated in Figure 9.12. These modules leverage OSGi to obtain runtime support for modularity. Also shown is a configuration file that will be used to help us realize Container Independence.

Listing 9.8 illustrates the start method of a class in the service module that is registered as an OSGi service, enabling other classes to discover the class when requesting the service. As shown, the code is heavily dependent on the OSGi framework, and this prohibits the code from being used outside the context of an OSGi runtime.

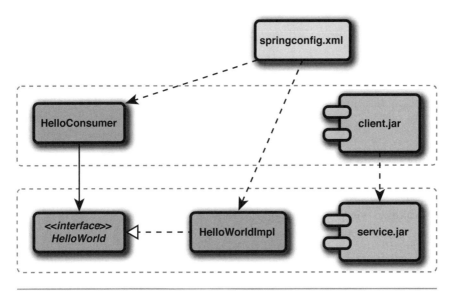

Figure 9.12 Simple client module using a service module

Listing 9.8 Heavy Container Dependencies

```
import java.util.Properties;
import com.extensiblejava.hello.service.HelloService;
import org.osgi.framework.BundleActivator;
import org.osgi.framework.BundleContext;
import org.osgi.framework.ServiceListener;
import org.osgi.framework.ServiceEvent;
import org.osgi.framework.ServiceRegistration;

public class HelloServiceImpl implements
   HelloService, BundleActivator {

   private ServiceRegistration registration;

   public void start(BundleContext context) {
      Properties props = new Properties();
      props.put("Language", "English");
      registration =
         context.registerService(
         HelloService.class.getName(),
         this, props);
      }
```

```
        public String sayHello() {
        return "Hello World!! ";
    }

    public String sayGoodbye() {
        return "Goodbye World!!";
    }
}
```

Any client that hopes to use this class that has been registered with the OSGi service registry also needs to leverage the OSGi framework. Listing 9.2 illustrates a sample client in the client module that interacts with OSGi to obtain a reference to the service registered in Listing 9.9.

Listing 9.9 Heavyweight Client

```
package com.extensiblejava.hello.client;

import com.extensiblejava.hello.service.HelloService;

import org.osgi.framework.BundleActivator;
import org.osgi.framework.BundleContext;
import org.osgi.framework.ServiceReference;
import org.osgi.util.tracker.ServiceTracker;

public class HelloConsumer implements BundleActivator {

    private ServiceTracker helloWorldTracker;
    private HelloService helloService;

    public void setService(HelloService helloService) {
        this.helloService = helloService;
    }

    public void removeService() {
        this.helloService = null;
    }

    public void start(BundleContext context)
        throws Exception {
        helloWorldTracker = new ServiceTracker(context,
            HelloService.class.getName(), null);
        helloWorldTracker.open();
        HelloService hello = (HelloService)
        helloWorldTracker.getService();
```

```
        if (hello == null) {
            System.out.println(
      "Hello service unavailable on HelloConsumer start");
        } else {
            System.out.println(hello.sayHello());
        }
    }

    public void stop(BundleContext context) {
        HelloService hello = (HelloService)
      helloWorldTracker.getService();
        if (hello == null) {
            System.out.println(
      "Hello service unavailable on HelloConsumer stop");
        } else {
            System.out.println(hello.sayGoodbye());
        }

        helloWorldTracker.close();
    }
}
```

The heavyweight nature of this code prevents it from being used outside the context of the OSGi framework and also prohibits unit testing. Keeping our exact same module structure, as illustrated in Figure 9.12, we leverage Spring DM to remove all dependencies on the OSGi framework. Listings 9.10 and 9.11 show the updated code that leverages Spring DM, illustrating that all OSGi dependencies have been removed. To achieve this, we need to deploy the Spring DM modules to the OSGi runtime and have also introduced the appropriate configuration file that informs Spring DM how to treat these modules. Listing 9.12 shows the configuration file.

Listing 9.10 Independent HelloServiceImpl Class

```
package com.extensiblejava.hello.service.impl;

import java.util.Properties;
import com.extensiblejava.hello.service.HelloService;

public class HelloServiceImpl implements HelloService {

    public String sayHello() {
        return "Hello OSGi Spring World!! ";
    }
```

```
    public String sayGoodbye() {
        return "Goodbye OSGi Spring World!!";
    }
}
```

Listing 9.11 Independent Consumer Class

```
package com.extensiblejava.hello.client;

import com.extensiblejava.hello.service.HelloService;

public class HelloConsumer {
    private HelloService hello;

    public void setHelloService(HelloService hello) {
        this.hello = hello;
    }

    public void start() throws Exception {
        System.out.println(hello.sayHello());
    }

    public void stop() throws Exception {
        System.out.println(hello.sayGoodbye());
    }

}
```

Listing 9.12 Spring XML Configuration File

```
<osgi:reference id="helloService" interface="com.
extensiblejava.hello.service.HelloService"/>

<bean name="helloConsumer" class="com.extensiblejava.hello.
client.HelloConsumer"
        init-method="start" destroy-method="stop">
        <property name="helloService" ref="helloService"/>
</bean>
```

WRAPPING UP

Container dependencies result in heavyweight modules that are difficult to reuse and maintain. Eliminating these dependencies helps improve the ease with which modules can be tested. Modules with no container dependencies are also portable across runtime environments and can be used in a variety of different contexts. Dependency injection is a common technique used to help ensure modules aren't container dependent.

INDEPENDENT DEPLOYMENT

STATEMENT

Modules should be independently deployable units.

DESCRIPTION

outgoing dependencies, 116

Cohesive Modules, 139

For a module to be independently deployable, it cannot have any outgoing dependencies on any other module. Some modules are naturally more independent than others. For instance, it would be relatively easy to create an independent module to perform various mathematical and statistical functions, mainly because there are few external forces that impact how the module needs to behave. However, you cannot always expect to eliminate all outgoing dependencies. In most interesting systems, cohesive modules collaborate and work together to provide the complex behavior exhibited by business applications, and there are many more forces that can affect how an object behaves. Although we strive to reduce coupling as much as possible, some coupling must exist in order for a network of objects to work together. Without some coupling, your system would not be interesting.

Given that some degree of coupling is necessary, it's also likely that collaborating objects are spread throughout and across many different modules. To obtain high degrees of maintainability, and a glimmer of hope for reusability, it's important to minimize the coupling between modules.

IMPLEMENTATION VARIATIONS

Abstract Modules pattern, 222

Modules need to interact because it's the sum of these interactions that result in a system's desired behavior. If it's required that two modules must interact, you can create an interface or abstract class within a module that defines the dependent module's extension points. Implementations can be plugged into the module at runtime. This will eliminate compile-time dependencies and offers significant flexibility at runtime, since a module can work with many different implementations.

External Configuration pattern, 200

There are two ways to wire together modules at runtime when the modules have no compile-time dependencies. First, you can use a factory to programmatically wire them by configuring the classes of a module with implementations that implement or extend an abstraction defined by the module. Another way is to externalize the wiring using External Configuration.

Acyclic Relationships introduces escalation, demotion, and callback, which are three different ways to break cyclic relationships among modules. Escalation and callback can also be used to break a dependency altogether. Since demotion pushes the dependency to a lower-level module, it cannot be used to break a dependency, though it can be used to reduce the weight of a module.

Acyclic Relationships pattern, 146

A driving force behind the need to make a module independently deployable is how frequently a module is reused. Modules not intended for reuse don't need their dependencies managed as carefully. It's important to balance techniques that manage dependencies with techniques to maintain simplicity. Favoring simplicity initially will make a module easier to use, while a more flexible design will help increase reuse.

reuse versus use, 62

This isn't to say that dependency management is less important for these modules. But if you're not planning to reuse the module, the driving force behind dependency management becomes maintainability. And when you want higher degrees of maintainability, your best option is to usually focus on testability.

The problem we'll quickly encounter with developing reusable modules is that it's very difficult to create a reusable module until that module has been used a number of different times in a variety of different contexts. Do you attempt to develop a module so that's it's reusable right away, or do you design the module only for its initial use and then refactor that module as additional reuse is necessary? The challenge in designing a reusable module initially is that you are forced to predict how others are going to want to use that module. You'll find that you're either paralyzing your development by attempting to fight through problems to which you cannot yet know the answer or, worse yet, that you're solving the wrong problems altogether.

architectural flexibility, 33

Instead of attempting to predict reuse, develop the module for its specific initial need, and as other uses are identified and known, modify the module to accommodate these needs by applying various patterns. While not perfect, you'll find it's easier to take something simple that works and make it work better than it is to take something that is insanely complex and difficult to understand and try to reuse it. It's likely you're going to find that you have to modify the module anyway, resulting in the same type of refactoring that you'd do with a simpler approach, except that your refactoring is going to be more difficult because of the initial complexity. To summarize, it's better to start simple and grow the module as the need arises rather than starting complex based on a perceived need.

CONSEQUENCES

reuse versus use, 62

A large number of module dependencies are costly. They inhibit reusability and restrict testability. But independence comes with its own price. It can make your module harder for other developers to use, and that can be frustrating. Of course, the complexity incurred because of the additional flexibility isn't all bad, since without the flexibility, other developers wouldn't have the option of using the module since it wouldn't give them the behavior they need anyway.

Levelize Modules pattern, 157

flexibility breeds complexity, 34

In most situations, you'll want to make sure that most modules are as independently deployable as possible. This is especially important for lower-level modules. Taken to an extreme, you could make almost every module in your application stand-alone. However, the complexity such a solution would require likely will outweigh any advantage.

SAMPLE

Let's consider a payroll system where an `Employee` class has a `pay` method on it that will calculate the pay for that instance of `Employee`. The `pay` method needs to interact with a legacy payroll system that feeds a downstream financials system, generates a paystub, and stores an image of the paystub in an enterprise document management system. Figure 9.13 shows the diagram for this system.

In the `Employee` class shown in Listing 9.13, we import the `Payroll` class, which is the facade to the legacy payroll system. For the sake of example, I've kept the `pay` method simple, but there could many other aspects to the pay method that we'd want to test.

Listing 9.13 Employee Class with Payroll Import

```
package com.extensiblejava.employee;
import com.extensiblejava.payroll.Payroll;
import java.math.*;
public class Employee {
    private Name name;
```

```
    private BigDecimal salary;
    public Employee(Name name, BigDecimal salary) {
        this.name = name;
        this.salary = salary;
    }
    public PayCheck pay() {
        Payroll payroll = new Payroll(salary);
        return new PayCheck(payroll.run());
    }
}
```

About all that I can do is test that the **PayCheck** is not null, since I don't know what to expect back from the **Payroll** system. To check for a specific value, I'd be required to understand the payroll calculation process, which I'm not interested in when testing only the **Employee**. Listing 9.14 shows the **EmployeeTest** class.

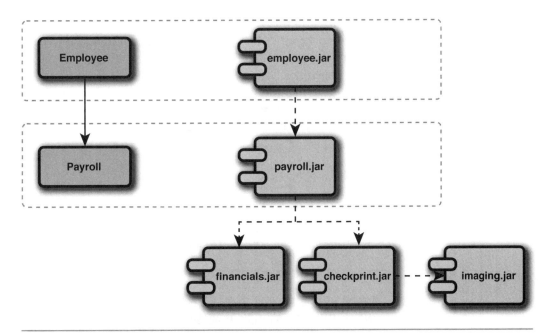

Figure 9.13 Initial diagram for an employee payroll system

Listing 9.14 EmployeeTest Class

```
package com.extensiblejava.test;
import junit.framework.TestCase;
import com.extensiblejava.employee.*;
import java.math.BigDecimal;
   public class EmployeeTest extends TestCase {
      public static void main(String[] args) {
         junit.textui.TestRunner.run(EmployeeTest.class);
      }
   public void testEmployeePay() {
      Employee employee = new Employee(new Name(),
         new BigDecimal("20000.00"));
      PayCheck payCheck = employee.pay();
      assertNotNull(payCheck);
   }
}
```

At this point, I'm not able to reuse `Employee` without also bringing along `Payroll` and all of its dependencies. In other words, reusing the **employee.jar** module requires all other modules. Ultimately,
this design has some pretty severe limitations. To clean things up, I want
to eliminate the dependency of my `Employee` class, and more importantly my **employee.jar** module, on the legacy payroll system. To do
this, I create an interface named `PayrollRunner` that represents the
`Employee` view of how pay must be calculated. The `PayrollRunner`
interface, shown in Listing 9.15, is in the **employee.jar** module.

Listing 9.15 PayrollRunner Interface

```
package com.extensiblejava.employee;
import java.math.BigDecimal;
public interface PayrollRunner {
   public BigDecimal runPayroll(BigDecimal salary);
}
```

Now, instead of `Employee` using the `Payroll` class directly, as it
did previously, I'll inject an implementation of the `PayrollRunner`
into the **pay** method of `Employee`, as shown in Listing 9.16.

Listing 9.16 Employee Class with PayrollRunner Injected

```
package com.extensiblejava.employee;
import java.math.*;
public class Employee {
   private Name name;
   private BigDecimal salary;
   public Employee(Name name, BigDecimal salary) {
      this.name = name;
      this.salary = salary;
   }
   public PayCheck pay(PayrollRunner runner) {
      return new PayCheck(runner.runPayroll(this.salary));
   }
}
```

The class implementing the `PayrollRunner` interface is the `PayFacade` class, which has been place in the new `payfacade.jar` module and which controls the interaction with the legacy payroll system. Essentially, the initial dependency between the `employee.jar` module and the `payroll.jar` module has been escalated. Figure 9.14 shows the final module diagram. *escalation and callback, 147*

Listing 9.17 shows the `PayFacade` class.

Listing 9.17 PayFacade Class

```
package com.extensiblejava.facade;
import com.extensiblejava.employee.*;
import com.extensiblejava.payroll.*;
import java.math.BigDecimal;
public class PayFacade implements PayrollRunner {
   public BigDecimal runPayroll(BigDecimal salary) {
      Payroll payroll = new Payroll(salary);
      return payroll.run();
   }
}
```

This eliminates any outgoing dependency of my `employee.jar` module, making it an independent module. It's also a bit easier to test my `Employee` class, and ultimately my `employee.jar` module, since I'm not forced to also test the heavier-weight payroll process in conjunction with `Employee`. I'm also able to create a mock implementation of

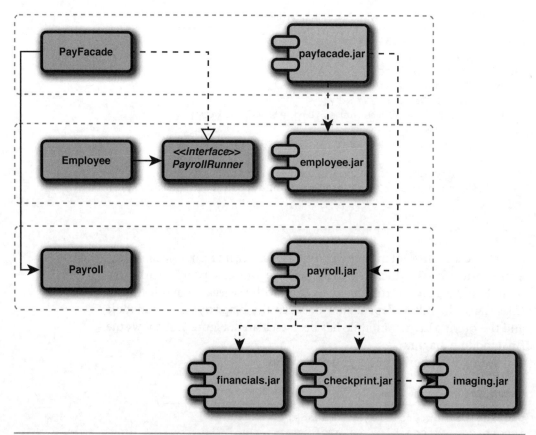

Figure 9.14 Diagram with independent employee modules

the `PayrollRunner` that can be used in the test case, as shown in Listing 9.18.

Listing 9.18 EmployeeTest Class with PayrollRunner

```
package com.extensiblejava.test;
import junit.framework.TestCase;
import com.extensiblejava.employee.*;
import java.math.BigDecimal;
public class EmployeeTest extends TestCase {
    public static void main(String[] args) {
        junit.textui.TestRunner.run(EmployeeTest.class);
    }
```

```
public void testEmployeePay() {
    PayrollRunner runner = new PayrollRunner() {
        public BigDecimal runPayroll(BigDecimal salary) {
            return new BigDecimal("500.00");
        }
    };
    Employee employee = new Employee(new Name(),
        new BigDecimal("20000.00"));
    PayCheck payCheck = employee.pay(runner);
    assertEquals(payCheck.getPay(),
        new BigDecimal("500.00"));
    }
}
```

There are two interesting comments regarding the structure. First, we've used the `PayrollRunner` to allow the `Employee` class to call back on the implementation when the pay calculation must be performed. Second, by using this callback, we have eliminated any relationship between `Employee` and `Payroll`. Note that we could have placed the `PayrollRunner` implementation in the `payroll.jar` module. However, this would have created a dependency from `Payroll` to `Employee`, which may be undesirable. To this end, the relationship between `Payroll` and `Employee` has been escalated to the `payfacade.jar` module.

WRAPPING UP

It's not possible for every module in your software system to maintain its independence. Some degree of coupling between modules is always necessary for any complex system. However, some modules are better reuse candidates than others, and it's these modules where we should focus our efforts. Because we don't always recognize which modules these might be early in the development life cycle, it's likely that we'll need to refactor using some of the other patterns in the book to increase the independence of those modules.

REFERENCE

Lakos, John. 1996. *Large-Scale C++ Software Design*. Reading, MA: Addison-Wesley.

USABILITY 10 PATTERNS

Although coupling is an important measurement, cohesion is equally important. It's easy to create and manage module dependencies if I throw all of my classes in a couple of JAR files. But in doing so, I've introduced a maintenance nightmare. In this chapter, we'll see patterns that help ensure our modules are cohesive units that balance reuse with use. It's interesting that you'll find some contention between the dependency patterns and usability patterns. I talk about this contention, what you can do to manage it, and when you want to do it. The usability patterns include the following:

- **Published Interface**: Makes a module's published interface well known.
- **External Configuration**: Modules should be externally configurable.
- **Default Implementation**: Provide modules with a default implementation.
- **Module Facade**: Create a facade serving as a coarse-grained entry point to another fine-grained module's underlying implementation.

PUBLISHED INTERFACE

STATEMENT

Make a module's published interface well known.

DESCRIPTION

design
encapsulation, 37

A module should encapsulate implementation details so that other modules do not need to understand how a module is implemented in order to leverage the capabilities of the module. Ideally, a module will expose an application programming interface (API) that other modules are able to use to interact with the module. The API that a module exposes should also be easy to understand. A module's API is its published interface. More formally, a module's published interface is defined as the following:

> A Published Interface consists of the public methods within the public classes within the exported packages that other modules are able to invoke.

Unfortunately, Java doesn't allow you to define a module's exported packages, so enforcing a published interface using standard Java is not possible. Because of this shortcoming of the Java language, a module's published interface is polluted by other public methods on public classes within a module.

In Figure 10.1, the operations defined on the `Service` interface in the `service.jar` module represents the module's published interface. The `ServiceImpl` class provides the implementation. The `Client` class within the `client.jar` module receives a reference to an instance of the `Service` interface type and therefore cannot invoke public methods on `ServiceImpl` that aren't defined on `Service`. Of course, downcasting to `ServiceImpl` would allow the `Client` class to invoke the `method3` operation. It's easy to see why enforcing a published interface using standard Java is not possible.[1]

---

1. It's not possible with standard Java. But with a framework like OSGi, it works beautifully.

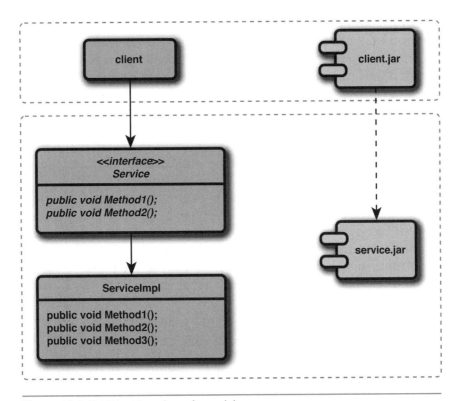

Figure 10.1 Published Interface of a module

IMPLEMENTATION VARIATIONS

There are two ways to use standard Java to enforce restricting access to methods within a module:

- Define a method as private within a class by using the private visibility modifier on the method definition.
- Define a class as private within a package by using no visibility modifier on the class declaration.

Each of these approaches have limitations if our desire is to allow all other classes within a module to invoke a method but prohibit access to the method from outside the module. Let's see an example.

In Figure 10.1, there is no way to enforce restricting access to the public methods on the `ServiceImpl` class if we want to provide access to those methods to all other classes within the `service.jar` module. If `method3` is public, consumers of `service.jar` are able to cast any instances of type `Service` down to a `ServiceImpl` type and invoke `method3`. Revising the method definition of `method3` so that it's private will not work either, since no other class within the `service.jar` module would be able to invoke it. Finally, we could limit visibility of the `ServiceImpl` class by making it private, but that doesn't absolutely enforce encapsulation either, as we demonstrated in the example in Section 4.4.1. All of our options to define a published interface using standard Java are suboptimal.

Using standard Java, the easiest way to prevent external classes from accessing a class or method you do not want published is to use interfaces. The interface defines methods you want to expose, while the implementation within the module can define additional public methods. Users of the module should interact with the interface, not the implementation. Without casting, the module's user will not be able to invoke these methods on the implementing class. This allows you to, a certain extent, hide public methods that you do not want invoked outside of the module since module users will not know the concrete type of the class they are working with. Of course, with some investigative digging, they can always find out the name of the implementing class, and there isn't much you can do to enforce access restriction.

The strongest way to enforce access restriction is to define implementation classes at package scope. These implementation classes then implement an interface that is referenced by external module users. Unfortunately, this strongest form of enforcement is not always feasible, given that other packages within the module may need to reference the implementing class to invoke its methods or create instances. However, it's a good idea to begin with this approach and then loosen it access as the needs demand.

An informal way to define your module's Published Interface is to express the desired published API in the module's JavaDoc or in a UML diagram. When using JavaDoc, a common practice is to clearly express the class or method you prefer developers not use. If you want to discourage external classes from using an internal class, you'll be required to present an interface for external classes to use, similar to what was discussed in the previous paragraph. This is the approach often used by the JDK itself. The `java.rmi.server.RemoteObjectInvocationHandler` class, used with Java's dynamic proxy feature in J2SE 1.5, is an example of using an interface to shield a public implementation class, while expressing in the JavaDoc that this class is desirably used only internally.

Combined with variations of each of the previous, a Module Facade serves as a single point of entry to your module. In most situations, a facade will increase the ease with which other developers can integrate the module into their environments. The facade may also serve as the factory responsible for creating the module's internal implementation classes.

Module Facade pattern, 212

Given these variations, I recommend going with package scope classes initially. As the visibility of these classes move beyond their package, begin by exposing these methods via an interface. If you find the module needs additional behavior beyond that of what module users will need, then allow classes within the module to work with the concrete type or define another interface within the module used by classes inside the module. With each of these approaches, I suggest making your intent clear in the documentation you create, including the JavaDoc. Last, a Module Facade is useful to help increase the usability of your module, but by itself it is not a robust stand-alone solution and should be combined with the package scope or interface-based approach.

OSGi

Admittedly, the approaches described have a nasty code smell because we are working around the shortcomings of the Java language. If you're using a framework that enables modularity on the Java platform, defining a module's published interface is much easier.

For instance, the OSGi framework allows you to manage type visibility of a module by restricting access to specific packages. To access a class encapsulated within an OSGi bundle, the package containing the class must be exported by the module. Because of this, it's easy to restrict access to public methods on public classes within a module by simply not exporting the packages containing those classes. Therefore, it's important that classes with methods you want to expose are placed in different packages than classes you hope to encapsulate. If you do this through Abstract Modules, you'll gain even more flexibility. Many of the remaining examples in this book that use OSGi also apply the Published Interface pattern, especially the samples in Part III that focus exclusively on OSGi.

design encapsulation for a published interface, 37

Abstract Modules pattern, 222

CONSEQUENCES

reuse versus
use, 62

The greatest advantage of defining a module's Published Interface is that you're making the module easier to use by other developers. Even though a module may be well-designed and offer valuable behavior, a cluttered API will undoubtedly scare developers away. Unquestionably, offering a thinner and lighter module interface will allow developers to more quickly understand how to integrate the module. Keep in mind that with standard Java, there is no way to hide public methods within a module unless the class containing those public methods is defined at package scope, which is not always reasonable. Quite simply, Java has no language construct to accommodate this. However, efforts to define a module's Published Interface are undoubtedly still valuable.

Each of the previous implementation variations has a different set of consequences. While defining package scope classes strictly enforces internal usage of the class, package scope may be too limiting. If classes in other packages within the module need to use the class, package scope will not work.

External
Configuration
pattern, 200

Exposing only interfaces, on the other hand, allows you to expose only the methods you want. However, you can never prevent another developer from using the implementation class directly, since the implementing class is public. Using interfaces has another limitation, too. For classes within the module to invoke methods on the implementation, it requires that the module's internal classes work with a concrete type, preventing the module from working with alternative implementations of the interface, which can make External Configuration difficult.

Ultimately, you're giving up internal module flexibility for external module usability. The consequences of this decision must be given careful consideration. Additionally, if the implementing class within the module is in a separate package from the module's classes that need to use it, the implementation class must be declared public, and you can never really prevent other developers from using it directly, assuming they learn of the implementation class. However, the implementation class is still pretty well insulated, and it's likely you can prevent most honest developers from referencing it directly.

Expecting to enforce your Published Interface via JavaDoc is difficult at best. While undoubtedly the easiest approach, there is no way to ensure developers follow this recommendation. Use caution when adopting an approach relying solely on any form of documentation. Likewise, a Module

Facade is not a stand-alone solution, since the facade will likely expose a module's expected implementation classes via the facade's return types. However, a facade offers advantages in enhancing the usability of a module, as well as the ease with which developers can learn about the module.

SAMPLE

Let's consider the domain objects for an application that must allow a customer to place orders. A customer has a list of filled and unfilled orders. For all new orders, the customer is given a discount, which is calculated based on the total number of items ordered by the customer. Any new orders placed will count toward this discount.

The Customer class has a createNewOrder method on it that accepts the quantity of items ordered and the charge amount of the order. This method creates a new order, adds that new order to the list of already placed orders, and then calculates the discount for that new order based upon all of the orders. The method then updates the new order with the discount amount. Unfortunately, since the Customer and Order are in separate Java packages, the setDiscountAmount method must be made public, making it accessible to not only Customer but also any other classes within the system. The code in Listing 10.1 shows the Customer class and highlights the declaration of the Order array and invocation of the setDiscountAmount method.

Listing 10.1 Customer Class

```
package com.extensiblejava.customer;
import com.extensiblejava.order.*;
import java.math.BigDecimal;
public class Customer {
   private String fullName;
   private Order[] orders;
   private OrderBuilder builder;
   public Customer(String fullName, OrderBuilder builder) {
      this.fullName = fullName;
      this.builder = builder;
   }
   public String getName() { return this.fullName; }
   public Order[] getOrders() {
      if (this.orders == null) {
         this.orders = builder.build();
      }
```

```
            return this.orders;
        }
        public Order createNewOrder(Integer productQuantity,
            BigDecimal chargeAmount) {
            int numOrders = this.getOrders().length + 1;
            Order[] newOrders = new Order[numOrders];
            System.arraycopy(this.orders, 0, newOrders, 0,
                this.orders.length);
            newOrders[numOrders - 1] = new Order(productQuantity,
                chargeAmount);
            this.orders = newOrders;
            BigDecimal discount = this.calculateDiscount();
            this.orders[numOrders - 1].
                setDiscountAmount(discount);
            return this.orders[numOrders - 1];
        }
        private BigDecimal calculateDiscount() {
            Order[] orders = this.getOrders();
            int totalQuantity = 0;
            for (int i = 0; i < orders.length; i++) {
                totalQuantity += orders[i].getProductQuantity().
                    intValue();
            }
            if (totalQuantity < 10) {
                return new BigDecimal("0.05");
            } else if ( (totalQuantity >= 10) &&
                        (totalQuantity < 100) ) {
                return new BigDecimal("0.10");
            } else if (totalQuantity >= 100) {
                return new BigDecimal("0.25");
            }
            return new BigDecimal("0.00");
        }
    }
```

In Listing 10.2, we see that the `CustomerTest` test case can update
the discount amount for this order, something we do not want to allow.
The discount amount is a derived attribute that we do not want exposed.

Listing 10.2 CustomerTest Test Class

```
package com.extensiblejava.customer.test;
import junit.framework.*;
import junit.textui.*;
import com.extensiblejava.customer.*;
```

```
import com.extensiblejava.order.*;
import java.math.BigDecimal;

public class CustomerTest extends TestCase {
   public static void main(String[] args) {
      String[] testCaseName = {
         CustomerTest.class.getName() };
      junit.textui.TestRunner.main(testCaseName);
   }
   protected void setUp() {}
   public void testCustomerLoad() throws Exception {
      CustomerBuilder builder =
         new DefaultCustomerBuilder();
      Customer customer = builder.build();
      assertNotNull(customer);
      assertEquals("John Doe", customer.getName());
   }
   public void testCustomerOrderLoad() throws Exception {
      CustomerBuilder builder =
          new DefaultCustomerBuilder();
      Customer customer = builder.build();
      Order[] orders = customer.getOrders();
      assertEquals(orders.length, 3);
   }
   public void testPlaceOrder() {
      CustomerBuilder builder =
         new DefaultCustomerBuilder();
      Customer customer = builder.build();
      Order order = customer.createNewOrder(
         new Integer(3), new BigDecimal("50.00"));
      order.setDiscountAmount(
         new BigDecimal("0.50"));
      assertEquals(order.getDiscountAmount(),
         new BigDecimal("0.50"));
   }
}
```

Figure 10.2 shows the relationships between the classes and corresponding modules. Just as any class within the `custtest.jar` module has access to the public methods on the `Order` class, so, too, would any other consuming module.

So, how can we prevent anything except `Customer` or other internal module classes from invoking `setDiscountAmount`? First, we'll

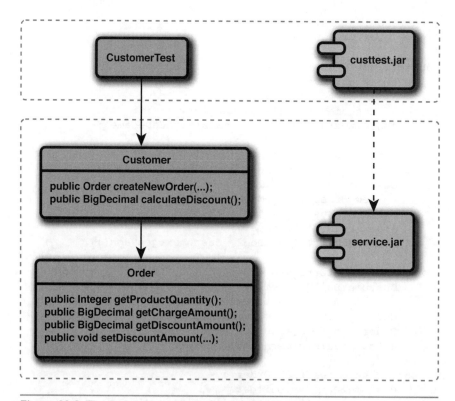

Figure 10.2 The Order class with public methods exposed

introduce a `Customer` interface to ensure we expose only the methods we want to publish. Listing 10.3 illustrates the `Customer` interface.

Listing 10.3 Customer Interface

```
package com.extensiblejava.customer;
import com.extensiblejava.order.*;
import java.math.BigDecimal;
public interface Customer {
   public String getName();
   public Order[] getOrders();
   public Order createNewOrder(Integer productQuantity,
                               BigDecimal chargeAmount);
}
```

Likewise, we also create an Order interface. Note the omission of the setDiscountAmount method on Order in Listing 10.4.

Listing 10.4 Order Interface

```
package com.extensiblejava.order;
import java.math.BigDecimal;
public interface Order {
   public Integer getProductQuantity();
   public BigDecimal getChargeAmount();
   public BigDecimal getDiscountAmount();
}
```

Now, we refactor the original Customer class and rename it to DefaultCustomer while implementing the Customer interface, as shown in Listing 10.5. Likewise, we refactor the original Order class and rename it to DefaultOrder while implementing the Order interface.

The DefaultCustomer implementation has also been changed slightly. It now directly instantiates the concrete DefaultOrder class, allowing it to call the setDiscountAmount method. However, because the array of Orders is of type Order, no consumer can invoke the setDiscountMethod unless it downcasts the Order to a DefaultOrder. Downcasting is certainly something we want to avoid. Again, the significant difference is that createNewOrder returns an array of type Order. Internally, the method still works with DefaultOrder instances. This exposes only the Order interface but allows the Customer to work directly with the implementation.

Listing 10.5 Refactored DefaultCustomer Class

```
public class DefaultCustomer implements Customer {
...
   public Order createNewOrder(Integer productQuantity,
                               BigDecimal chargeAmount) {
     int numOrders = this.getOrders().length + 1;
     Order[] newOrders = new Order[numOrders];
     System.arraycopy(this.orders, 0, newOrders, 0,
        this.orders.length);
     DefaultOrder newOrder =
        new DefaultOrder(productQuantity, chargeAmount);
     newOrders[numOrders - 1] = newOrder;
     this.orders = newOrders;
```

```
        BigDecimal discount = this.calculateDiscount();
        newOrder.setDiscountAmount(discount);
        return this.orders[numOrders - 1];
    }
...
}
```

The `CustomerTest` test case, shown in Listing 10.6, can no longer call the `setDiscountAmount` method because it is bound to the `Order` interface, not the `DefaultOrder` implementation. Attempting to invoke the `setDiscountAmount` method will now result in a compiler error because only internal module classes know of the `DefaultOrder` and its methods.

Listing 10.6 Refactored CustomerTest Class

```
package com.extensiblejava.customer.test;
import junit.framework.*;
import junit.textui.*;
import com.extensiblejava.customer.*;
import com.extensiblejava.customer.impl.*;
import com.extensiblejava.order.*;
import java.math.BigDecimal;
public class CustomerTest extends TestCase {
    public static void main(String[] args) {
        String[] testCaseName = {
            CustomerTest.class.getName() };
        junit.textui.TestRunner.main(testCaseName);
    }
...
    public void testPlaceOrder() {
        CustomerBuilder builder =
            new DefaultCustomerBuilder();
        Customer customer = builder.build();
        Order order = customer.createNewOrder(
            new Integer(3), new BigDecimal("50.00"));
        //No longer allowed.
        //order.setDiscountAmount(new BigDecimal("0.50"));
        assertEquals(order.getDiscountAmount(),
            new BigDecimal("0.25"));
    }
}
```

When `Customer.createNewOrder` is called, I require `product-Quantity` and `chargeAmount` to be passed in. I don't want people changing these values on my `Order` instance either, so the `Order` instance must be created with these values passed to the constructor. Since the `Customer` is a factory for the `Order` instances, I'm protected. The final structure is illustrated in Figure 10.3, which shows that the `set-DiscountAmount` method is encapsulated within the module.

WRAPPING UP

Without a module system, such as OSGi, implementing and enforcing a Published Interface is unwieldy at best. It can leave a certain code smell you may not especially enjoy. With OSGi, however, we can enforce a Published Interface using OSGi μServices. An OSGi bundle exports public packages, and the published interface of a bundle represents the public methods on the public classes that are exported from a module and subsequently registered with the OSGi Service Registry. Sadly, without a module system, we are left with a relatively sloppy and smelly alternative.

OSGi μServices, 278

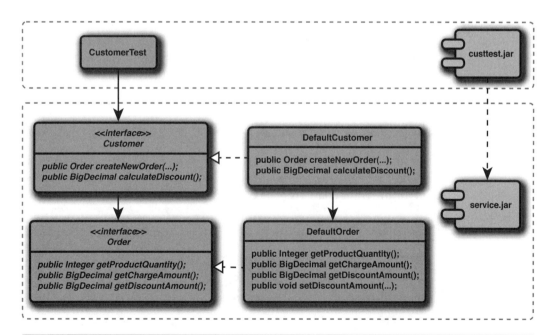

Figure 10.3 Encapsulate DefaultOrder implementation with Order interface

EXTERNAL CONFIGURATION

STATEMENT

Modules should be externally configurable.

DESCRIPTION

module weight, 64 When a module is deployed to its runtime environment, it must often be initialized before it can be used. For instance, initializing a module with the necessary user ID and password might be necessary before the module can access data from a database. But we also want to avoid tightly coupling the configuration information to the module. Doing so will tightly couple the module to a single environmental context and limit the likelihood that the module can be reused in alternative contexts.

External configuration allows a module to be configured across environmental contexts. Figure 10.4 illustrates External Configuration, where an XML configuration file is used by the `Client` class to configure the `client.jar` module. Note that the configuration information responsible for initializing the `client.jar` module is separate from the `Client` class representing the behavior of the module. The ability to configure a module to its environmental context increases our ability to reuse the module across contexts. New consumers of the `client.jar` module will now have the ability to configure the module so that it can be used in different environments.

IMPLEMENTATION VARIATIONS

There are different ways to configure a module for its environmental context. Foremost, we may want separate configuration files that can be used for different contexts. The configuration file can be included in the

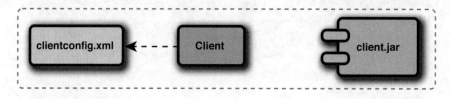

Figure 10.4 External Configuration

module, included in a separate module, or both. The option we choose depends upon the flexibility desired.

In Figure 10.4, we saw that the configuration information was included within the module. The advantage of including the configuration file within the module is that it's easy to use the module within its default context. In other words, you won't need to specify the configuration information. The module knows how to initialize itself in that context. Unfortunately, the disadvantage is that this default configuration will likely not work in alternative contexts.

Figure 10.5 illustrates a configuration file that is not deployed within the module but is provided to the module separately upon initialization. The advantage with this second approach is that the module is no longer coupled to its environment and can be reused across context. However, each time the module is used in a new environment, the configuration information must be provided. There is no default.

A flexible alternative is to provide a default configuration file within the module but allow for the module to be configured with an alternative configuration file. In some cases, though, including a default configuration isn't possible since there is no default environmental context. For instance, many popular logging frameworks, such as Log4J, require developers to define the logging framework parameters before the framework is configured properly to work within the system. However, there is generally no default configuration provided because there is no default environmental context that is known to the developers of the module.

Including a default configuration file within the module is one aspect of providing a module's Default Implementation. In some cases, you may choose to break configuration out into multiple configuration files. Some

Default Implementation pattern, 206

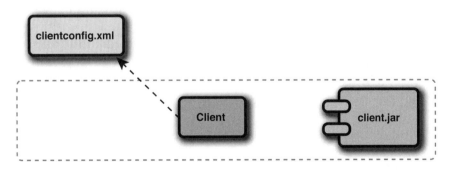

Figure 10.5 External Configuration file

initialization activities will be static, while others will vary depending on the environment. We'll see an example of this in the "Sample" section.

CONSEQUENCES

reuse versus use, 62

flexibility and complexity, 34
Failing to provide external configuration results in a heavyweight module that is tightly coupled to a single environmental context. On the other hand, external configuration makes it more difficult to use a module since the module must be configured to its context before it can be used. Configuring a module demands that developers spend time understanding the proper configuration options. In general, we can say this:

> External Configuration increases module reuse but decreases use.

Developers must be cognizant of this trade-off and recognize where configuration is necessary versus where it's overhead. When possible, providing a default configuration for the module is desirable since it increases module reuse across multiple environmental contexts.

For instance, a module that provides connection pooling capabilities can be reused across contexts if the user ID and password combination used to connect to the database is contained within a configuration file instead of within source code inside the module. On the other hand, external configuration makes it more difficult to use a module since the module must be configured to its context before it can be used.

SAMPLE

Many systems require a `userid` and `password` (that is, credentials) combination to connect to external resources. To ensure a module can be deployed across a variety of contexts, it's important to drive the initialization of the module using configuration.

Listing 10.8 illustrates a simple bean that is configured with a `userid` (UID) and `password` (PWD) combination. We desire to initialize the `InjectedBean` class with the `uid` and `pwd` from an external configuration file.

Listing 10.7 Simple Bean Configured with UID/PWD Combination

```
package com.extensiblejava.main;

public class InjectedBean implements InjectedInterface {
   private String uid;
   private String pwd;

   public void setUid(String uid) { this.uid = uid; }
   public void setPwd(String pwd) { this.pwd = pwd; }
   public void injection() { System.out.println("uid: "
      + uid + " pwd: " + pwd); }
}
```

To drive the initialization of the uid and pwd combination, we define a Resource.properties file that contains this information, as shown in Listing 10.8.

Listing 10.8 Resource.properties with UID and PWD Combination

```
app.uid=springuid
app.pwd=springpwd
```

Now, we need to initialize the InjectedBean in Listing 10.7 with these values. To do this, we'll leverage the Spring framework. Listing 10.9 illustrates the Spring configuration file that does this. Note that the configuration file references the attributes of the Resources.properties file. As an alternative, we could have avoided using the Resources.properties file and placed the uid and pwd combination directly into the Spring configuration file. However, the Spring configuration file is included and deployed within the module while the Resource.properties file resides on the file system. This allows us to modify module configuration without updating the Spring configuration file and rebuilding the module.

Listing 10.9 Spring Configuration File

```
<beans>
   <bean id="firstBean"
    class="com.extensiblejava.main.FirstBean">
      <constructor-arg>
         <ref bean="injectedBean"/>
```

```
        </constructor-arg>
    </bean>

    <bean id="injectedBean"
     class="com.extensiblejava.main.InjectedBean">
        <property name="uid" value="${app.uid}"/>
        <property name="pwd" value="${app.pwd}"/>
    </bean>

    <bean id="placeholderConfig"
     class="org.springframework.beans.factory.
            config.PropertyPlaceholderConfigurer">
        <property name="location"
         value="com/extensiblejava/main/Resource.properties"/>
    </bean>
</beans>
```

Figure 10.6 illustrates the resulting structure, with the default configuration included in the **reuse.jar** module, along with the external **Resource.properties** file that is used to configure the module with the appropriate **uid** and **pwd** combination.

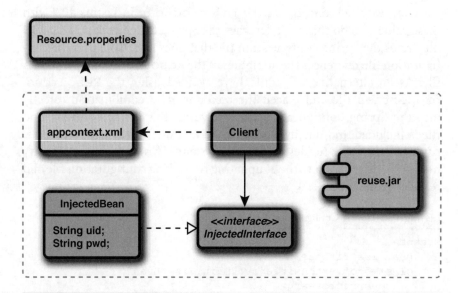

Figure 10.6 External Configuration

WRAPPING UP

External Configuration helps increase the reusability of a module by allowing developers to configure the module to context. Unfortunately, excessive configuration requirements can increase the difficulty developers have in using a module. A balance must be sought when using external configuration to ensure the optimal solution. When possible, providing a default implementation will help achieve the balance necessary.

DEFAULT IMPLEMENTATION

STATEMENT

Provide modules with a default implementation.

DESCRIPTION

reuse versus use, 62

To maximize reuse, a module must be flexible enough so that it can function in a variety of different operating environments. Yet, for a module to be usable, it must be independently deployable. To address this tension, a module can be given a Default Implementation with well-defined extension points so that the module can be extended when necessary. This balances the desire for use with the desire for reuse.

Figure 10.7 shows Default Implementation. The `default.jar` module contains the `DefaultImpl` class, which is the default implementation for the `DefaultInterface`. The `default.jar` module contains the appropriate configuration to use this default implementation. The `betterimpl.jar` module also uses the `default.jar` module but provides its own implementation of `DefaultInterface`, as well as the appropriate configuration to configure the `default.jar` module.

IMPLEMENTATION VARIATIONS

Abstract Modules pattern, 222

Separate Abstractions pattern, 237

Sometimes the default implementation may reside within the module. Other times, it may reside in a separate module. If the default implementation resides in the same module, consider applying the Abstract Modules pattern. If the implementation resides in a separate module, consider the Separate Abstractions pattern.

External Configuration pattern, 200

In addition to the behavior of the module (that is, the default implementation), we must also account for module configuration. Ideally, a module is externally configurable so that it can be used in a variety of contexts. When defining the default implementation for a module, a default configuration should also be provided.

As a result of providing external configuration and a default implementation, the module can be simply dropped into the environmental context for which it was designed, helping to maximize module usability. In situations where the module behavior is desired in an environmental context for which the module was not originally designed, developers

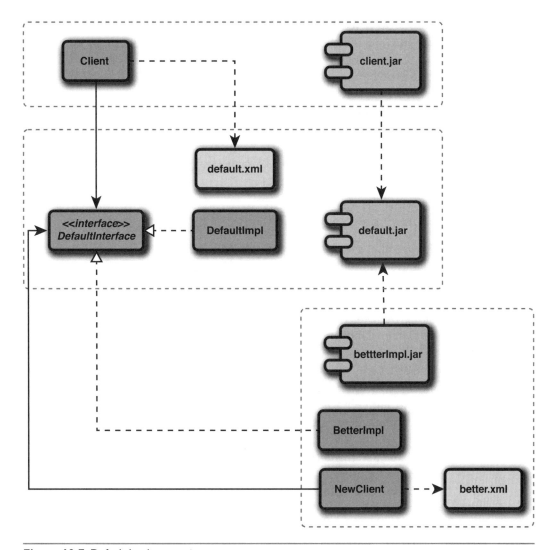

Figure 10.7 Default Implementation

can create a new implementation with appropriate configuration for the desired context, helping to maximize reusability.

For instance, in Figure 10.7, the `default.xml` file is placed in `default.jar`, allowing the `default.jar` module to be used in its default operating environment without the `client.jar` module.

Another alternative is to place the `default.xml` file in the `client.jar` module. Then, using the `default.jar` module in an alternative scenario will require us to appropriately configure the module. In other words, the module can never be used without the `client.jar` module unless we provide an alternative configuration.

Implementation Factory pattern, 229

Default Implementation often demands abstractions and the concrete implementations of those abstractions, so wiring together the instances within the modules is necessary. This can be performed using factory classes or a framework such as Spring. Consider an Implementation Factory to address these challenges.

CONSEQUENCES

Separate Abstractions pattern, 237

Most modules will have a default implementation. Without any implementation, a module is essentially only a specification and requires us to provide our own implementation any time we want to use the module. Certainly this is useful in some cases, especially where Separate Abstractions is desirable.

Abstract Modules pattern, 222

Default Implementation is one way to develop a plug-in architecture. The module containing the default implementation has extension points that are pluggable. In Figure 10.7, it's possible to plug in alternative behaviors into the `default.jar` module and then configure the module appropriately based on the new implementation. In other words, the default implementation is the implementation of the interfaces within a module. If this is an Abstract Module with no other modules dependent upon the implementation classes, we can provide new implementations of the abstractions that are plugged into the module at runtime.

Failure to accommodate both behavior and configuration when creating a default implementation will compromise the integrity of the system. It's relatively easy to create the extension points by implementing the necessary interfaces, but a way to configure the module is also very important.

SAMPLE

In Figure 10.8, `DefaultCalculator` is the default implementation of `DiscountCalculator` within the `customer.jar` module. In this example, the configuration for the `customer.jar` module lives within the `custtest.jar` module. Initially, the `custtest.jar` module is

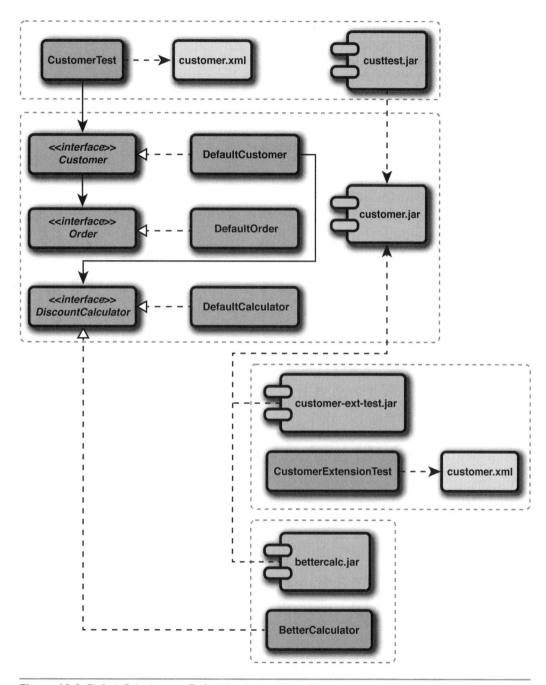

Figure 10.8 DefaultCalculator as Default Implementation for customer.jar module

the only client of the customer.jar module. The bettercalc.jar module provides a new implementation for the DiscountCalculator class and can be used by other clients to perform a different calculation than provided by the DefaultCalculator. In this example, we place the configuration files in the client modules, meaning that customer.jar must always be configured by the client, even though it does provide its own default implementation. All configuration is done using the Spring framework.

Listing 10.10 illustrates the Spring customer.xml file in the custtest.jar module, where we can see that it references the DefaultCalculator class, which is contained within the customer.jar module.

Listing 10.10 customer.xml File in the custtest.jar Module

```
<beans>
    <bean name="customerManager"
     class=
     "com.extensiblejava.customer.impl.CustomerManagerImpl">
        <constructor-arg>
            <ref bean="customerBuilder"/>
        </constructor-arg>
    </bean>

    <bean name="customerBuilder"
     class=
     "com.extensiblejava.customer.impl.
      DefaultCustomerBuilder">
        <constructor-arg>
            <ref bean="orderBuilder"/>
        </constructor-arg>
        <constructor-arg>
            <ref bean="discountCalculator"/>
        </constructor-arg>
    </bean>

    <bean name="orderBuilder"
     class=
     "com.extensiblejava.order.impl.DefaultOrderBuilder"/>
    <bean name="discountCalculator"
     class=
     "com.extensiblejava.calculator.impl.DefaultCalculator"/>
</beans>
```

Listing 10.11 illustrates the `customer.xml` file within the `customer-ext-test.jar` module, where we see that the new `BetterCalc` implementation is used.

Listing 10.11 customer.xml File in the customer-ext-test.jar Module

```
<beans>

    <bean name="customerManager"
     class=
     "com.extensiblejava.customer.impl.CustomerManagerImpl">
        <constructor-arg>
            <ref bean="customerBuilder"/>
        </constructor-arg>
    </bean>

    <bean name="customerBuilder"
     class="com.extensiblejava.customer.impl.
           DefaultCustomerBuilder">
        <constructor-arg>
            <ref bean="orderBuilder"/>
        </constructor-arg>
        <constructor-arg>
            <ref bean="betterCalculator"/>
        </constructor-arg>
    </bean>

    <bean name="orderBuilder"
     class="com.extensiblejava.order.impl.
           DefaultOrderBuilder"/>
    <bean name="betterCalculator"
     class="com.extensiblejava.calculator.better.
           BetterCalculator"/>
</beans>
```

WRAPPING UP

Default Implementation helps balance the tension between reuse and use. Modules can easily be used because they provide a default implementation but are extensible in that new implementations can be provided if they must be used in an operating environment for which they weren't initially designed. In addition to providing new behavior for a module through implementing interfaces, module configuration should also be given careful consideration.

MODULE FACADE

STATEMENT

Create a facade serving as a coarse-grained entry point to another fine-grained module's underlying implementation.

DESCRIPTION

weight and granularity of modules, 63

We create fine-grained and lightweight modules to increase module reuse. Unfortunately, fine-grained modules can also be difficult to use because the user must understand the API of several different modules and use them in conjunction with each other to accomplish a particular task. Additionally, lightweight modules must also be configured to an environmental context. Because of this, fine-grained and lightweight modules are generally more difficult to use.

A Module Facade is useful to provide a higher-level API that coordinates the work of a set of fine-grained modules. The Module Facade emphasizes usability, whereas the underlying fine-grained modules emphasize reusability. Figure 10.9 illustrates a Module Facade.

IMPLEMENTATION VARIATIONS

Oftentimes, configuring fine-grained modules can be a burden, especially when multiple fine-grained modules are used in conjunction but forces prevent module designers from combining the fine-grained module into a single coarse-grained entity. In these situations, a Module Facade can be used to expose a subset of the functionality contained within a group of fine-grained modules. A Module Facade allows a group of fine-grained modules to operate as a coarse-grained module.

External Configuration pattern, 200

A Module Facade is useful to encapsulate the configuration for a group of fine-grained and lightweight modules. With a Module Facade, we are able to maintain the balance between creating fine-grained and lightweight modules that are highly reusable while also providing an easy way for developers to use a group of modules. By encapsulating configuration information in a Module Facade, developers don't need to worry about knowing how to configure a module.

Multiple facades might exist for a group of lightweight and fine-grained modules. In many ways, this is similar to the separation we try

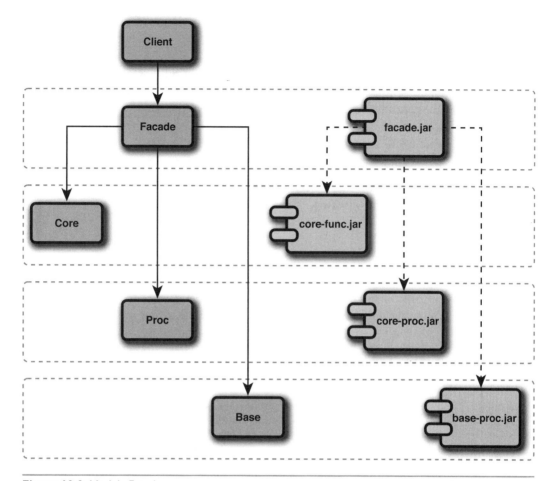

Figure 10.9 Module Facade

to achieve between an application's user interface and its domain logic. Ideally, we can create a new user interface for an existing set of business logic. Such is the goal of a Module Facade, except that the facade often-times encapsulates environmental context so that a group of modules can be easily reused in that context. But new contexts will likely require new facades. This is okay, especially if the group of modules are reused multiple times within that context.

A Module Facade might also augment a group of modules with additional behavior based on a particular context. For instance, business

Acyclic Relationships pattern, 146

logic that is performed only in specific situations can be encapsulated in a Module Facade to ensure that the modules for which it serves as the facade maintain their high degree of reusability. A Module Facade can alter or augment the API of its underlying modules, possibly decorating those modules with additional behavior based on the context. A Module Facade can also act as a mediator to help break the dependencies between a set of modules. This is quite similar to the concept of escalation that we discussed in Acyclic Relationships.

Published Interface pattern, 188

It's likely we'll use a Module Facade in conjunction with other patterns. For instance, the classes inside the Module Facade may have a Published Interface. We might choose to create a facade abstraction so that new facades can easily be created.

CONSEQUENCES

outgoing dependencies, 67

While a Module Facade is useful to augment the functionality of a group of underlying modules, it's likely that the Module Facade will have many outgoing dependencies on these modules. In other words, the Module Facade is generally tightly coupled to other modules. In addition to higher coupling, the Module Facade also encapsulates contextual behavior and configuration. Each diminishes the likelihood that the Module Facade is reusable across a variety of contexts. Instead, it's used to configure a group of modules in a particular context.

In general, a Module Facade makes a group of underlying modules easier to use, but the modules themselves are typically not highly reusable. Instead, a facade maintains the reuse of the group of modules for which it serves as a facade.

Because a Module Facade has many outgoing dependencies, any fine-grained modules that the Module Facade depends upon must be deployed whenever the coarse-grained module facade is deployed. A Module Facade can help increase the ease of use while maintaining the reusability surrounding its underlying modules, but the increase of dependencies that accompany a Module Facade can also increase the complexity surrounding deployment. In other words, when deploying the Module Facade, you'll have to manage all of its dependent modules.

Test Module pattern, 263

Testing a module facade in isolation is also difficult, since the purpose of the module facade is to treat an underlying group of modules as a cohesive unit. Regardless, a module facade is an excellent way to make it much easier to use a group of underlying fine-grained and lightweight modules.

SAMPLE

Listing 10.12 illustrates a `Loan` interface that calculates the payment schedule for an applicant's loan based on the present value of the loan, the interest rate, and the term. There are also options to obtain the monthly payment, final payment, cumulative interest and principal, and the total sum of the payments made.

Listing 10.12 Loan Interface

```
package com.extensiblejava.loan;

import java.math.*;

public interface Loan {
    public PaymentSchedule calculatePaymentSchedule(
        BigDecimal presentValue, BigDecimal rate, int term);
    public BigDecimal getMonthlyPayment();
    public BigDecimal getFinalPayment();
    public BigDecimal getCumulativeInterest();
    public BigDecimal getCumulativePrincipal();
    public BigDecimal getTotalPayments();
}
```

Clients that want to use the `Loan` interface are able to invoke the appropriate methods. The system is also highly modular, with the `Loan` interface existing in the `loan.jar` module. The implementation for the `Loan` exists in separate modules so that we can maintain the implementation separate from the interface. Figure 10.10 shows the module structure .

At some point, the implementation classes must get instantiated and wired together. Spring is used to accomplish the instantiation and wiring. This allows the modules to be reused across a variety of contexts, with the client responsible for providing the Spring configuration. The client provides the configuration so that we have flexibility in choosing which implementations get wired. Were we to embed the configuration within the module, it might be difficult to reuse the module because the module itself would contain contextual information. But requiring each client to wire the modules together is now a burden that the client must assume responsibility for. By introducing a Module Facade that provides default wiring, we have the best of both: highly reusable fine-grained and lightweight modules, as well as modules that are easy to use. Figure 10.11 shows the module structure with the module facade containing the Spring configuration file.

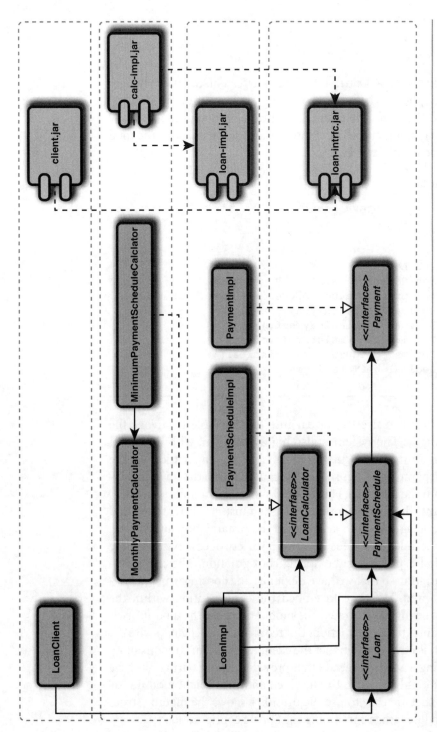

Figure 10.10 Modules of the Loan system

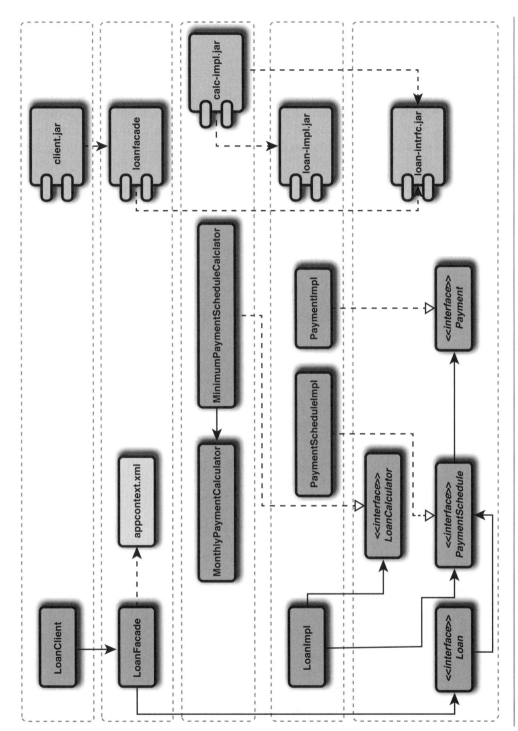

Figure 10.11 Loan system with Module Facade

Listing 10.13 shows the `LoanFacade` class that configures the loan modules. Client classes are now able to easily invoke the `LoanFacade` without any knowledge of the configuration overhead. If the `Loan-Facade` doesn't provide the correct configuration for a new context, a new facade can be created that provides the correct configuration or a new client can provide its own configuration.

Listing 10.13 LoanFacade Class

```java
package com.extensiblejava.facade;

import java.math.*;
import com.extensiblejava.loan.*;
import com.extensiblejava.calculator.*;
import org.springframework.context.*;
import org.springframework.context.support.*;

public class LoanFacade {

    public PaymentSchedule calculatePaymentSchedule(
        BigDecimal presentValue, BigDecimal rate, int term) {
        ApplicationContext appContext =
            new FileSystemXmlApplicationContext(
            "com/extensiblejava/facade/AppContext.xml");
        Loan loan = (Loan) appContext.getBean("loan");
        PaymentSchedule paymentSchedule =
            loan.calculatePaymentSchedule(
            presentValue, rate, term);
        return paymentSchedule;
    }

    public BigDecimal getMonthlyPayment(
        BigDecimal presentValue, BigDecimal rate, int term) {
        ApplicationContext appContext =
            new FileSystemXmlApplicationContext(
            "com/extensiblejava/facade/AppContext.xml");
        Loan loan = (Loan) appContext.getBean("loan");
        PaymentSchedule paymentSchedule =
            loan.calculatePaymentSchedule(
            presentValue, rate, term);
        BigDecimal monthlyPayment = loan.getMonthlyPayment();
        return monthlyPayment;
    }
}
```

WRAPPING UP

Developing systems with a modular architecture is tenuous. On one hand, developers strive to create fine-grained and lightweight modules that are highly reusable. On the other hand, developers want to ensure that modules are easy to use across a wide variety of contexts. A Module Facade allows developers to create a coarse-grained and heavyweight module that configures and coordinates the activities of a group of lightweight and fine-grained modules, allowing developers to strike the right balance between reuse and use.

reuse versus use, 62

EXTENSIBILITY PATTERNS

11

A goal in designing software systems is the ability to extend the system without modifying the existing codebase. Abstraction plays a central role in accomplishing this goal, but simply adding new functionality to an existing system is only part of the battle. We also want to be able to deploy those new additions without redeploying the entire application. The extensibility patterns focus on helping us achieve this goal. The extensibility patterns include

- **Abstract Modules**: Depend upon the abstract elements of a module.
- **Implementation Factory**: Use factories to create a module's implementation classes.
- **Separate Abstractions**: Place abstractions and the classes that implement them in separate modules.

ABSTRACT MODULES

STATEMENT

Depend upon the abstract elements of a module.

DESCRIPTION

When you design the dependencies between modules, depending on only the abstract elements increases flexibility. It gives you the ability to more easily extend and maintain areas of your application by defining new modules with classes that implement or extend the abstraction. Most importantly, clients of the modules now have the freedom to receive different implementations because they are no longer coupled to an implementation but instead are coupled to an abstraction (such as an abstract class or interface).

In Figure 11.1, you see the `client.jar` module is dependent on the `service.jar` module. Examining the contents of `client1`, notice that the dependency of the `Client` class is on the `Service` interface. This is supported by the associated code. Therefore, the `client.jar` module is dependent upon only the abstract elements in `service.jar` module. As much as possible using standard Java, this relationship is enforced and cannot be violated because the `ServiceImpl` class is given only package scope.

The stability of a module is a metric used to help determine the likelihood that a module will experience change (Martin 2000). Stable modules resist change and are desirably the most heavily depended-upon modules in the system. In Figure 11.1, you see the `service.jar` module used

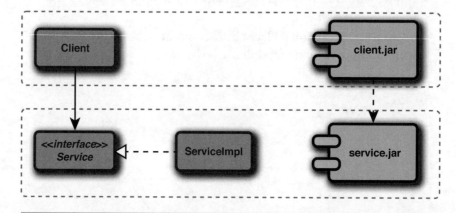

Figure 11.1 Depending on the abstract elements of a module

by the other module. The `service.jar` module should be as stable, or resistant to change, as possible.

IMPLEMENTATION VARIATIONS

Depending on only the abstract elements of a module carries a price. Creating the implementing class can no longer be done by using the `new` keyword to create an instance of the implementing class. Instead, you have to consider some of the following options:

- **Object factory**: To avoid dependencies on the concrete elements of a module, an object factory can be used to create the appropriate concrete instances. This offers a few advantages. First, the factory is the only area of the application referencing the concrete class. Adding new concrete classes that extend the abstraction is much easier. Second, if there are rules associated with creating the instances, these rules are well encapsulated within the factory. If the rules change, you'll have a single maintenance point.

- **Dynamic creation**: In some situations, you'll find that using the `Class` class is more appropriate than an object factory. I've found this approach to work best in a couple of cases. In a Web application, if I need to create certain classes at server start-up, I use the `Class` class and specify the concrete class to instantiate in a start-up properties file. This allows me to create new classes that can be plugged into my application when the server starts up by simply defining the new class and then specifying its fully qualified name in the appropriate properties file. The second scenario is when I'm using an Abstract Factory [GOF]. Specifying how the appropriate concrete factories get created is also useful to specify in a properties file. In most other cases, I'll use the object factory approach. Many dependency injection frameworks, such as Spring, rely on dynamic creation.

- **OSGi µServices**: If you're using a framework such as OSGi, µServices provide the ability to dynamically instantiate the appropriate classes registered as µService when an OSGi bundle is activated.

OSGi µServices, 278

Abstract classes or interfaces should absorb most incoming dependencies, whereas outgoing dependencies should originate from concrete classes. Although simpler, you'll want to avoid a heavily depended-upon module with a lot of concrete classes because a single change can have a significant ripple effect across all dependent modules. You'll also want to

module dependencies, 48

avoid modules with a lot of abstract classes that have no incoming dependencies. First, if all classes are abstract, there is no behavior. Second, having no incoming dependencies implies nothing uses the module. Abstract Modules and Separate Abstractions clearly illustrate the value of a dependency on only the abstract elements of a package.

CONSEQUENCES

Modules heavily depended upon have many incoming dependencies. In other words, you may have many modules that all depend on a single module. On one hand, this is a good thing because you've managed to maximize reuse of the module with many incoming dependencies. But reuse has its challenges. If the modules you're reusing heavily require a change, the ramifications of that change can ripple throughout all dependent modules. Changing a heavily reused module can be quite a maintenance headache.

minimizing the impact of change dependencies, 57

If you have to change a stable module, you'll experience a ripple effect throughout much of the application. Unless it's a simple change, the ripple effect is almost certain to cause a problem elsewhere. Of course, you'll probably have a gut feeling telling you what to expect of your change, and you should listen. The more you have to change stable modules, the less maintainable you'll find the application.

Test Module pattern, 263

A module can undergo two types of changes: to its interface or to its implementation. If you change the interface of the module, it impacts other modules that rely on that interface. Changing an implementation that has been encapsulated within the module should be less risky, because change is isolated to the individual module. A Test Module helps you verify that your changes didn't unexpectedly break anything.

Levelize Modules pattern, 157

Some modules within an application are very widely used. A module that can be used by any other module is a low-level module. An example of a low-level module is one containing utility classes that provide helpful methods to manipulate strings and format dates. You have to be cautious when changing low-level modules, even if your change is confined to the implementation details. A small problem can cause widespread failure.

SAMPLE

An architectural benefit we often try to achieve when leveraging the object-oriented paradigm is to define abstractions that allow us to mix and match different implementations at runtime. Doing this requires that we avoid dependencies on the implementation classes and instead depend only on the abstractions. Modularity can help us take this benefit one step further. With modularity, we have the benefit of using different implementation classes, as well as potentially using completely different modules that provide different implementations of an abstraction. Such flexibility requires that we depend only on a module's abstract elements.

Figure 11.2 illustrates a `loan.jar` module that is used by an `applicant.jar` module. The `Applicant` class within the `applicant.jar`

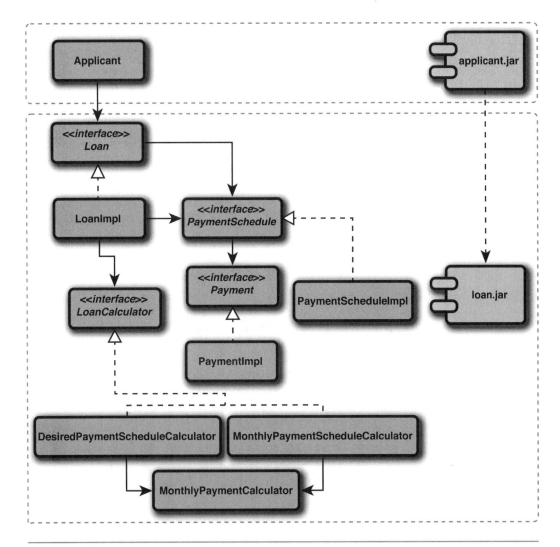

Figure 11.2 Abstract Loan module

module depends only upon the `Loan` and `PaymentSchedule` interfaces within the `loan.jar` module. By avoiding dependencies on concrete classes within `loan.jar`, we have the flexibility to introduce new implementations by creating another module that implements the necessary interfaces. It also allows us to create a `TestModule` so that we can independently test the `applicant.jar` module without requiring the implementation classes in the `loan.jar` module.

Listing 11.1 illustrates the `Applicant` class, where we can see the `Loan` interface is injected to the constructor. Once the `Applicant` instances obtains its reference to the `Loan` abstraction, the `Loan` `.calculatePaymentSchedule()` method is called, which returns the `PaymentSchedule`. Because the `Applicant` depends only on abstractions within the `loan.jar` module, we have the flexibility to create a new module that implements the `Loan` and `PaymentSchedule` interfaces, followed by injecting the alternative `Loan` implementation into the `Applicant` class. And this flexibility comes without the requirement of modifying anything within the `applicant.jar` module.

Listing 11.1 Applicant Class

```
package com.extensiblejava.applicant;

import com.extensiblejava.loan.*;

public class Applicant {
   Loan loan;
   PaymentSchedule paymentSchedule;

   public Applicant (Loan loan) {
      this.loan = loan;
      this.paymentSchedule =
         this.loan.calculatePaymentSchedule();
   }

   public Loan obtainLoanInformation () {
      return loan;
     //determine if applicant can afford the payments
     //by running a credit check.
   }
}
```

Listing 11.2 illustrates the `Loan` interface, while Listing 11.3 illustrates the `PaymentSchedule` interface. Note that the `PaymentSchedule` interface requires a `Payment` type be passed to its `addPayment` method. The `Payment` is also an interface, ensuring that if any class using the `loan.jar` module remains coupled only to abstractions.

Listing 11.2 Loan Interface

```
package com.extensiblejava.loan;</pre>

package com.extensiblejava.loan;

import java.math.*;

public interface Loan {
    public PaymentSchedule calculatePaymentSchedule();
    public BigDecimal getMonthlyPayment();
    public BigDecimal getFinalPayment();
    public BigDecimal getCumulativeInterest();
    public BigDecimal getCumulativePrincipal();
    public BigDecimal getTotalPayments();
}
```

Listing 11.3 PaymentSchedule Interface

```
package com.extensiblejava.loan;
public interface PaymentSchedule {
    public void addPayment(Payment payment);
    public Iterator getPayments();
    public Integer getNumberOfPayments();
}
```

There are a myriad of implementation details that are important to discuss. The method used to inject the `Loan` interface into the `Applicant` instance is of utmost importance and is one of the primary strengths of a dependency injection framework like Spring. Even greater flexibility can be realized if using a modularity framework like OSGi. OSGi offers the dependency injection capabilities of Spring while bringing the runtime dynamism that would allow us to install new modules we create that implement the `Loan` interface without restarting our system. This allows `Applicant` to dynamically discover new modules that implement the `Loan` and `PaymentSchedule` interfaces.

OSGi, 271

WRAPPING UP

If Acyclic Relationships is arguably the most important pattern, Abstract Modules arguably yields the most flexibility. While the resulting design is a bit more complex, you'll find you can achieve some pretty amazing results when applying patterns in conjunction with Abstract Modules. When layering an application using Physical Layers, your resulting module structure should be unidirectional. That is, it should adhere to Acyclic Relationships. But in some cases, you might have a strong desire to violate your layered relationships because of the perceived need to reference a method on a class in an upper-level layer. In Manage Relationships, we saw how we can alter our module dependency structure by moving classes to specific modules.

Implementation Factory and Separate Abstractions, the next two patterns discussed, offer additional perspectives surrounding how we can ensure module relationships maintain the degree of flexibility necessary that will maximize extensibility. Using the sample code from Abstract Modules, we'll show how we can use Spring to inject the `Loan` interface in the `Sample` in the sample code for Implementation Factory. We'll illustrate how we can bring even greater flexibility to our `Loan` system in Separate Abstractions. Colocate Exceptions will complete the design. Part III shows how OSGi μServices can bring a significant degree of flexibility to the `Loan` sample.

As you've seen with most of the modularity patterns thus far, they are rarely used independently. Instead, multiple patterns are often used in conjunction with each other to realize the flexibility desired. The patterns are presented independently, however, because each pattern also introduces an extra level of complexity that may not always be warranted.

IMPLEMENTATION FACTORY

STATEMENT

Use factories to create a module's implementation classes.

DESCRIPTION

A class dependent on an abstraction should avoid referencing any of the implementing classes; otherwise, any time a new implementation class is defined, the class dependent on the abstraction also needs to be changed:

> If a class depending on an abstraction must be changed when creating a new implementation of the abstraction, the design is flawed.

Because a client class cannot create an implementation class if we want the two classes abstractly coupled, we must find an alternative. The alternative is to use an Implementation Factory. Figure 11.3 illustrates the Implementation Factory pattern. As shown here, the `Implementation-Factory` class is responsible for creating the `ServiceImpl` class and

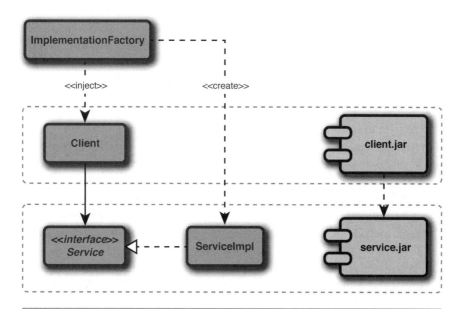

Figure 11.3 Implementation Factory pattern

injecting the `ServiceImpl` instance created into the `PaymentTest` class as a `Service` interface type.

IMPLEMENTATION VARIATIONS

Abstract Modules pattern, 222

One of the challenges we face with Abstract Modules is how the object relationships are established at runtime. There are different approaches to creating an Implementation Factory and establishing the appropriate object references, also known as *wiring*. The two most common approaches are dependency injection and lookup. Dependency injection is favorable over lookup or locator because it ensures that the client class has no direct dependency on the factory and has no indirect dependencies on the implementing classes.

There are different ways to implement the factory that creates the implementation classes and wires them together via dependency injection. As shown in Figure 11.3, the factory might be a class that abstracts away the creation process. The GOF creational patterns are each examples, in different configurations, of ways that a factory can be used to create implementations and wire together instances of the classes created. A dependency injection framework is another way to implement an Implementation Factory. Popular dependency injection frameworks include the Spring and Google Guice frameworks.

OSGi blueprint services, 278

Modeled directly after Spring, OSGi Blueprint Services offer a dynamic way to wire together instances of classes within the OSGi framework. The notion of OSGi μServices lends further benefit by offering significant runtime dynamism. An example illustrating the flexibility of OSGi and μServices can be found in Chapter 16, "OSGi and Groovy."

An Implementation Factory is often used with Abstract Modules and Separate Abstractions because the purpose of these two patterns is to create highly extensive modular systems with modules that are coupled only through abstractions. When these patterns are used, it's imperative that we avoid inadvertently coupling the modules while creating and wiring together the instances within them. The Implementation Factory solves this challenge. But, it also begs the question, "Where does the factory live?"

Manage Relationships pattern, 116

We already stated that the creation process must be encapsulated within its own class, as we saw in Figure 11.3. But, when allocating the classes to the modules, we must also determine where the factory class should live. In general, the factory class must live external to the module whose class it creates as well as the module into which it is injecting those classes. Any other approach results in coupling the two modules, even though the classes involved during the creation process might exhibit a flexible structure. In Module Relationships, we explored how class structure can be flexible while module structure might still be inflexible. Certainly, both are desirable. At this point, we make the following statement about where the factory must reside:

design encapsulation, 37

> The factory class must not be in the same module as the class instances it creates or in the same module as the class into which it's injecting those instances.

So, where does it live? If the factory is a class, it should live in a separate module. But typically, we don't create our own factory classes anymore. More likely we'll use a dependency injection framework. And many dependency injection frameworks wire together instances based on an XML configuration. In these cases, we have a bit more flexibility since the class isn't directly referenced as a class data type but is inferred dynamically based on its fully qualified class name. Since this avoids the tight coupling we are trying to avoid, the configuration can live within one of the modules. As new modules are introduced that must use different implementations, they can include their own configuration files. Alternatively, we can include the configurations in separate modules and replace only those modules with new configurations as necessary.

CONSEQUENCES

An Implementation Factory contributes to a more complex system structure. Either more classes are necessary or a dependency injection framework where configuration files define the wiring must be used. Additionally, an Implementation Factory implies that classes are coupled abstractly. Certainly, if classes weren't coupled abstractly, there would be no need for an Implementation Factory. Classes could easily create other concrete instances.

Abstract coupling offers significant flexibility. To realize the flexibility offered by other patterns such as Abstract Modules and Separate Abstractions, Implementation Factory is not only desirable but required. Ensuring that the factory, and corresponding modules, are designed correctly

abstract coupling example, 50

implies that the factory be given consideration as a critical factor when designing the structure and dependencies of the modules.

To illustrate the disadvantages of lookup, consider Figure 11.3. The `ImplementationFactory` class holds a reference to the `Payment-Test` class and injects the `ServiceImpl` instance into the `Payment-Test`. If a lookup approach had been used, the `PaymentTest` would have referenced the `ImplementationFactory` class directly, likely calling a method on `ImplementationFactory` that returned a reference to a `Service` type.

Although behaviorally identical, there are several structural disadvantages of lookup when compared to dependency injection. When new implementations of `Service` are created, the Implementation Factory must also be modified to create these new instances. Since the `Client` class depends on the `ImplementationFactory` class, there is risk that the ripple affect of change could adversely affect `Client` class. Another very apparent disadvantage is that it's difficult to independently test the `Client` class because of its dependence on `ImplementationFactory` and, indirectly, on all implementations of the `Service` interface.

SAMPLE

The loan sample in Abstract Modules illustrated how we increase extensibility by depending only upon the abstract elements of a module. However, we did not discuss how the `Loan` implementation is actually created, and we were left wondering how to create the implementation class without referencing the concrete class within the either the `applicant.jar` or `client.jar` module. Figure 11.4 illustrates how we create the `Loan` implementation using the `SpringAppContext.xml` file referenced by the `Client` class in the `client.jar` module.

The class created by `SpringAppContext.xml` is injected into the `Applicant` class by the `Client` class. Listing 11.4 illustrates the bean definitions in the `SpringAppContext.xml` file. As can be seen, the `LoanImpl` class is injected into the `Applicant` class constructor. We also see that when the `LoanImpl` class is created, we pass a `LoanCalculator` to its constructor. The `LoanCalculator` constructor is configured with the information necessary to create the `PaymentSchedule` instance.

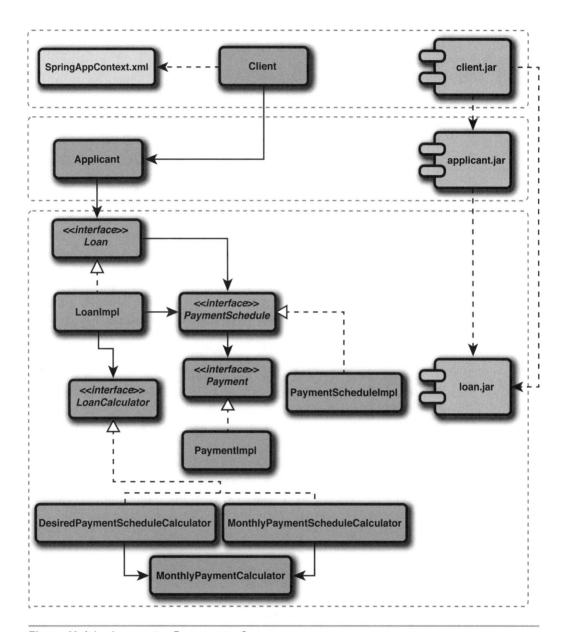

Figure 11.4 Implementation Factory using Spring

Listing 11.4 SpringAppContext.xml File

```xml
<beans>
   <bean id="applicant"
    class="com.extensiblejava.applicant.Applicant">
      <constructor-arg>
         <ref bean="loan"/>
      </constructor-arg>
   </bean>

   <bean id="loan"
      class="com.extensiblejava.loan.impl.LoanImpl">
      <constructor-arg>
         <ref bean="loanCalculator"/>
      </constructor-arg>
   </bean>

   <bean id="loanCalculator"
    class="com.extensiblejava.calculator.
          MinimumPaymentScheduleCalculator">
      <constructor-arg type="java.math.BigDecimal"
                       value="15000.00"/>
      <constructor-arg type="java.math.BigDecimal"
                       value="12.0"/>
      <constructor-arg type="int" value="60"/>
   </bean>

</beans>
```

Listing 11.5 shows the `Client` class. The `Client` class uses the Spring framework to obtain its reference to the `SpringAppContext.xml` configuration file. It then uses the configuration file to obtain its reference to the `LoanImpl` class, but as a `Loan` interface data type.

Listing 11.5 Client Class

```java
package com.extensiblejava.client;

import java.math.*;
import com.extensiblejava.applicant.*;
import com.extensiblejava.loan.*;
import com.extensiblejava.calculator.*;
import com.extensiblejava.applicant.*;
import org.springframework.context.*;
import org.springframework.context.support.*;
```

```
public class Client {
   public static void main(String args[]) {
      ApplicationContext appContext = new
      FileSystemXmlApplicationContext(
      "com/extensiblejava/someclient/SpringAppContext.xml");
      Applicant applicant = (Applicant)
      appContext.getBean("applicant");
      Loan loan = applicant.obtainLoanInformation();
      BigDecimal monthlyPayment = loan.getMonthlyPayment();
      System.out.println(monthlyPayment);
   }
}
```

Listing 11.6 shows the Applicant class. The Applicant class shown here is equivalent to the Applicant class shown in Listing 11.1 of the Abstract Modules "Sample" section, illustrating the behavioral similarity.

Listing 11.6 Applicant Class

```
package com.extensiblejava.applicant;

import com.extensiblejava.loan.*;

public class Applicant {
   Loan loan;
   PaymentSchedule paymentSchedule;

   public Applicant (Loan loan) {
      this.loan = loan;
      this.paymentSchedule =
         this.loan.calculatePaymentSchedule();
   }

   public Loan obtainLoanInformation () {
      return loan;
      //determine if applicant can afford the
      //payments by running a credit check.
   }
}
```

Listing 11.7 shows the LoanImpl, which implements the Loan interface. The LoanImpl instance is injected into the Applicant instance by the `Client` instance as a `Loan` interface data type. The `LoanImpl` accepts a `LoanCalculator`, which we saw in the `SpringApp-Context.xml` file in Listing 11.4. The `LoanCalculator`, which we'll omit here, is also an interface. At runtime, this sample uses the `Minimum-PaymentScheduleCalculator` implementation, which is configured with the loan parameters.

Listing 11.7 LoanImpl Class

```
package com.extensiblejava.loan.impl;

import java.math.*;
import java.util.*;
import com.extensiblejava.loan.*;

public class LoanImpl implements Loan {
   private LoanCalculator loanCalculator;
   private PaymentSchedule paymentSchedule;

   public LoanImpl(LoanCalculator loanCalculator) {
      this.loanCalculator = loanCalculator;
   }
      //...rest of Loan interface implementation.
}
```

Again, Listing 11.4 illustrates how the instances are wired, and Spring manages the creation of the instances, thereby allowing our code to maintain abstract references to each other, ultimately allowing the `applicant.jar` module to reference only the abstract elements of the `loan.jar` module.

WRAPPING UP

Any time types are coupled abstractly, it's imperative that we introduce a mechanism for creating the implementation classes. This is a well-known challenge for which multiple options are available when using an object-oriented programming language. Yet, maintaining a flexible module structure implies that we must not only have a creation mechanism in place but that we also bundle the modules accordingly to ensure we take advantage of the flexible class structure and creation mechanisms we use. Next, in Separate Abstractions, we'll introduce how our module structure can be made even more flexible.

SEPARATE ABSTRACTIONS

STATEMENT

Place abstractions and the classes that implement them in separate modules.

DESCRIPTION

Providing new implementations of the abstractions within a module allow you to create new modules with implementations that extend the behavior of the system. Abstract Modules accommodates this scenario. However, in certain situations, you may want to replace an existing behavior of the system with new behavior altogether. Unfortunately, with Abstract Modules, the abstractions and implementations live within the same module, preventing you from replacing the default behavior.

Abstract Modules pattern, 222

By separating the abstractions from the implementations, placing each in different modules, you allow yourself the flexibility to provide new implementations that completely replace the existing implementation. Figure 11.5 illustrates Separate Abstractions. The `Service` interface and `ServiceImpl` are placed in separate modules. New service

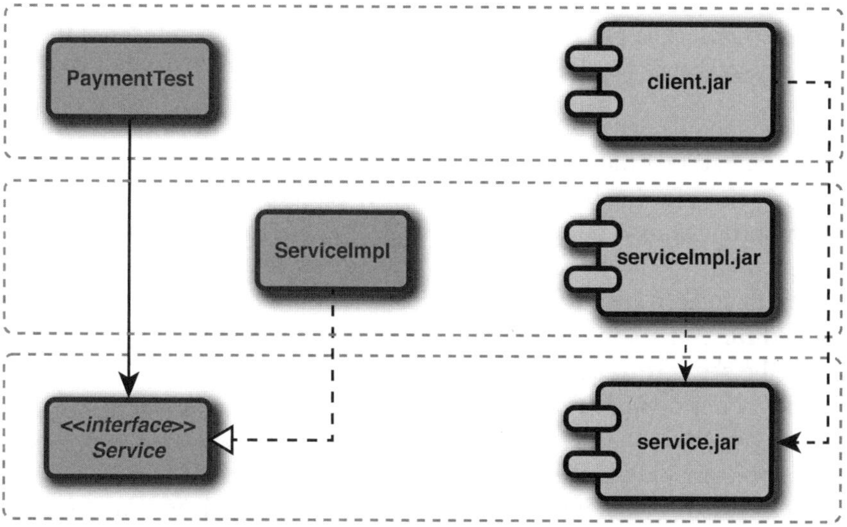

Figure 11.5 Separate Abstractions pattern

implementations can be created and placed in their own modules, allowing you to remove any existing service implementations without modifying the existing system.

IMPLEMENTATION VARIATIONS

The two key ingredients when using Separate Abstractions is deciding where you should place the abstraction and where you should place the implementation. Because there could be many different implementations, the key to making this decision is figuring out the module dependencies, keeping in mind that the modules containing the implementation will be dependent on the module containing the abstraction. In general, use the following principle:

> Keep the abstraction closer to the classes that depend upon it and further from the classes that extend or implement it.

Here are some general guidelines to help you accommodate this goal:

- If all the classes that depend upon the abstraction live in a single module, then place the classes and the abstraction in the same module.
- If all the classes that depend upon the abstractions live in multiple modules, then place the abstraction in a module separate from the classes that depend upon it.

Implementation Factory pattern, 229   The module depending on the abstraction needs to be injected with an implementation of the abstraction or have some way to look up the implementation at runtime. In other words, creating the appropriate implementation is an important consideration. Otherwise, the module that is dependent on the abstraction will also be dependent on the implementation, which compromises the integrity. For instance, in Figure 11.5, if the `PaymentTest` class created the `ServiceImpl` class, the `client.jar` module would depend upon the `serviceimpl.jar` module. New implementations of the service would then necessitate modifying the `client.jar` module to create a new instance of the new implementation. The implementation mechanism you choose must avoid coupling modules unnecessarily.

inverting relationships, 122   Placement of the abstractions allows you to invert or eliminate the relationships between modules. As shown in Figure 11.6, if the abstraction and classes dependent on the abstraction live in a module separate from

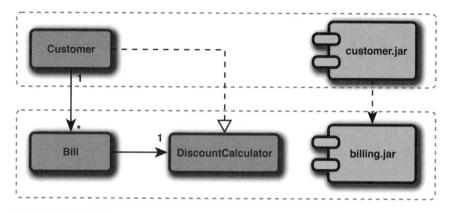

Figure 11.6 Abstraction and dependent classes in the same module

the implementation, then the module containing the implementation is dependent upon the module containing the classes and the abstraction. However, if the abstraction lives in its own module, there is no relationship between the module containing the implementation and the module containing the classes dependent on the abstraction, as shown in Figure 11.7. In the latter case, the module containing the abstractions serves as a specification module or a contract between the other two modules.

Figure 11.6 illustrates how the abstraction and class dependent on the abstraction reside in the same module. Figure 11.7 illustrates separating the abstraction to a different module, effectively eliminating the relationship between the `billing.jar` module and `customer.jar` module altogether.

When assembling modules, you may find that two otherwise independent modules share a common state. You'll likely want to avoid having each module initialize and manage that state separately because of overhead and possibly unreliable processing. Doing so also incurs an unnecessary performance burden. If the state that each module relies upon is simply data that each requires to perform some processing, then it's fairly easy to populate a bean defined by each module and pass the bean into the class requiring that data. This is an example of demotion, which was discussed in Acyclic Relationships.

Acyclic Relationships pattern, 146

With Separate Abstractions, you are massaging the relationships between modules. We saw an example of how module relationships can be inverted in the Manage Relationships pattern "Sample" section, including

Manage Relationships pattern, 116

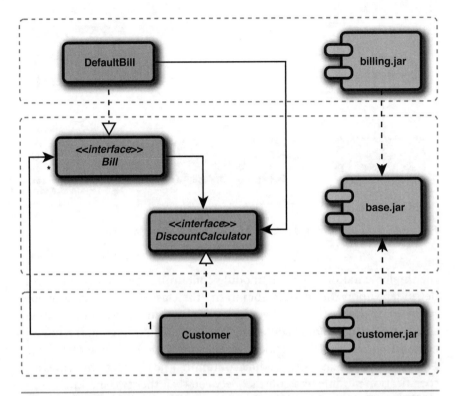

Figure 11.7 Abstraction, implementation, and dependent classes in separate modules

ways to invert and eliminate the relationships between modules. Placement of the abstraction allows you to invert or eliminate these module relationships.

CONSEQUENCES

Separate Abstractions help you eliminate module relationships. Unfortunately, Separate Abstractions results in a more complex structure to manage. With Separate Abstractions, you are faced with the dilemma of flexibility versus complexity. Separate Abstractions is more flexible but also more complex. When using Separate Abstractions, you've decided that the extra flexibility is worth the price of additional complexity.

In some cases, with a well-designed class structure, you can separate the abstractions without making any coding changes at all. However, you'll still have to deal with managing more module dependencies, albeit the dependency structure will be more flexible. Separate Abstractions is a way to manage module relationships.

Keep in mind, however, that with Abstract Modules, the intent is to depend upon the abstract elements of a module that make it easier to extend an existing module with new functionality. With Separate Abstractions, you are interested not only in extending a module with new functionality but also in replacing the existing implementation of a module. For instance, in Figure 11.6, the `billing.jar` module is not an Abstract Module because the `customer.jar` module is not dependent upon abstractions in the `billing.jar` module. However, the `billing.jar` module can easily be extended with new functionality.

Abstract Modules pattern, 222

The trade-off between Abstract Modules and Separate Abstractions is subtle. With Abstract Modules, you have fewer module dependencies to manage, although module relationships may be more brittle. With Separate Abstractions, module relationships are flexible, but you have more relationships to manage. Fortunately, if you already have Abstract Modules, you can often transition to Separate Abstractions by simply separating the abstractions and implementations into different modules.

Sample

In Abstract Modules, we depend upon the abstract elements of a module. In Implementation Factory, we used a factory to create the implementation class. Now, by separating the interfaces from their implementation and placing the classes in separate modules, we can completely eliminate module dependencies between all modules that contain concrete classes. Here, we'll continue with our loan sample to illustrate Separate Abstractions.

In Manage Relationships, we saw how we can invert and eliminate module relationships. Now we'll partition our loan classes into a separate set of modules and eliminate the relationships between all modules with concrete classes. As it turns out, because I have a flexible class structure for the loan sample, I can do this by simply bundling two interfaces into a single module and the implementation classes out into their own separate set of modules. Figure 11.8 shows the new module structure, with the same class structure. The only other modification I've made is to modify my build script.

Manage Relationships Pattern, 116

As we can see here, the `loan-intrfc.jar` module contains only interfaces. Then, we'll separate classes responsible for calculating the loan

Cohesive Modules pattern, 139

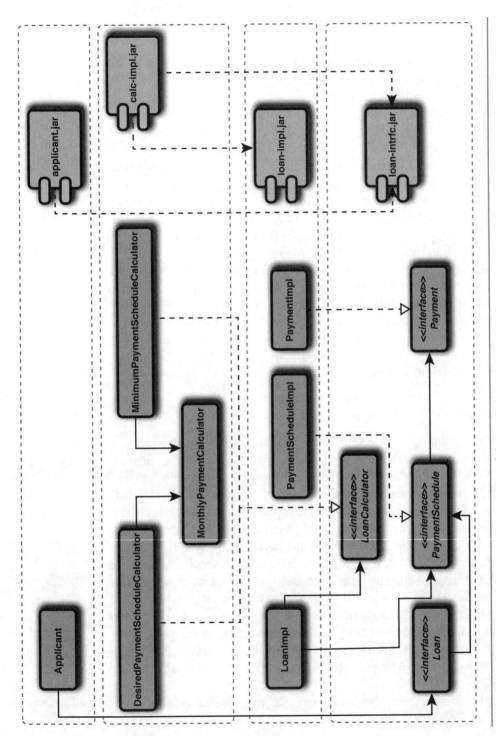

Figure 11.8 Separating Abstractions to another module

payments into the `calc-impl.jar` module and put the classes that contain the loan information in the `loan-impl.jar` module. We do this to give us the flexibility of creating new loan or calculation modules, allowing the two to evolve independent of each other. Unfortunately, the `calc-impl.jar` module is still dependent on the `loan-impl.jar` module, representing a flaw in our design. Separating `calc-impl.jar` and `loan-impl.jar` functionality into separate modules in an example of the Cohesive Modules pattern. In the "Sample" section for Colocate Exceptions, we'll fix the flaw and eliminate the relationship between these two modules. We'll also show the final version of this sample code managed by an OSGi framework using OSGi µServices.

Colocate Exceptions pattern, 246

OSGi µServices, 278

Listing 11.8 illustrates a section of the `dist` build target that creates the modules. Note the modules that are created and the classes that are allocated to the modules.

Listing 11.8 build.xml File

```
<target name="dist" depends="compile">
   <jar jarfile="${bindist}/loan-impl-${version}.jar"
    basedir="${build}"
    includes = "com/extensiblejava/loan/impl/**"/>
   <jar jarfile="${bindist}/loan-intrfc-${version}.jar"
    basedir="${build}"
    excludes="com/extensiblejava/calculator/test/**
             com/extensiblejava/calculator/**
             com/extensiblejava/loan/impl/**
             com/extensiblejava/applicant/**
             com/extensiblejava/someclient/**
             com/extensiblejava/test/**"/>
   <jar jarfile="${bindist}/calc-test-${version}.jar"
    basedir="${build}"
    includes="com/extensiblejava/calculator/test/**"/>
   <jar jarfile="${bindist}/applicant-test-${version}.jar"
    basedir="${build}"
    includes="com/extensiblejava/applicant/test/**"/>
   <jar jarfile="${bindist}/alltests-test-${version}.jar"
    basedir="${build}"
    includes="com/extensiblejava/test/**"
    excludes ="com/extensiblejava/applicant/test/**
              com/extensiblejava/calculator/test/**"/>
   <jar jarfile="${bindist}/applicant-${version}.jar"
    basedir="${build}"
    includes="com/extensiblejava/applicant/**"
    excludes="com/extensiblejava/applicant/test/**"/>
```

```
    <jar jarfile="${bindist}/calc-impl-${version}.jar"
     basedir="${build}"
     includes="com/extensiblejava/calculator/**"
     excludes="com/extensiblejava/calculator/test/**"/>
    <jar jarfile="${bindist}/client-${version}.jar"
     basedir="${build}"
     includes="com/extensiblejava/someclient/**"/>
</target>
```

Wrapping Up

Separate Abstractions allows us to create a highly flexible and extensible system. Depending only on the abstract elements of a module and using an Implementation Factory help ensure that we realize the intended benefits of Separate Abstractions. It also exemplifies another important point: Module patterns are rarely used in isolation and are almost always used in conjunction with design patterns as well as multiple modularity patterns.

Reference

Martin, Robert C. 2000. *Design Principles and Design Patterns*. www.objectmentor.com/resources/articles/Principles_and_Patterns.pdf

UTILITY PATTERNS

12

The utility patterns aid modular development. Unlike the other patterns, they don't emphasize reuse, extensibility, or usability. Instead, the utility patterns support the other patterns and discuss ways that modularity can be enforced and help address quality-related issues. The utility patterns include the following:

- **Colocate Exceptions**: Exceptions should be close to the class or interface that throws them.
- **Levelize Build**: Execute the build in accordance with module levelization.
- **Test Module**: Each module should have a corresponding test module.

COLOCATE EXCEPTIONS

STATEMENT

Exceptions should be close to the class or interface that throws them.

DESCRIPTION

Sadly, dealing with exceptions in enterprise software systems is often an afterthought. But, the allocation of exceptions to modules has significant implications on the modularity and, more specifically, the dependencies between modules within our software system. Placing the exception close to a class that catches it often causes a cyclic dependency between the module containing the class that throws the exception and the module containing the class that catches the exception. Exceptions should always be placed in a module closer to the class that throws the exception than a module closer to the class that catches the exception. This helps maintain your desired module dependency structure. Figure 12.1 illustrates this scenario.

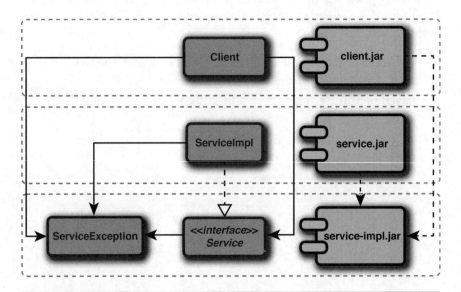

Figure 12.1 Colocate exceptions

IMPLEMENTATION VARIATIONS

Whereas Separate Abstractions says that interfaces should be close to the classes that use them, exceptions should be close to the class that throws them. If multiple classes from separate modules throw the same exception, then demotion should be used to manage the dependencies between the two modules. In other words, the exception should be demoted to a module upon which the other modules that throw, and catch, the exception depend upon.

Separate Abstractions pattern, 237

demotion, 147

CONSEQUENCES

Neglecting to place an exception in the appropriate module will result in undesired dependencies between modules. For instance, if the exception is placed in the same module as the class that catches that exception, then the module with classes throwing the exception will depend upon the module where the exception is caught. It's likely that this will result in a cyclic dependency between two or more modules. For instance, in Figure 12.1, had the `ServiceException` been placed in the `client.jar` module, both the `service-impl.jar` and `service.jar` modules would be dependent on the `client.jar`. Figure 12.2 shows the resulting

cyclic dependencies, 50

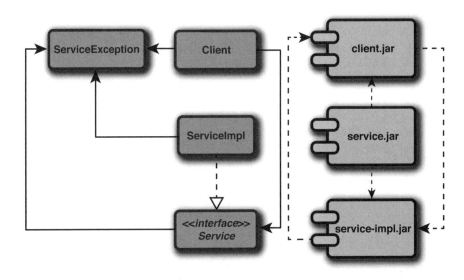

Figure 12.2 Incorrect placement of exceptions

structure. A clear cyclic dependency exists between the `client.jar` and `service-impl.jar` modules.

SAMPLE

So far, we used variations of the loan sample application for a few patterns. But each implementation has had subtle flaws (though we haven't necessarily pointed these out). Although we accomplished the goal of the pattern, other areas of our module structure still suffered from design deficiencies. Now, we illustrate the gold standard for the loan sample. Part III continues this sample and shows how we can leverage OSGi and the flexibility it brings to the application.

Figure 12.3 illustrates the final module structure. Notice the `CalculationException` that is located within the `loan-intrfc.jar`. This is necessary for two primary reasons. First, the `LoanCalculator` interface throws the exception, as illustrated in Listing 12.1. If we placed `CalculationException` in the `calc-impl.jar` module, the `loan-intrfc.jar` module would depend on the `calc-impl.jar` module. Second, if we placed the exception in any other module, our `loan-intrfc.jar` module would depend on that module. Because `LoanFacade` and any client will always depend on the `loan-intrfc.jar` module, placing `CalculationException` in this module is the safest place.

Listing 12.1 LoanCalculator Throws CalculationException

```
package com.extensiblejava.loan;

import java.math.*;

public interface LoanCalculator {
   public Loan calculateLoan(BigDecimal presentValue,
                             BigDecimal rate,
                             int term)
                             throws CalculationException;
}
```

Module Facade pattern, 212

Test Module pattern, 263
Another significant flaw in the design has also been corrected. In Module Facade, the `calc-impl.jar` module is dependent upon the `loan-impl.jar` module. Two modules with concrete classes dependent on one another results in a brittle structure. Changing the `loan-impl.jar` module may cause a ripple effect that impacts the `calc-impl.jar` module.

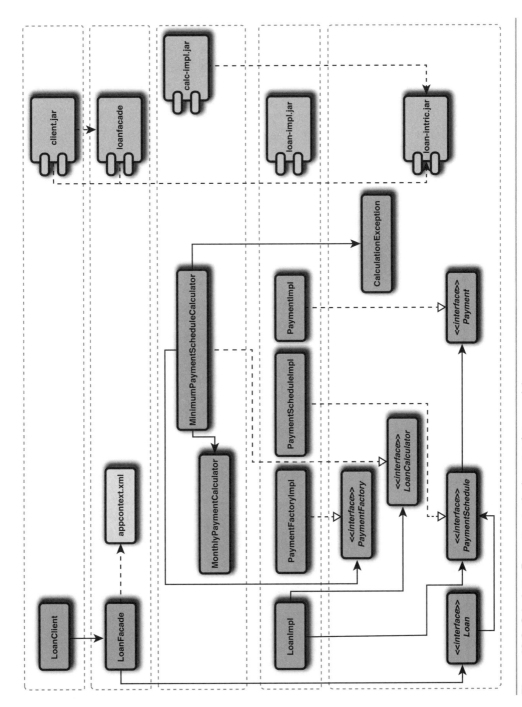

Figure 12.3 CalculationException in the loan-intrfc.jar module

After removing this dependency, as illustrated in Figure 12.3, the `calc-impl.jar` module now only depends on `loan-intrfc.jar` module. We accomplished this by introducing the `PaymentFactory` interface in the `loan-intrfc.jar` module with the implementation residing in the `loan-impl.jar` module. The `PaymentFactory` is sent to the `MinimumPaymentScheduleCalculator` class, which can use the factory to create the appropriate implementations instead of creating them using the new keyword. This new structure will be beneficial when creating a Test Module. Listing 12.2 shows the `PaymentFactoryImpl` code. Listing 12.3 shows the `MinimumPaymentScheduleCalculator`, which uses the `PaymentFactoryImpl` to create the `PaymentSchedule` and `Payment` instances.

Listing 12.2 PaymentFactoryImpl Class

```
package com.extensiblejava.loan.impl;
import java.math.*;
import com.extensiblejava.loan.*;

public class PaymentFactoryImpl implements PaymentFactory {
   public PaymentSchedule createPaymentSchedule()
      { return new PaymentScheduleImpl(); }

   public Payment createPayment(BigDecimal principal,
                                BigDecimal interest)
      { return new PaymentImpl(principal, interest); }
}
```

Listing 12.3 calculatePaymentSchedule Method in MinimumPaymentScheduleCalculator Class

```
public PaymentSchedule calculatePaymentSchedule(BigDecimal
presentValue, BigDecimal rate, int term)
   throws CalculationException {
   try {
      PaymentSchedule paymentSchedule =
         this.paymentFactory.createPaymentSchedule();
      BigDecimal adjustedRate = rate.
         divide(new BigDecimal("1200"), 2,
         BigDecimal.ROUND_UNNECESSARY);
      MonthlyPaymentCalculator paymentCalculator =
         new MonthlyPaymentCalculator();
```

```
BigDecimal monthlyPayment =
   paymentCalculator.calculatePayment(presentValue,
   rate, term);
BigDecimal loanBalance =
   new BigDecimal(presentValue.toString());
while (loanBalance.doubleValue() >
      monthlyPayment.doubleValue())
{
   BigDecimal interest =
      loanBalance.multiply(adjustedRate);
   interest =
      interest.setScale(2, BigDecimal.ROUND_HALF_UP);
   BigDecimal principal =
      monthlyPayment.subtract(interest);
   principal = principal.
      setScale(2, BigDecimal.ROUND_HALF_UP);
   Payment payment =
      this.paymentFactory.createPayment(principal,
      interest);
   paymentSchedule.addPayment(payment);

   this.cumulativeInterest =
      this.cumulativeInterest.add(interest).
      setScale(2, BigDecimal.ROUND_HALF_UP);
   this.cumulativePrincipal =
      this.cumulativePrincipal.add(principal).
      setScale(2, BigDecimal.ROUND_HALF_UP);
   loanBalance = loanBalance.subtract(principal);
}

BigDecimal interest =
   loanBalance.multiply(adjustedRate).
   setScale(2, BigDecimal.ROUND_HALF_UP);
BigDecimal principal = loanBalance.
   setScale(2,BigDecimal.ROUND_HALF_UP);
this.cumulativeInterest =
   this.cumulativeInterest.add(interest).
   setScale(2, BigDecimal.ROUND_HALF_UP);
this.cumulativePrincipal =
   this.cumulativePrincipal.add(principal).
   setScale(2, BigDecimal.ROUND_HALF_UP);
Payment payment = this.paymentFactory.
   createPayment(principal, interest);
paymentSchedule.addPayment(payment);
return paymentSchedule;
```

```
    } catch (Exception e) {
        throw new CalculationException(e);
    }
}
```

WRAPPING UP

It's easy to compromise a well-designed structure by incorrectly allocating exceptions to the incorrect modules. The result is undesirable dependencies between modules and possibly cyclic dependencies. The design of exceptions should not be an afterthought, and allocating exceptions to their appropriate modules is an important design decision that helps maintain the system's integrity.

LEVELIZE BUILD

STATEMENT

Execute the build in accordance with module levelization.

DESCRIPTION

An automated and repeatable build is a critical aspect to most successful development projects. First and foremost, an automated and repeatable build forces you to integrate early and integrate often, so you're guaranteed to always have a system that works. Of course, you must follow a couple of rules:

- Any compile error that ever creeps in must be immediately resolved. Because you should be using a version control system, the projects comprising your application should always be free of any compilation errors.
- Any unit test that fails must be immediately fixed. Unit and acceptance tests should be run after each change you make, and if you ever find that a test fails, you should treat this failure with the same urgency you'd give a compile error.

Although pretty simple, these two rules are key elements because they are part of what defines an automated and repeatable build. So here, in order, are the characteristics of defining an automated and repeatable build:[1]

- It must be a clean compile, meaning that no compiler-generated syntactical errors occur. While it's acceptable to encounter certain warnings, such as those generated by deprecated method usage, you should strive to remove these warnings before future builds.
- The build should be done using the most current version of all source files. There are occasions where you'll want to compile older versions of code to revert to a previous version. Typically, when compiling these older versions, you'll use the source files consistent with the version of the application you're building.

---

1. Martin Fowler describes the five steps to a successful build in his seminal article on the topic, which can be found at http://martinfowler.com/articles/originalContinuousIntegration. html#WhatIsASuccessfulBuild. This list is a slight variation of his five steps.

- A clean build implies that all application source files are compiled. Conditional compiles or partial builds do not prove the syntactical correctness of the entire application. You do not need to compile existing binary modules.

- The build should generate all files representing the units of deployment. For Java applications, this means all `.jar`, `.war`, and `.ear` files should be created.

- The build should verify that the application is functionally correct, meaning all unit tests for the application should be run. If all unit tests pass successfully, the build is successful.

A rather significant aspect of an automated and repeatable build is that it be separated and performed outside the confines of your favorite integrated development environment (IDE). Most IDEs allow you to perform conditional compiles, as well as full compiles within the environment. Performing the build within an IDE leaves too many loopholes open for individual developers to produce inconsistent results. In fact, without a repeatable build script, it would be very difficult to enforce the module relationships that compose your application.

The most common manifestation of an automated and repeatable build is a full classpath build, where all source files are compiled as part of the same target. Since all source is included within a single build step, you're also required to include all dependent modules in the classpath of that target. In doing so, you lose your ability to enforce module dependencies as part of the build process, and the module dependencies that you expect to exist may not be entirely accurate. With a full classpath build, there is no good way to enforce your module dependency structure.

When you levelize your build, however, it allows you to build each module independently as part of a module specific target, where each target has its own build classpath. Because each target specifies its own classpath, you are required only to include dependent modules for the source being built instead of all modules for the complete application. Any developer creating a dependency on a module not in the target's build classpath will cause a compilation error to occur when the build process executes, essentially enforcing your desired module dependencies.

Levelize Modules pattern, 157

Acyclic Relationships pattern, 146 Levelize Build can be performed only if modules themselves have been levelized and all relationships between modules are acyclic. Cycles existing between any two modules will require that each module be built at the same time. Given any two or more modules, if a cycle exists in the dependency structure among any of those modules, then there is no way to get the binary form of one module without also having the binary form of all dependent modules. Because of the cycle between the modules, you'll be required to build all as part of the same target. Figure 12.4 illustrates Levelize Build.

IMPLEMENTATION VARIATIONS

Levelize Build can be more complex than performing a full classpath build. If you're using a build tool like Ant, you'll find that you have many more build targets—effectively, one for each module. Like most complex development issues, breaking down the problem can help simplify it significantly. Modularizing your build scripts by breaking a single complex script into multiple simpler scripts is beneficial.

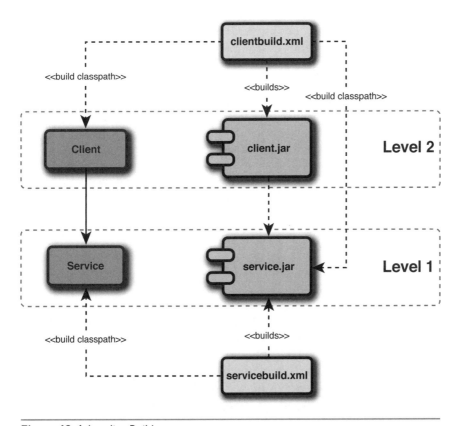

Figure 12.4 Levelize Build

A logical way to break up the build script is to define a separate build script for each module. These module-specific build scripts can also build the test module and even run the test cases. A simplified main build script can be set up to call each of the module build scripts. Additionally, you also have the ability to independently build each module, as well as include the module in other application build scripts.

other tools for modular design, 106

Another option worth considering is using a tool, such as JarAnalyzer, to help enforce levelization of modules. JarAnalyzer offers you the ability to create tests cases that can verify module dependencies. Although you aren't actually performing the build with JarAnalyzer, you still verify levelization of modules by defining test cases that verify the module relationships that span module boundaries. The basic idea is that within your test case, you specify the module dependency constraints, and if any relationships exist that violate the constraints in the test case, the test will fail. So if a new relationship is introduced between module boundaries that isn't allowed, the test case, and ultimately the build, will fail. With this approach, you can actually perform a full classpath build and allow JarAnalyzer to enforce the levelization for you.

> **Note**
>
> I favor a Levelize Build because managing module relationships by defining module dependency constraints can become tedious, especially early in the life cycle when the application structure is subject to wide refactorings that can significantly affect the structure.

Levelize Build also allows you to break large builds down into a set of smaller builds. Ultimately, if build performance is a concern, this separation will allow you to build modules at the same level in parallel with each other. When doing this, lower-level modules are built first, followed by upper-level modules.

CONSEQUENCES

enforcing modularity, 26

Managing dependencies between modules is important, but enforcing the dependencies can be a rather daunting task, especially for large development teams. An elegant conceptual design can quickly evolve into a tangled mess during implementation where not one developer understands how the initial high-level vision has manifest itself in code. Although you may have made it clear what dependency relationships you expect, undesirable dependencies have a way of creeping into your application. Levelize Build helps enforce module relationships.

Levelize Build forces you to think about module dependencies. Early in the development life cycle, you have to define your module dependencies to create the build script. As development progresses, it can be tempting to introduce new dependencies on other modules. However, with Levelize Build, you'll also be forced to modify the build script each time a new module dependency is introduced. Because any new dependency requires a change to the build script, defining any new dependency must be a very conscious decision on the part of a developer. Levelize Build makes it a bit more effort to introduce new dependencies. Introducing new dependencies is an important enough design and architectural decision to warrant this extra effort.

SAMPLE

Recall from Manage Relationships how we eliminated the dependencies between two modules by allocating an abstract class to its own module. Figure 12.5 illustrates this. After we have a module structure that is acyclic, we can use Levelize Build.

Manage Relationships pattern, 116

Let's examine how Levelize Build can help enforce the module relationships. Figure 12.5 shows an initial build script, which performs a full classpath build. Although the result will be the same as the final solution discussed later, there is no way to enforce the relationships using a full classpath build, as shown in Listing 12.4. In the following snippet from our Ant build script, the path ID specifies the location for all application and test source code, as well as the location of Struts and the Servlet API.

Listing 12.4 Full Classpath Build

```
<project name="Comp" default="compile" basedir=".">

    <property name="src" location="${basedir}/src"/>
    <property name="build" location="${basedir}/build"/>
    <property name="lib" location="${basedir}/lib"/>
    <property name="buildstats" location="${basedir}/stats"/>
    <property name="dist" location="${basedir}/bin"/>
    <property name="version" value="1.0"/>

    <path id="project.class.path">
        <pathelement path="${src}"/>
```

```
        <pathelement path="${lib}/junit.jar"/>
    </path>

    <target name="clean">
        <delete dir="${build}"/>
        <delete dir="${buildstats}"/>
        <delete dir="${dist}"/>
    </target>

    <target name="init" depends="clean">
        <mkdir dir="${build}"/>
        <mkdir dir="${buildstats}"/>
        <mkdir dir="${dist}"/>
    </target>

    <target name="compile" depends="init">
        <javac srcdir="${src}" destdir="${build}">
            <classpath refid="project.class.path"/>
        </javac>

        <jar jarfile="${dist}/bill.jar" basedir="${build}"
includes="com/kirkk/bill/**"/>
        <jar jarfile="${dist}/cust.jar" basedir="${build}"
includes="com/kirkk/cust/**"/>
        <jar jarfile="${dist}/base.jar" basedir="${build}"
          includes="com/kirkk/base/**"/>
        <jar jarfile="${dist}/billtest.jar" basedir="${build}"
          includes="com/kirkk/test/**"/>

        <junit printsummary="yes" haltonfailure="yes">
            <classpath>
                <pathelement path="${dist}/bill.jar"/>
                <pathelement path="${dist}/cust.jar"/>
                <pathelement path="${dist}/base.jar"/>
                <pathelement path="${dist}/billtest.jar"/>
                <pathelement path="${lib}/junit.jar"/>
            </classpath>
            <test name="com.kirkk.test.AllTests"
              outfile="junitresults">
                <formatter type="plain"/>
            </test>
        </junit>
    </target>
</project>
```

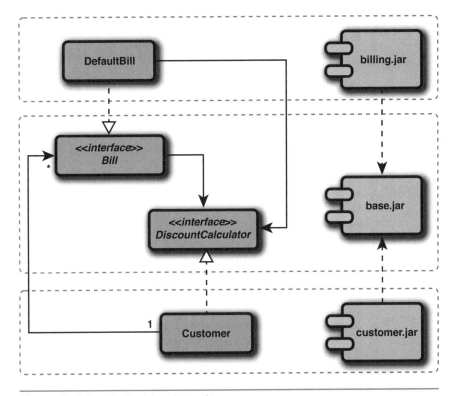

Figure 12.5 Acyclic Module relationships

Listing 12.5 shows the levelized version, which does the exact same thing, except it enforces the module dependencies. The build script is also markedly longer. Each module has its own compilation target. After completion, the binaries are placed into a module. Subsequent targets that rely on a module already built include that module in the build classpath. The build will fail if the build classpath isn't correct, essentially enforcing module dependencies.

Listing 12.5 Levelize Build

```
<project name="Comp" default="testcompile" basedir=".">

    <property name="src" location="${basedir}/src"/>
    <property name="build" location="${basedir}/build"/>
    <property name="buildsrc"
              location="${basedir}/buildsrc"/>
```

```
<property name="lib" location="${basedir}/lib"/>
<property name="buildstats" location="${basedir}/stats"/>
<property name="dist" location="${basedir}/bin"/>
<property name="version" value="1.0"/>

<target name="clean">
   <delete dir="${build}"/>
   <delete dir="${buildsrc}"/>
   <delete dir="${buildstats}"/>
   <delete dir="${dist}"/>
</target>

<target name="init" depends="clean">
   <mkdir dir="${buildstats}"/>
   <mkdir dir="${dist}"/>
</target>

<target name="basecompile" depends="init">
   <mkdir dir="${build}"/>
   <mkdir dir="${buildsrc}"/>
   <copy todir="${buildsrc}">
      <fileset dir="${src}">
         <include name="com/kirkk/base/**"/>
      </fileset>
   </copy>

   <javac srcdir="${buildsrc}" destdir="${build}">
      <classpath>
         <pathelement path="${buildsrc}"/>
      </classpath>
   </javac>

   <jar jarfile="${dist}/base.jar" basedir="${build}"
    includes="com/kirkk/base/**"/>

   <delete dir="${buildsrc}"/>
   <delete dir="${build}"/>
</target>

<target name="billcompile" depends="basecompile">
   <mkdir dir="${build}"/>
   <mkdir dir="${buildsrc}"/>
   <copy todir="${buildsrc}">
      <fileset dir="${src}">
         <include name="com/kirkk/bill/**"/>
      </fileset>
   </copy>
```

```
<javac srcdir="${buildsrc}" destdir="${build}">
    <classpath>
        <pathelement path="${buildsrc}"/>
        <pathelement path="${dist}/base.jar"/>
    </classpath>
</javac>

<jar jarfile="${dist}/bill.jar" basedir="${build}"
  includes="com/kirkk/bill/**"/>

    <delete dir="${buildsrc}"/>
    <delete dir="${build}"/>
</target>

<target name="custcompile" depends="billcompile">
    <mkdir dir="${build}"/>
    <mkdir dir="${buildsrc}"/>
    <copy todir="${buildsrc}">
        <fileset dir="${src}">
            <include name="com/kirkk/cust/**"/>
        </fileset>
    </copy>

    <javac srcdir="${buildsrc}" destdir="${build}">
        <classpath>
            <pathelement path="${buildsrc}"/>
            <pathelement path="${dist}/base.jar"/>
        </classpath>
    </javac>

    <jar jarfile="${dist}/cust.jar" basedir="${build}"
      includes="com/kirkk/cust/**"/>

    <delete dir="${buildsrc}"/>
    <delete dir="${build}"/>
</target>

  <target name="testcompile" depends="custcompile">
    <mkdir dir="${build}"/>
    <mkdir dir="${buildsrc}"/>
    <copy todir="${buildsrc}">
        <fileset dir="${src}">
            <include name="com/kirkk/test/**"/>
        </fileset>
    </copy>
```

```
<javac srcdir="${buildsrc}" destdir="${build}">
   <classpath>
      <pathelement path="${buildsrc}"/>
      <pathelement path="${dist}/base.jar"/>
      <pathelement path="${dist}/cust.jar"/>
      <pathelement path="${dist}/bill.jar"/>
      <pathelement path="${lib}/junit.jar"/>
   </classpath>
</javac>

<jar jarfile="${dist}/billtest.jar" basedir="${build}"
 includes="com/kirkk/test/**"/>

<junit printsummary="yes" haltonfailure="yes">
   <classpath>
      <pathelement path="${dist}/bill.jar"/>
      <pathelement path="${dist}/cust.jar"/>
      <pathelement path="${dist}/base.jar"/>
      <pathelement path="${dist}/billtest.jar"/>
      <pathelement path="${lib}/junit.jar"/>
   </classpath>
   <test name="com.kirkk.test.AllTests"
    outfile="junitresults">
      <formatter type="plain"/>
   </test>
</junit>
<delete dir="${buildsrc}"/>
<delete dir="${build}"/>
</target>
</project>
```

WRAPPING UP

Levelize Build helps enforce the module structure within an application. If undesirable dependencies are introduced between modules, the build will fail. Unfortunately, because the build has knowledge of the module structure, if the structure changes, the build must also change. This cost, however, is worth the price of admission, which is enforceable module dependencies.

TEST MODULE

STATEMENT

Each module should have a corresponding test module.

DESCRIPTION

Unit testing is one of the most important activities you should perform as a developer. A Test Module is a way to organize your unit tests into a module that corresponds to the module containing the classes under test. Figure 12.6 illustrates a Test Module. The `testclient.jar` module is responsible for testing the behavior of the `client.jar` module.

IMPLEMENTATION VARIATIONS

It is tempting for a Test Module to define dependencies on other modules that contain implementations for classes within the module under test. Resisting this temptation is important. Defining additional dependencies on other modules within a Test Module will save you a bit of time in creating the test cases, but it will also compromise the integrity of your test. By using classes in other modules as your stubs, you cannot be certain that a failing test case is the result of a flaw in the module under test or a bug in the classes you are using as your stubs.

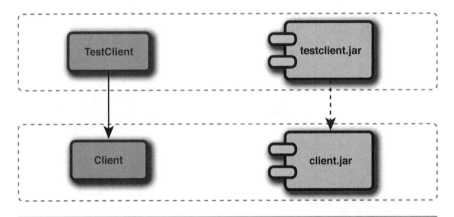

Figure 12.6 Test module

Abstract Modules
pattern, 222

Allowing the Test Module to depend on other system modules also increases the complexity of the dependency structure of your test suite. Instead, the Test Module should provide mocks for the abstractions that it needs, as shown in Figure 12.7. Here, the use of Abstract Modules makes it easy to create a Test Module with its own mock implementation of the `Service` interface.

There are some cases where a Test Module will want to introduce additional dependencies. For instance, if the module under test relies heavily upon database interaction or your goal is to test the integration of two modules working together, then separate these module integration tests from the module unit tests.

In some cases, you may want to share some utility classes across Test Modules. In this situation, you can either duplicate the utility classes or create a lower-level test utility module that contains the test utility classes.

Acyclic Relationships
pattern, 146

Recall that levelizing your module hierarchy requires that you have Acyclic Relationships between all modules. A Test Module should also

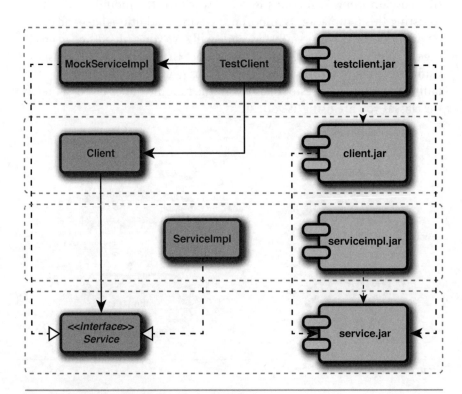

Figure 12.7 Test Module with Abstract Module

have Acyclic Relationships. If you find that the Test Module is more than a single level higher than the module it's testing, it's a good indication that the Test Module is using another module's classes as stubs for the module under test. You must carefully consider the placement of integration, design, performance, and functional tests. It's likely that these types of tests will introduce undesirable Test Module dependencies.

CONSEQUENCES

Test modules increase testability by allowing you to test modules independent of each other. Once a module functions correctly as an independent unit, any error is the result of integration with other modules. A Test Module allows you to ensure that a module works correctly as a standalone entity. Application-level integration tests can be helpful in the situation where you want to test module integration.

Creating a robust suite of tests has other significant advantages. A Test Module helps you design your system. Because modules should be independently testable, a natural byproduct of a Test Module is that you'll emphasize managing module dependencies. When refactoring your code or adding new functionality to an existing code base, a suite of tests can be repeatedly run to guarantee that your changes haven't broken anything that once worked. A Test Module also helps you understand the Published Interface of a module, since it's the interface a Test Module verifies. *module dependencies, 48*

Published Interface pattern, 188

Because you will always run the risk that changes can break the system, a Test Module allows you to automate execution of the module test cases. This offers a guarantee that if a change does break an individual module, it will be caught quickly because it's easy to execute the Test Module as a regression test.

Other types of Test Module can also be useful. A design test allows you to make assertions about the design metrics of the system. Tools such as JarAnalyzer can be used to create tests that check for dependencies between modules. Performance tests allow you to verify the response time of a test. Structuring your test cases into specific test modules allow you to effectively organize the different suites of test cases that you want to run. *JarAnalyzer and other tools, 106*

SAMPLE

Recall the example using a Callback in the discussion on the Acyclic Relationships pattern. Figure 12.8 illustrates the relationship between the *callback example, 154*

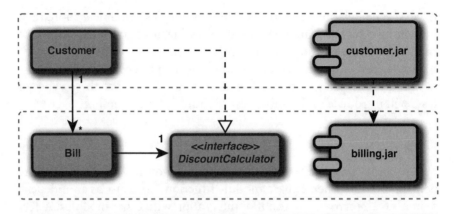

Figure 12.8 Module relationships

customer.jar and billing.jar modules resulting from the relationship between the Customer and Bill classes.

Based on these module relationships, we can already create a separate test module for the billing.jar module. Listing 12.6 illustrates the test case to test the payment functionality of Bill.

Listing 12.6 Testing Payment Functionality of Bill Class

```
package com.kirkk.test;

import junit.framework.TestCase;
import java.math.BigDecimal;
import java.util.*;
import com.kirkk.cust.*;
import com.kirkk.bill.*;

public class BillTest extends TestCase {

    public PaymentTest(String arg0) {
        super(arg0);
    }

    public void testPayment() {
        Customer customer = new Customer();
        customer.createBill(new BigDecimal(500));

        Iterator bills = customer.getBills().iterator();
```

```
    while (bills.hasNext()) {
        Bill bill = (Bill) bills.next();
        BigDecimal paidAmount = bill.pay();
        assertEquals("Paid amount not correct.",
            new BigDecimal(485).setScale(2), paidAmount);
    }
  }
}
```

This test case results in the relationships between modules shown in Figure 12.9, where we can now see the `billingtest.jar` test module. At this point, the `PaymentTest` is actually an integration test because it uses `Customer` to test `Bill`.

Ideally, the `billtest.jar` module won't depend on `customer.jar` to test `billing.jar`. We would also like to create a Test Module for `customer.jar`. So, we need to eliminate the dependency between `billing.jar` and `customer.jar` altogether. To do this, we'll move the `DiscountCalculator` to a new `base.jar` module and refactor the `Bill` class to an interface. The `Bill` interface will also be placed in the `base.jar` module. Figure 12.10 illustrates the new structure.

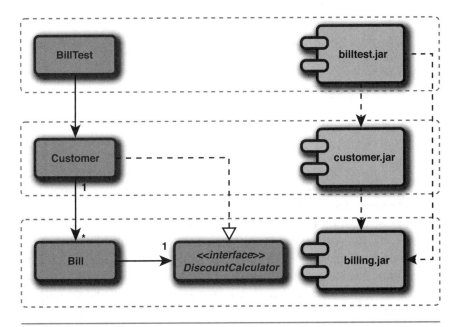

Figure 12.9 BillTest module

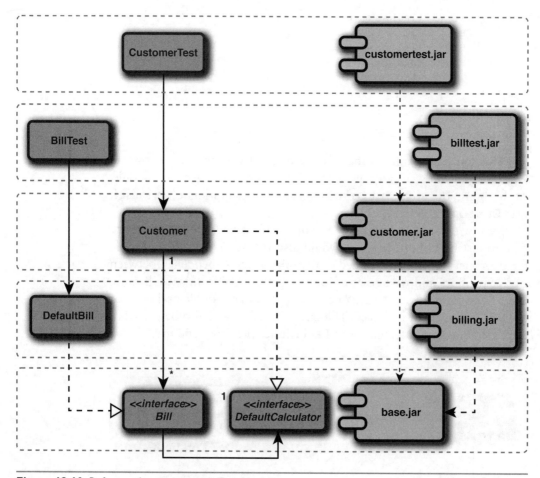

Figure 12.10 Refactored structure with Test Modules

We've also refactored the `BillTest` class so that it no longer depends on `Customer` for testing the new `DefaultBill` class. Listing 12.7 shows the refactored `BillTest` class. Notice that the `BillTest` is no longer dependent on `Customer`. Instead, it uses a mock object setup as an anonymous inner class that serves as the `DiscountCalculator` instance. This helps remove the dependency on the `customer.jar`. The `CustomerTest` would use the `Bill` interface instead of the `Default-Bill` to ensure the dependency between `customer.jar` and `bill.jar` is eliminated.

Listing 12.7 Refactored BillTest Class

```
package com.kirkk.test;

import junit.framework.TestCase;
import java.math.BigDecimal;
import java.util.*;
import com.kirkk.bill.*;
import com.kirkk.base.*;

public class BillTest extends TestCase {
public PaymentTest(String arg0) {
     super(arg0);
}
public void testPaymentWithoutCustomer() {
   Bill bill = new DefaultBill(new DiscountCalculator() {
      public BigDecimal getDiscountAmount() {
         return new BigDecimal(0.1);
      }
   }, new BigDecimal(500));
   BigDecimal paidAmount = bill.pay();
   assertEquals("Paid amount not correct.",
      new BigDecimal(450).setScale(2), paidAmount);
}
}
```

WRAPPING UP

Like unit testing, where classes are ideally tested in isolation, a Test Module allows you to test modules in isolation. A Test Module can help identify undesirable module dependencies. Then, utilizing other patterns, these dependencies can be broken if that's the desirable course of action. Unlike unit testing, a test module is a coarse-grained test that tests at the module level. A Test Module also provide excellent insight on how to configure a module and interact with its Published Interface.

POMA AND OSGi III

OSGi is the dynamic module system for the Java platform. Part III provides a brief introduction to OSGi. Following this introduction, we'll examine the loan sample we discussed in several of the pattern sample code sections throughout Part II. Specifically, we'll begin with the final version of the Loan sample from the Colocate Exceptions sample code. In doing so, you should experience several of the benefits that runtime support for modularity provides, further entrenching the concepts discussed in Part I.

Part III is a departure from the higher-level concepts presented thus far and is the perfect companion to the earlier discussions in Parts I and II that demonstrate how the patterns can be applied using OSGi. Possibly more important, though, Part III demonstrates that by applying the patterns presented in Part II, it's a technology exercise to bring the system under the control of OSGi. That is, once you've designed a modular software system, adopting a framework that supports and enforces modularity is much easier than if the system doesn't have a modular architecture.

INTRODUCING 13 OSGi

OSGi is the dynamic module system for the Java platform. It is a standard specification that is developed by a consortium of industry vendors and managed by the OSGi Alliance. OSGi is a mature and stable specification. In fact, most application platforms now allow enterprise developers to leverage OSGi in building their own enterprise applications. This chapter introduces the fundamentals of OSGi, discusses its advantages, and briefly explores the patterns in the context of OSGi.

For years, OSGi technology has flourished in the embedded systems and networked devices market. Until recently, it's remained a relatively obscure technology for the enterprise developer. Today, OSGi is emerging as a viable and valuable technology in the enterprise.

13.1 Some History

In 2003, the Eclipse team began looking for ways to make Eclipse a more dynamic rich client platform and increase the platform's modularity. Eventually, the team settled on the OSGi framework as the runtime module system (code-named the project Equinox) and, in June 2004, released Eclipse 3.0. This newest version of Eclipse sported a runtime model based on OSGi. OSGi was no longer a technology isolated to use in embedded software and networked devices but had now become the foundation upon which all Eclipse plug-ins would be developed, as well as the platform upon which thousands of software developers would use the Eclipse IDE to develop software.

Eclipse adoption of OSGi marked a significant milestone for the OSGi Alliance, as adoption by a major product and brand such as Eclipse thrust it into the spotlight for many commercial software companies. Today, almost all major vendors build their application platforms atop OSGi, and most application servers used within the enterprise currently support it.

13.2 BENEFITS OF OSGi

OSGi is a dynamic module system for Java. OSGi enables the development of modular applications on the Java platform and provides several benefits.

13.2.1 MODULAR DEVELOPMENT

The OSGi framework defines a unit of modularization called a *bundle*. A bundle is nothing more, and nothing less, than a Java JAR file. A JAR file is a valid OSGi bundle if it contains resources that provide functionality and a Manifest file containing metadata about the bundle. The resources can be Java classes, HTML, images, servlets, and even JSP. The metadata is defined using required and optional key-value pairs. Since all developers are familiar with JAR files, creating a valid OSGi bundle is relatively straightforward. OSGi changes the deployment model for enterprise applications. Traditional thinking is centered around Web application development, and teams devote valuable resources to identifying functionality contained within Web applications, and inter-Web-app communication. With OSGi, you won't develop traditional Web applications. Instead, you'll develop bundles that are assembled into an application, so your development philosophy turns from application-centric to module-centric. While we've been attempting to design modular software for a long time, OSGi enforces the design of modular software through these bundles and managed dependencies.

13.2.2 MANAGED DEPENDENCIES

module dependencies, 48 OSGi accepts reality that the JAR file is the predominant method of reuse and deployment with Java. OSGi treats a JAR as a first-class module. The

Manifest within an OSGi bundle defines export packages that other bundles can use, as well as import packages used by the bundle. Think of this as public and private access to the packages within a JAR file. With OSGi, you can now truly establish a module's published interface simply through how classes are allocated to packages and the packages made visible through export by a bundle. OSGi offers local transparency for its bundles, because you don't need to include JAR files on the runtime classpath. Instead, exported packages within an OSGi bundle can be used by other bundles running on the OSGi platform. Optionally, some OSGi implementations may provide a Security layer that allows access to a bundle if permission has been granted.

*Published
Interface, 188*

13.2.3 Module Platform

OSGi is a service platform because it reduces coupling between bundles. Yet, viewing OSGi as only a service platform tends to lump it in with all other service (as in SOA) solutions. OSGi is also a true module platform that hits a sweet spot not presently accommodated for in enterprise Java development or SOA. OSGi is not a distributed service technology. Instead, OSGi bundles are deployed and communicate within a single JVM, making interbundle communication in-process and lightweight. OSGi bundles are true software modules. The OSGi platform contains a framework specification, making it similar to any other specification you've worked with in Java, like the Servlet API, JDBC, and so on. There will be numerous implementations of the OSGi specification, but your code should only ever refer to the OSGi package structure (`org.osgi.*`). Additionally, when you compile, you'll want to compile against the specification, not the specific implementation you choose to use.

13.2.4 Versioned Bundles

When exporting and importing packages from other bundles, you can specify a version number. Because bundles can be versioned, you can deploy multiple versions of the same bundle on the OSGi platform without experiencing fatal errors, such as a `ClassCastException` commonly experienced when the same class definition is deployed multiple times within the same JVM.

13.2.5 DYNAMIC (RE)DEPLOYMENT

Separate Abstractions, 237
OSGi allows you to deploy bundles individually, without performing a restart. When functionality within a bundle changes, you simply redeploy that bundle to the appropriate OSGi platform, and clients of that bundle automagically discover it through the packages it exports and its version. There's no need to redeploy entire applications. This offers tremendous flexibility if you separate implementation from specification in your application bundles, by allowing you to completely swap implementation without any interruption to other deployed bundles.

13.2.6 ENVIRONMENTAL CONTROL

Because OSGi is a managed container environment, you have the ability to install, start, stop, update, and uninstall individual bundles.

13.3 DIGESTING OSGI

Let's take a moment to digest exactly what OSGi entails and examine what it means for the enterprise developer in the trenches. We no longer need to emphasize development and deployment of individual Web applications. Instead, we develop enterprise software systems as a composition of software modules that can be assembled dynamically to form a complete system. The challenge of interapplication communication is a nonissue, because individual modules can expose resources that serve content to the user and consume behavior exposed by other modules. We no longer need to redeploy an entire suite of enterprise software systems because of a behavioral change in a single JAR file. Instead, simply update the JAR file on the OSGi platform.

Extending the software system to support new processes is as simple as deploying or redeploying only the necessary modules, without any interruption to critical processes. An SOA built on Web services is also assembled from the same software modules by simply building a service protocol layer on top of the appropriate modules. It's possible to assemble a rich client application from the same software modules. Additionally, it's possible to allow separate modules within an OSGi container to utilize the behavior of different versions of the same module.

Because module dependencies are explicitly stated, the module structure of the application is well understood. At the very least, this minimizes the risk of change as the ramification of change can be more accurately assessed. Because OSGi bundle collaboration is in-process, granularity of modules can be established that allow teams to maximize module reuse without incurring performance degradation because of excessive inter-module collaboration. Overall, OSGi has eliminated many architectural challenges with enterprise software development and has established more refined techniques for deploying and managing enterprise software.

When you add it all up, OSGi fills an important technology gap between SOA and object-oriented design on the Java platform. For some time, we've been able to build flexible and extensible class structures in Java. With technologies such as enterprise Java beans (EJB) (primarily session and message beans) and Web services, we've had a service deployment model. But we've lacked a robust module model. Chapter 3 talked about architecture and modularity. OSGi helps us architect all the way down. OSGi is a key technology filling an important void in enterprise software development.

architecture all the way down, 30

13.4 OSGi Bundle

An OSGi bundle is a standard Java JAR file that is packaged with a manifest file. The manifest file contains descriptive metadata that the OSGi framework uses to initialize the bundle. If a JAR file doesn't contain a manifest, it isn't recognized as a valid OSGi bundle.

13.4.1 Bundle State

All bundles managed by the OSGi framework have a corresponding bundle life cycle. At any point in time, an OSGi bundle exists in one of the following states:

- **Installed:** The OSGi bundle is successfully installed, but dependencies have not been resolved.

- **Resolve:** All required OSGi bundle dependencies have been resolved. However, its services have not been started and are not yet available.

- **Starting:** A bundle is starting, and its services will soon be available.

- **Active**: A bundle has successfully started, and its services are now available for use.

- **Stopping:** A bundle is stopping. Its services are no longer available.

- **Uninstalled:** A bundle has been uninstalled.

13.4.2 OSGI μSERVICES

The OSGi Service Platform defines a service registry that contains references to Java objects that have been registered as OSGi services. So as not to confuse OSGi services with Web services, we typically refer to OSGi services as μServices, since they are services that run within a single instance of the Java Virtual Machine (JVM).

OSGi creates and manages the full service life cycle by registering all μServices with the OSGi service registry. Once a μService is registered with the service registry, classes contained with OSGi bundles are able to use the μService. A μService has two important aspects: the service interface and the service implementation.

design
encapsulation
example, 37

The service interface is a Java interface or abstract class that exposes as few implementation details about the μService as possible. Other bundles use the OSGi μService by requesting a reference to the μService from the service registry using a keyword under which the μService has been registered. Often, the name of the interface is used to register the μService. The μService is defined in the service implementation and is encapsulated within the OSGi bundle.

Separate
Abstractions
pattern, 237

module weight, 64

Many different μService implementations can be registered with the OSGi service registry using the same service interface name. The μService instances implementing the interface can be registered and unregistered without restarting the JVM. If the interface and each implementation reside in different OSGi bundles, the bundles can be uninstalled, and new bundles can be installed that extend the behavior of the application dynamically. In fact, this separation of interface and implementation is the intent behind Separate Abstractions. There are a few different ways to use μServices with OSGi. The first is to code directly to the OSGi API, which is inflexible because it results in heavyweight modules. The others are to use Blueprint Services or Declarative Services:

- **Blueprint Services**: As much as possible, developers want to avoid dependencies on the OSGi framework within their code. Based on the Spring framework, Blueprint Services allows the developer to achieve this goal. Interaction with the framework itself is confined to configuration, allowing a developer to focus less on writing the plumbing code surrounding OSGi services and more on writing application business logic.

- **Declarative Services**: Declarative Services is a component model that makes it easier to publish and consume OSGi µServices. Like Blueprint Services, Declarative Services allow you to leverage OSGi while minimizing dependencies on the OSGi framework API.

13.5 OSGi Runtime Management

The OSGi framework provides an API that allows developers to manage OSGi bundles. In fact, these management capabilities are implemented by the OSGi framework using OSGi µServices.

Managing the OSGi framework can be done once the framework is available within the application or platform. Many OSGi frameworks, such as Equinox and Felix, provide command-line controls that facilitate starting, stopping, installing, and uninstalling OSGi bundles. Additionally, application developers can use the OSGi API to perform these management tasks programmatically.

13.6 The Two Facets of Modularity, Revisited

Chapter 2 discussed the two facets of modularity: the development model and the runtime model. The development model is comprised of the programming model and the design paradigm. Although the patterns in this book help address the design paradigm surrounding modularity, the OSGi framework addresses the runtime model, while the OSGi framework API, Blueprint Services, and Declarative Services address the programming model.

development model, 22

13.7 OSGi and the Patterns

When runtime support for modularity is provided by the target platform, the benefits of modular software are even more pronounced. Today, the de facto standard platform for modularity is OSGi, with most major application platform vendors supporting OSGi. Soon, we'll walk through some sample code that illustrates how the patterns can be applied using OSGi.

You're certainly free to jump ahead right now. But if you want to learn a bit more about the patterns in connection with OSGi, then read on.

As illustrated throughout this book, many of the patterns can be applied using all of the tools at your disposal today. You don't necessarily need a runtime module system to develop modular software applications. But a runtime module system, such as OSGi, certainly can help. To explore how OSGi can help, let's look at some of the features of OSGi and how they aid the use of the patterns.

Not all the modularity patterns are discussed in this section, because the topic of patterns and OSGi can fill its own book! Regardless, after reading the following sections, you'll have a better understanding of how the patterns can be used with OSGi.

13.7.1 MANAGING DEPENDENCIES

In OSGi, you are required to export any packages that you want to make visible outside of a bundle. These package exports are declared in the bundle manifest file. Likewise, when a bundle wants to use some other bundle, you are required to import any packages that you'll be dependent upon. Again, this import package information belongs in the bundle manifest. Here are just a few of the ways package exports and imports can help when using the patterns.

13.7.1.1 The Manage Relationships Pattern

When you deploy the bundle, the OSGi framework enforces type visibility of a module's classes using the manifest and its exported packages. Exporting and importing packages offers a way for you to Manage Relationships because the OSGi framework won't allow you to use a bundle if you haven't imported any of its packages.

13.7.1.2 The Published Interface Pattern

Relying solely on Java, it's not possible to hide types within a module. With OSGi, you can hide a type within a module simply by not exporting the package containing the type.

13.7.1.3 The Physical Layers Pattern

Because we must import all the packages that a bundle uses, we can verify via the manifest that we haven't imported any presentation classes.

13.7.2 DYNAMISM

OSGi allows you to hot deploy modules without restarting the system. This brings great dynamism to the environment. Here are just a few ways this dynamism can help when using the patterns.

13.7.2.1 The Module Reuse Pattern

If we emphasize reusability at the module level, the dynamism of OSGi allows us to easily deploy the reusable modules to an existing system.

13.7.2.2 The Abstract Modules Pattern

By depending upon the abstract elements of a module, we can define new implementations of the abstraction in new modules and deploy those new modules to a running system without disruption.

13.7.2.3 The Separate Abstraction Pattern

An extension of Abstract Modules, if we separate our abstractions from the modules containing the implementation, not only can we deploy new implementations, but we can also undeploy existing modules containing implementations that are no longer used.

13.7.2.4 The Independent Deployment Pattern

If we have independently deployable modules, we can easily deploy them to a running system without disruption.

13.7.3 BLUEPRINT SPECIFICATION

The OSGi Blueprint allows us to use OSGi without worrying about the OSGi programming model. In other words, the Blueprint allows us to keep our code independent of the OSGi API. Here are just a few ways the OSGi Blueprint Specification can help when using the patterns.

13.7.3.1 The Container Independence Pattern

This is what the Blueprint Specification is all about: remaining independent of the OSGi API.

13.7.3.2 The External Configuration Pattern

The Blueprint specification allows us to define a module's OSGi services without coupling the module itself, or the class acting as a service, to the OSGi API. Blueprint Services allow us to define the module configuration.

13.7.3.3 The Implementation Factory Pattern

OSGi Blueprint or Declarative Services serves as a factory for OSGi μServices and allows us to wire these services together at runtime. The result is a model that is familiar to experienced developers who already use the Spring framework.

THE LOAN SAMPLE AND OSGI

14

In the Colocate Exceptions pattern, we created a simple loan system. In this chapter, we look at the modules in the Loan system, refactor them into OSGi bundles, and then deploy them to an OSGi environment. You may be surprised at how easy it is to take a system with a modular design and leverage the advantages of a modularity framework like OSGi. As you'll see, because we already had a modular software system, not a single coding change is necessary to take advantage of OSGi.

14.1 GETTING STARTED

Figure 14.1 illustrates the classes and modules in the final structure of our loan system from the Colocate Exceptions "Sample" section. The immediate goal is to refactor these modules so that they'll execute in an OSGi environment. To do this, we need to do a few things. First, we need to include within each module a bundle manifest file that contains the metadata used by the OSGi runtime. This metadata informs the runtime of the module dependencies, visibility of its internal types, and more. Second, we need to register each module's services with the OSGi service registry. We use Spring DM to do this, which is the reference implementation for the OSGi Blueprint Services.

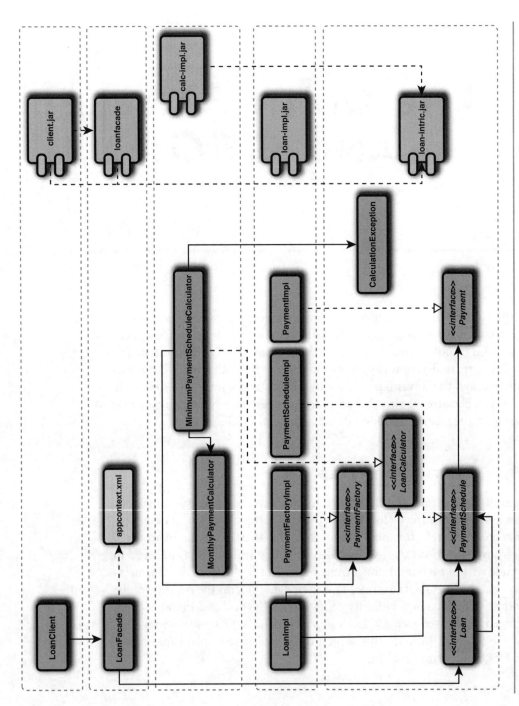

Figure 14.1 Loan sample modules

After we convert our modules to OSGi bundles, we'll deploy them to an OSGi environment to see firsthand the benefits of a runtime environment that supports modularity. Throughout the following exercises, we'll be sure to point out the relevant modularity patterns we've used and how they've helped us. As you'll see, not only do the modularity patterns provide guidance that help us create more modular software, but they also provide a vocabulary that allow us to communicate the design decisions we've made.

14.2 THE MANIFESTS

The first thing we need to do is create the manifest files for each of our bundles. Let's start with the `loan-itrfc.jar` module. Because `loan-intrfc.jar` has only incoming dependencies but no outgoing dependencies, it is a Level 0 module. The Levelize Module pattern informs us of this information.

Levelize Modules pattern, 157

Because OSGi bundles can interact only with the visible types of other OSGi bundles, we are required to export the packages that we want to make available to other OSGi bundle and import the packages that encapsulate the behaviors of other OSGi bundles. In this case, because `loan-intrfc.jar` doesn't depend on anything, we only have to define its exports. Listing 14.1 shows the bundle manifest for the `loan-intrfc.jar` bundle.

Listing 14.1 Manifest.mf for loan-intrfc.jar Bundle

```
Manifest-Version: 1.0
Bundle-ManifestVersion: 2
Bundle-Name: Loan Interface
Bundle-SymbolicName: loaninterface
Bundle-Version: 1.0.0
Export-Package: com.extensiblejava.loan
Spring-Context: *;timeout:-30
```

The metadata contained in the `Manifest.mf` file in Listing 14.1 represents only a small subset of all the OSGi header information that you are able to express. For more information on all these headers, see the OSGi specifications.[1] Most important to us for this example is that we export

---

1. You can find the OSGi specifications at http://www.osgi.org.

the `com.extensiblejava.loan` package, so any classes or interfaces in that package can be referenced by any other bundle in the system.

The next module we focus on is the `loan-impl.jar` module. Recall that the classes in the `loan-impl.jar` module implement the interfaces in the `loan-intrfc.jar` bundle, and we'll explicitly state this dependency in the bundle manifest for `loan-impl.jar`. Referencing Figure 14.1, we clearly see that the `loan-impl.jar` module has no incoming dependencies. In other words, we don't need to export any packages. Listing 14.2 illustrates the bundle manifest for the `loan-impl.jar` bundle.

Listing 14.2 Manifest.mf for loan-impl.jar

```
Manifest-Version: 1.0
Bundle-ManifestVersion: 2
Bundle-Name: Loan Implementation
Bundle-SymbolicName: loanimpl
Bundle-Version: 1.0.0
Import-Package: com.extensiblejava.loan
```

GitHub repository information, 13

Defining the bundle manifests for the remaining modules are each done in the same fashion, so we'll skip this trivial exercise and move on. If you're interested, you can reference the remaining manifests by reviewing the sample code on GitHub.

14.3 µSERVICES

OSGi µServices, 278

Defining the bundle manifests is only the first step in setting up our modules to run in an environment that supports OSGi. Defining our OSGi µServices is the next step. Services bring dynamism to the environment. It's possible to wire together instances using dependency injection the same way we do in Java without OSGi. However, the benefit of services is the dynamism they bring to the environment and the resulting encapsulation of implementation details. We'll see an example of this later.

14.3.1 BLUEPRINT SERVICES

design encapsulation, 37

We can expose our bundle's API as services in two ways. First, we can implement interfaces from the OSGi API, providing an implementation that will register the service and make it available within the container.

Unfortunately, this will couple the bundles to the OSGi framework, which is something we want to avoid.

Our other option is to use Blueprint Services. In this example, we'll use Spring DM, which is the reference implementation for the Blueprint. Using Spring DM allows us to maintain our Container Independence, allowing us to test and execute our system outside the confines of the OSGi framework.

Container Independence pattern, 170

When using Spring DM, we specify two main configuration criteria. First, we need to specify the bean wiring configuration, just as we do with Spring if we weren't using OSGi. Second, we use Spring to declare our OSGi μServices. We'll place these two different configurations in two separate files so that we ensure ourselves that our system will execute outside the context of the OSGi framework.

14.3.2 THE LOAN BEAN CONFIGURATION

Again, let's start by first defining the bean configurations for our bundles, and we'll begin with the `loan-impl.jar` bundle. Note that we do not need to provide any Spring configuration for the `loan-intrfc.jar` bundle because it doesn't expose any services. The `loan-intrfc.jar` bundle is strictly the contract through which all other bundles communicate.

To ensure that each module is capable of standing on its own, we want to avoid defining a single configuration file for the entire system. To accomplish this, we'll place each bean configuration in the same module as the beans we are configuring. This will help us ensure Independent Deployment by providing a Default Implementation.

Independent Deployment pattern, 178

Before we see the bean configuration, let's briefly review the wiring that will be necessary. The `PaymentFactoryImpl` class is responsible for creating the loan classes in the `loan-impl.jar` bundle. The `PaymentFactory` is passed to the `MinimumPaymentSchedule-Calculator`, which uses the factory to instantiate the appropriate implementation classes. The `MinimumPaymentScheduleCalculator`, which implements `LoanCalculator`, is passed to the `LoanFacade`. The `LoanFacade` class is used by the `LoanClient` to perform the actual calculations and obtain a reference to the `Loan`.

Default Implementation pattern, 206

We need to wire the following:

- `PaymentFactoryImpl` to the `MinimumPaymentScheduleCalculator`

- MinimumPaymentScheduleCalculator to LoanFacade
- LoanFacade to LoanClient

Once the wiring is complete, we can obtain the reference to the LoanFacade from the Spring container.

Listing 14.3 illustrates the loan.xml configuration for the loan-impl.jar bundle. Note that this is normal Spring configuration. No declaration is used that depends on the OSGi API.

Listing 14.3 loan-intrfc.jar Bundle Bean Configuration

```
<beans>
<bean id="paymentFactory"
   class="com.extensiblejava.loan.impl.PaymentFactoryImpl"/>
</beans>
```

Likewise, Listing 14.4 illustrates the bean configuration for the calc-impl.jar bundle.

Listing 14.4 loan-impl.jar Bundle Bean Configuration

```
<bean name="loanCalculator"
      class=
         "com.extensiblejava.calculator.
         MinimumPaymentScheduleCalculator">
      <constructor-arg ref="paymentFactory"/>
</bean>
```

Listing 14.5 illustrates the loan-facade.jar wiring.

Listing 14.5 loan-facade.jar Bundle Bean Configuration

```
<bean id="loanFacade"
      class="com.extensiblejava.facade.impl.LoanFacadeImpl">
   <constructor-arg ref="loanCalculator"/>
</bean>
```

At this point, we can compile and run our system from the command prompt. If you want to do this, navigate to the command line, execute the Ant build script, and navigate to the bin directory. Simply run the run.sh script, and you'll be prompted to enter the loan parameters.

When running this sample in the OSGi environment, however, we don't invoke a main method to initiate the process. Instead, we start a client bundle that will invoke the process. To accommodate this, we've created an alternative client bundle named `dumbclient.jar`. This new client will also register a service with the OSGi service register and will be fed the `LoanFacade` upon construction. Listing 14.6 shows the Spring bean configuration for our `dumbclient.jar` file. As can be seen, the `DumbClientImpl` is configured with a `LoanFacade`, which in turn is wired together with the other classes as appropriate. At this point, our application is almost ready to execute within an OSGi environment. Our only step is to expose the beans as OSGi Services.

Listing 14.6 dumbclient.jar Spring Bean Configuration

```
<bean name="LoanClient"
      class="com.extensiblejava.dumbclient.impl.
         DumbClientImpl"
      init-method="run" destroy-method="stop">
   <property name="loanFacade" ref="loanFacade"/>
</bean>
```

It's important to note that the `DumbClientImpl` isn't designed to execute outside the OSGi environment and the `dclient.jar` bundle exists only to invoke our loan functionality from within OSGi. Because of this, we define the appropriate initialization and destruction methods. The `init-method` parameter informs OSGi which method to call upon bundle activation, and the `destroy-method` parameter informs OSGi what to call when the bundle is stopped.

Listing 14.7 illustrates the `DumbClientImpl`. Note that on construction, the class will be wired together with a `LoanFacade`, the run method is invoked, and we calculate the `Loan` payment.

Listing 14.7 DumbClientImpl Class That Drives the Process

```
package com.extensiblejava.dumbclient.impl;

import java.math.*;
import com.extensiblejava.dumbclient.*;
import com.extensiblejava.loan.*;
import com.extensiblejava.facade.*;
import java.io.*;
import java.util.*;
```

```
public class DumbClientImpl implements LoanClient {
   private LoanFacade loanFacade;

   public void setLoanFacade(LoanFacade loanFacade) {
      this.loanFacade = loanFacade;
   }

   public void run() throws Exception {
      BigDecimal payment =
         this.loanFacade.getMonthlyPayment(
         new BigDecimal("15000"),
         new BigDecimal("12"), 60);
         System.out.println("Payment: " + payment);
   }

   public void stop() throws Exception {
      System.out.println("GOODBYE LOAN!");
   }
}
```

14.3.3 OSGi µSERVICE DECLARATIONS

Because the `PaymentFactoryImpl` is wired to the `Minimum-PaymentScheduleCalculator`, we want to expose the `Payment-FactoryImpl` as an OSGi µService. By doing this, we bring dynamicity to the environment. In other words, we can create new `PaymentFactory` implementations and plug them into our environment, and the application will automatically discover the new µService. We'll see an example of this in the next chapter. First, let's look at the µService configurations.

Listing 14.8 illustrates how we define the `PaymentFactoryImpl` and expose it as an OSGi service. We are saying that we want to use the `paymentFactory` bean and expose it as an OSGi µService.

Listing 14.8 PaymentFactoryImpl OSGi Service Configuration

```
<osgi:service id="PaymentFactory" ref="paymentFactory"
  interface="com.extensiblejava.loan.PaymentFactory"/>
```

The `calc-impl.jar` bundle requires two configurations. First, we want to expose the `MinimumPaymentScheduleCalculator` as an OSGi µService that can be consumed by the `LoanFacade`. We also want to obtain a reference to the `paymentFactory` μService we configured in Listing 14.8. Listing 14.9 illustrates this service configuration.

Listing 14.9 calc-impl.jar Service Configuration

```
<osgi:reference id="paymentFactory"
 interface="com.extensiblejava.loan.PaymentFactory"/>
<osgi:service id="LoanCalculator" ref="loanCalculator"
 interface="com.extensiblejava.loan.LoanCalculator"/>
```

Now, we need to follow the same steps to set up the `loan-facade.jar` configuration. Listing 14.10 shows this configuration. As we can see, the `loanFacade` is exposed as an OSGi μService, and the `loan-facade.jar` bundle obtains a reference to the `loanCalculator` it requires.

Listing 14.10 loanfacade.jar Service Configuration

```
<osgi:service id="LoanFacade" ref="loanFacade"
 interface="com.extensiblejava.facade.LoanFacade">
</osgi:service>
<osgi:reference id="loanCalculator"
 interface="com.extensiblejava.loan.LoanCalculator"/>
```

Keep in mind that these μService configurations are used only when these bundles are installed to the OSGi environment. In other words, it is these configurations that the OSGi framework uses to determine the μServices and the bean definitions they reference. The Spring configuration files represent the actual bean definitions.

Finally, we have to define the configuration for our client (see Listing 14.11). As shown, we simply state that the client needs a reference to the `loanFacade` service.

Listing 14.11 loanclient.jar Service Configuration

```
<osgi:reference id="loanFacade"
 interface="com.extensiblejava.facade.LoanFacade"/>
```

At this point, note that none of our code is coupled to the OSGi framework. Our bundles will run in an OSGi environment, and they will also run outside the environment. They can also be tested independently of OSGi.

14.4 INSTALLATION AND EXECUTION

It's now time to run the system. To do this, we need to start our OSGi container and install the application bundles. We use the Equinox framework for this example. If you're following along, navigate to the Colocate-Exceptions project and then the OSGi subdirectory. To start Equinox, navigate to the Equinox directory and issue this command:

```
java —jar org.eclipse.osgi_3.6.0.v20100517.jar  -console
```

At this point, you see yourself within the OSGi console. The Spring DM/Blueprint bundles are installed for us at start-up. To see how this was done, be sure to check out the `config.ini` file in the configuration subdirectory. Now, it's time to install our bundles. To do so, issue the commands shown in Listing 14.12.

Listing 14.12 Install the Bundles

```
install file:../bin/loggerconfig.jar
install file:../bin/loan-intrfc-1.0.jar
install file:../bin/loan-impl-1.0.jar
install file:../bin/calc-impl-1.0.jar
install file:../bin/loanfacade-1.0.jar
install file:../bin/dclient-1.0.jar
```

Now, start each bundle by using the `bundle-id` command (start the `dclient-1.0.jar` bundle last):

```
Start <bundle-id>
```

To get the `bundle-id`, use the following command:

```
ss
```

Note that upon starting the final bundle, `dclient-1.0.jar`, it printed out at the OSGi console the loan amount. In this sample, we don't prompt the user for input to determine whether they'd like to know the payment or see the full payment schedule. We'll leave that as an exercise for you. To do this, you can create your own client bundle and simply install it and start it. You'll be able to use all the existing bundles as they currently stand.

If you issue the `stop` command, you'll notice that `dclient-1.0` `.jar` shuts down. To stop `dclient-1.0.jar`, issue the following command:

```
stop <bundle-id>
```

14.5 CONCLUSION

The example in this chapter demonstrates two important points. First, it shows the benefits of a runtime module system by demonstrating how we can manage modules independently. Second, it illustrates how easy it can be to take a system with a modular design and leverage the advantages of a modularity framework like OSGi. In the next couple of chapters, we'll build on this example and show you the dynamism of the OSGi environment.

15 OSGi and Scala

Suppose that we want to implement the loan calculation so that it can execute in a highly concurrent environment. Scala is a functional language that excels in helping you create programs that run in a high concurrent environment. Let's see how to do this.

The goal at this point is to replace the Java implementation of `calc-impl.jar` with a Scala implementation.

15.1 Getting Started

Just as refactoring our modules to OSGi didn't require any coding changes, replacing `calc-impl.jar` will not require modifying our existing system. We did a good job creating Cohesive Modules with a Default Implementation. Independent Deployment was also a strength of our design. So, now that we want to create the Scala[1] module, we only need to write the Scala code to perform the loan calculation, define our bean configurations, and then define the µService. Because Scala is highly interoperable with Java code, it's fairly easy to ensure that everything plays together nicely.

---

1. Scala is a functional programming language for the Java platform. For more information on Scala, see www.scala-lang.org.

15.2 THE SCALA CODE

First, let's write the Scala code. Replacing the Java `calc-impl.jar` requires only that we implement the interfaces that fulfill the contract with the rest of the system. Effectively, this means we have to provide an implementation of `LoanCalculator`.

To make things easy, we'll adopt the same approach we used in the Java sample. We'll define a `MinimumPaymentScheduleCalculator` that implements the interface and a `MonthlyPaymentCalculator` to calculate the monthly payments for the loan. Listing 15.1 illustrates the `MonthlyPaymentCalculator`, and Listing 15.2 shows the `MinimumPaymentScheduleCalculator`.

Listing 15.1 The MonthlyPaymentCalculator in Scala

```
package com.extensiblejava.calculator.scala

import scala.math._

class MonthlyPaymentCalculator {
   def calculatePayment(presentValue:BigDecimal,
                        rate:BigDecimal,
                        term:Int): BigDecimal = {
      val dPresentValue = presentValue.toDouble
      val dRate = rate.toDouble / 1200

      val revisedRate = dRate + 1;
      val dTerm = term.toDouble

      val powRate = pow(revisedRate, dTerm)

      val left = powRate * dPresentValue
      val middle = dRate / (powRate - 1)
      val right = 1/(1);

      val payment = BigDecimal(left * middle * right).
                    setScale(2,
                    BigDecimal.RoundingMode.HALF_UP)
      payment
   }
}
```

Listing 15.2 The MinimumPaymentScheduleCalculator in Scala

```scala
package com.extensiblejava.calculator.scala

import com.extensiblejava.loan._
//import MonthlyPaymentCalculator._

class MinimumPaymentScheduleCalculator(
    paymentFactory:PaymentFactory) extends LoanCalculator {
    def calculateLoan(value:java.math.BigDecimal,
                      rate:java.math.BigDecimal,
                      term:Int): Loan = {

    Console.println(
        "---** IN SCALA CALCULATOR **---")
    val mc = new java.math.MathContext(2,
                java.math.RoundingMode.HALF_UP)
    val presentValue = BigDecimal(value)
    val presentRate = BigDecimal(rate).apply(mc)

    var cumulativePrincipal = BigDecimal("0.00")
    var cumulativeInterest = BigDecimal("0.00")

    val paymentSchedule =
        paymentFactory.createPaymentSchedule()
    val adjustedRate = (presentRate /
        (BigDecimal("1200")).
        setScale(2,BigDecimal.RoundingMode.HALF_UP))
    val calculator = new MonthlyPaymentCalculator()
    val monthlyPayment =
        calculator.calculatePayment(presentValue,
                                    presentRate,
                                    term)

    var loanBalance =
        BigDecimal(presentValue.bigDecimal)

    while (loanBalance.toDouble >
           monthlyPayment.toDouble) {
      val interest = (
        loanBalance.*(adjustedRate)).setScale(2,
           BigDecimal.RoundingMode.HALF_UP)
      val principal = (monthlyPayment.-(interest)).
           setScale(2,
                    BigDecimal.RoundingMode.HALF_UP);
```

```
            val payment =
               paymentFactory.
                  createPayment(principal.bigDecimal,
                                interest.bigDecimal);
               paymentSchedule.addPayment(payment);

            cumulativeInterest = cumulativeInterest.
                  +(interest).setScale(2,
                              BigDecimal.RoundingMode.HALF_UP);
            cumulativePrincipal = cumulativePrincipal.
                  +(principal).setScale(2,
                              BigDecimal.RoundingMode.HALF_UP);
            loanBalance = loanBalance.-(principal);
         }
         val interest = (loanBalance.*(adjustedRate)).
                           setScale(2,
                           BigDecimal.RoundingMode.HALF_UP)
         val principal = loanBalance.setScale(2,
                           BigDecimal.RoundingMode.HALF_UP)
         cumulativeInterest = cumulativeInterest.+(interest).
                           setScale(2,
                           BigDecimal.RoundingMode.HALF_UP)
         cumulativePrincipal = cumulativePrincipal.
                           +(principal).
                           setScale(2,
                           BigDecimal.RoundingMode.HALF_UP)
         val payment = paymentFactory.
                           createPayment(principal.bigDecimal,
         interest.bigDecimal)
         paymentSchedule.addPayment(payment)

         val loan = paymentFactory.createLoan(paymentSchedule,
                     cumulativeInterest.bigDecimal,
                     cumulativePrincipal.bigDecimal)
         loan

      }
   }
```

15.2.1 THE MANIFEST

Next, we have to create the manifest file for the new bundle. Because we're using Scala, our Scala code depends on the Scala API. Unlike Java, no Scala API is available in the OSGi environment. Therefore, we must deploy the Scala bundle, and because our calculation bundle depends on this Scala

API, we must import the Scala API packages in our bundle manifest. Listing 15.3 shows a snippet of this manifest file.

Listing 15.3 Partial Manifest.mf for the Scala Bundle

```
Manifest-Version: 1.0
Bundle-ManifestVersion: 2
Bundle-Name: Scala Calculator
Bundle-SymbolicName: scala calculator
Bundle-Version: 1.0.0
Import-Package: com.extensiblejava.loan,
 scala.annotation.unchecked;uses:="scala.reflec,scala";
 version="2.8.0.final",...
```

15.3 SCALA BEAN CONFIGURATION

Next, we have to define the Spring bean configuration. Because the Scala code is compiled to the same byte-code format that's used by the Java Virtual Machine (JVM) for Java code, the Spring bean configuration for our Scala code is the same as our Spring bean configuration for the Java code. The only difference is that we reference the Scala class, as shown in Listing 15.4.

Listing 15.4 Scala Bean Configuration

```
<bean name="loanCalculator" class=
"com.extensiblejava.calculator.scala.
 MinimumPaymentScheduleCalculator">
   <constructor-arg ref="paymentFactory"/>
</bean>
```

At this point, we can execute the system from the command line, outside the context of the OSGi framework, to illustrate that the functionality is exactly the same as it was with the Java implementation.

15.4 SCALA μSERVICE CONFIGURATION

Similarly, exposing our Scala class as an OSGi μService is done in a fashion that closely resembles the Java μService configuration. Listing 15.5 shows the Scala μService configuration.

Listing 15.5 Scala Service Configuration

```
<osgi:reference id="paymentFactory"
 interface="com.extensiblejava.loan.PaymentFactory"/>
<osgi:service id="LoanCalculator" ref="loanCalculator"
 interface="com.extensiblejava.loan.LoanCalculator"/>
```

15.5 BUILDING THE SCALA MODULE

Next, we'll build the Scala module. This can easily be done by using the scalac compiler and packaging the code into a bundle, just like we did when building the Java version of the calculator. First, we must ensure that the Scala library is on our build classpath. Then, we'll define an Ant task for the compilation step. Listing 15.6 illustrates the snippets of the build file that perform these tasks for us. Once the code is compiled, it can be packaged into a bundle using the same mechanisms as the Java code.

Listing 15.6 Scala Calculator Build Script

```
<path id="scala.class.path">
    <pathelement path="${scala.library.jar}"/>
    <pathelement path="${scala.compiler.jar}"/>
</path>

<taskdef resource="scala/tools/ant/antlib.xml"
        classpathref="scala.class.path"/>

<target name="compile" depends="init">
    <scalac srcdir="${scala.src}" destdir="${scala.build}">
        <classpath refid="project.class.path"/>
    </scalac>
</target>
```

15.6 INSTALLATION AND EXECUTION

Recall that our Scala implementation of the loan calculation imported the Scala API. Therefore, we have to install the Scala API bundle, as shown here (type on a single line):

```
install file:../../scala/lib/org.scala-ide.
            scala.library_2.8.0.final-p0002.jar
```

Now, install the Scala loan calculator implementation, as shown here:

```
install file:../../scala/bin/calc-iompl-scala-1.0.jar
```

Now, start it by executing the start command, as shown here:

```
start <bundle-id>
```

Next, stop the Java implementation of the loan calculation by using the following command with the `bundle-id` of the Java `calc-impl-1.0.jar` implementation:

```
Stop <bundle-id>
```

Now, start the `dclient-1.0.jar` module by executing the `start` command, as shown next. This calculates the loan using the Scala calculator:

```
Start <bundle-id>
```

You should see that the loan calculation was performed using the Scala implementation. We replaced the Java code with Scala, without modifying any other system components. Our modular architecture allowed us to do this, but OSGi has brought the dynamism necessary to allow the benefits of our modular architecture to carry over into the runtime environment.

15.7 Conclusion

In this chapter, we demonstrated the dynamism of OSGi and a runtime module system. We were able to develop a new module for calculating the loan using the Scala programming language and seamlessly, without any interruption, replace the Java implementation with the Scala implementation at runtime.

OSGI AND GROOVY

Like we did with Scala, let's say we want to use a dynamic language to improve the expressiveness and speed with which we develop the calculation implementation. In this case, we'll replace the Scala version of `calc-impl.jar` with a Groovy version.

16.1 GETTING STARTED

Similar to what we did for the Scala calculation module, creating a Groovy[1] version of the calculation won't require any modifications to our existing system either. We'll simply write the Groovy code, bundle the code into a `calc-impl-groovy.jar` module, and deploy it. Again, we did a good job creating Cohesive Modules with a Default Implementation. Independent Deployment was also a strength of our design. So, now that we want to create the Groovy module, we only need to write the Groovy code to perform the loan calculation, define our bean configurations, and then define the μService. Because Groovy is highly interoperable with Java code, it's fairly easy to ensure everything plays together nicely.

Independent Deployment pattern, 178

Cohesive Modules pattern, 139

Default Implementation pattern, 206

---

1. Groovy is a dynamic language for the Java platform. For more information on Groovy, see www.groovy.org.

16.2 THE GROOVY CODE

First, let's write the Groovy code. Replacing the Java `calc-impl.jar` or `calc-impl-scala.jar` module requires only that we implement the interfaces that fulfill the contract with the rest of the system. Effectively, this means we have to provide an implementation of the `LoanCalculator`.

To make things easy, we'll adopt the same approach we used in the Java and Scala samples. We'll define a `MinimumPaymentSchedule-Calculator` that implements the interface and a `MonthlyPayment-Calculator` to calculate the monthly payments for the loan. Listing 16.1 illustrates the `MonthlyPaymentCalculator`, and Listing 16.2 shows the `MinimumPaymentScheduleCalculator`.

Listing 16.1 MonthlyPaymentCalculator in Groovy

```
package com.extensiblejava.calculator.groovy

class MonthlyPaymentCalculator {

    def calculatePayment(presentValue, rate, term) {

        def dPresentValue = presentValue.doubleValue()
        def dRate = rate.doubleValue() / 1200

        def revisedRate = dRate + 1;
        def dTerm = term.doubleValue()

        def powRate = Math.pow(revisedRate, dTerm)

        def left = powRate * dPresentValue
        def middle = dRate / (powRate - 1)
        def right = 1/(1);

        def payment = new BigDecimal(left * middle * right).
            setScale(2, BigDecimal.ROUND_HALF_UP)
    }
}
```

Listing 16.2 MinimumPaymentScheduleCalculator in Groovy

```
package com.extensiblejava.calculator.groovy

import com.extensiblejava.loan.*
```

```
class MinimumPaymentScheduleCalculator
   implements LoanCalculator {
   def paymentFactory

   MinimumPaymentScheduleCalculator(pFactory) {
      paymentFactory = pFactory
   }

   def Loan calculateLoan(BigDecimal presentValue,
                          BigDecimal rate, int term) {

      println("---** IN GROOVY CALCULATOR **---")

      def cumulativePrincipal = new BigDecimal("0.00")
      def cumulativeInterest = new BigDecimal("0.00")

      def paymentSchedule =
         paymentFactory.createPaymentSchedule()
      def adjustedRate = (rate / (new BigDecimal("1200")).
         setScale(2,
                  BigDecimal.ROUND_HALF_UP))
      def calculator = new MonthlyPaymentCalculator()
      def monthlyPayment = calculator.calculatePayment(
                           presentValue, rate, term)

      def loanBalance = new BigDecimal(presentValue)

      while (loanBalance.doubleValue() >
             monthlyPayment.doubleValue()) {
         def interest = loanBalance.multiply(adjustedRate).
            setScale(2, BigDecimal.ROUND_HALF_UP)
         def principal = monthlyPayment.subtract(interest).
            setScale(2, BigDecimal.ROUND_HALF_UP)
         def payment = paymentFactory.createPayment(
                    principal, interest)
         paymentSchedule.addPayment(payment)

         cumulativeInterest = cumulativeInterest.
            add(interest).
            setScale(2, BigDecimal.ROUND_HALF_UP)
          cumulativePrincipal = cumulativePrincipal.
            add(principal).
            setScale(2,BigDecimal.ROUND_HALF_UP)
          loanBalance = loanBalance.subtract(principal)
      }
```

```
    def interest = loanBalance.multiply(adjustedRate).
        setScale(2, BigDecimal.ROUND_HALF_UP)
    def principal = loanBalance.
        setScale(2, BigDecimal.ROUND_HALF_UP)
    cumulativeInterest = cumulativeInterest.add(interest).
        setScale(2, BigDecimal.ROUND_HALF_UP)
    cumulativePrincipal = cumulativePrincipal.
        add(principal).setScale(2,BigDecimal.ROUND_HALF_UP)
    def payment = paymentFactory.createPayment(principal,
        interest)
    paymentSchedule.addPayment(payment)

    def loan = paymentFactory.createLoan(paymentSchedule,
            cumulativeInterest, cumulativePrincipal)
    loan


  }
}
```

16.2.1 THE MANIFEST

Next, we have to create the manifest file for the new bundle. Because we're using Groovy, our Groovy code depends on the Groovy API. Like Scala, no Groovy API is available in the OSGi environment. Therefore, we must deploy the Groovy bundle, and because our calculation bundle depends on this Groovy API, we must import the Groovy API packages in our bundle manifest. Listing 16.3 shows a snippet of this manifest file.

Listing 16.3 Partial Manifest.mf for the Groovy Bundle

```
Manifest-Version: 1.0
Bundle-ManifestVersion: 2
Bundle-Name: Groovy Calculator
Bundle-SymbolicName: groovy calculator
Bundle-Version: 1.0.0
Import-Package:
com.extensiblejava.loan,groovy.xml.streamingmarkupsupport;
version="1.7.6"...
```

16.3 GROOVY BEAN CONFIGURATION

Next, we have to define the Spring bean configuration. Because our Groovy code is compiled to the same byte-code format that's used by the

JVM for Java code, the Spring bean configuration for our Groovy code is the same as our Spring bean configuration for the Java code. The only difference is that we reference the Groovy class, as shown in Listing 16.4.

Listing 16.4 Scala Bean Configuration

```
<bean name="loanCalculator"
 class= "com.extensiblejava.calculator.groovy.
        MinimumPaymentScheduleCalculator">
   <constructor-arg ref="paymentFactory"/>
</bean>
```

At this point, we can execute the system from the command line, outside the context of the OSGi framework, to illustrate that the functionality is exactly the same as it was with the Java implementation.

16.4 Groovy Service Configuration

Similarly, exposing our Groovy class as an OSGi µService is done in a fashion that closely resembles the Java µService configuration. Listing 16.5 shows the Groovy µService configuration.

Listing 16.5 Groovy Service Configuration

```
<osgi:reference id="paymentFactory"
 interface="com.extensiblejava.loan.PaymentFactory"/>
<osgi:service id="LoanCalculator" ref="loanCalculator"
 interface="com.extensiblejava.loan.LoanCalculator"/>
```

16.5 Building the Groovy Module

Next, we'll have to build the Groovy module. This can easily be done by using the `groovyc` compiler and packaging the code into a bundle, just like we did when building the Java version of the calculator. First, we must ensure that the Groovy library is on our build classpath. Then, we'll define an Ant task for the compilation step. Listing 16.6 illustrates the snippets of the build file that perform these tasks for us. Once the code is compiled, it can be packaged into a bundle using the same mechanisms as the Java code.

Listing 16.6 Groovy Calculator Build Script

```
<path id="groovy.class.path">
   <pathelement path="${groovy.library.jar}"/>
   <pathelement path=
                "${groovy.dir}/lib/commons-cli-1.2.jar"/>
   <pathelement path="${groovy.dir}/lib/asm-3.2.jar"/>
   <pathelement path="${groovy.dir}/lib/antlr-2.7.7.jar"/>
</path>

<taskdef name="groovyc"
         classname="org.codehaus.groovy.ant.Groovyc"
         classpathref="groovy.class.path"/>

<target name="compile" depends="init">
   <groovyc srcdir="${groovy.src}"
            destdir="${groovy.build}">
      <classpath refid="project.class.path"/>
   </groovyc>
</target>
```

16.6 INSTALLATION AND EXECUTION

Recall that our Groovy implementation of the loan calculation imported the Groovy API. Therefore, we have to install the Groovy API bundle:

```
install file:<path to bundle>/groovy-all-1.7.6.jar
```

Now, install the Groovy loan calculator implementation by executing this command:

```
install file:../../groovy/bin/calc-impl-groovy-1.0.jar
```

Start the Groovy calculator by executing this command:

```
start <bundle-id>
```

Next, we should stop the Java and Scala implementation of the loan calculation using the following command with the `bundle-id` of the Java `calc-impl-1.0.jar` and Scala `calc-impl-scala-1.0.jar` implementations:

```
stop <bundle-id>
```

Now, start the `dclient-1.0.jar` bundle by using the following command. This should calculate the loan using the Groovy calculator:

```
start <bundle-id>
```

You see that the loan calculation was performed using the Groovy implementation. We replaced the Java and Scala code with Groovy, without modifying any other system modules. Our modular architecture allowed us to do this, but it's OSGi that has brought the dynamism necessary to allow the benefits of our modular architecture to carry over into the runtime environment.

16.7 CONCLUSION

In this chapter, we again demonstrated the dynamism of OSGi and a runtime module system. We were able to develop a new module for calculating the loan using the Groovy programming language and seamlessly, without any interruption, replace the Scala implementation with the Groovy implementation at runtime.

FUTURE OF **17** OSGi

OSGi is not new. It has been around since the late 1990s. Unfortunately, although OSGi is the only dynamic module system for the Java platform, adoption is not widespread. However, traction within the industry is building. Many products continue to emerge that leverage OSGi internally, and more are beginning to expose the virtues of OSGi to the developer community. But, there is a concern that OSGi will not have the disruptive impact of which it's capable. I assert that if OSGi does succeed, it won't be based on the technical merits of OSGi. It'll be because of something else. Something trendy. Something fashionable.

Now, I could be wrong. OSGi adoption is certainly increasing, albeit slowly. And as case studies begin to emerge that tout the cost reduction, improved responsiveness, and time-to-market advantages of OSGi, adoption will likely continue to rise.

But, adoption is one thing, disruption another, and I still have a hesitation. What if something trendier, more fashionable surfaces, and OSGi is pushed into the backwaters? Will it really have the impact it's capable of? You know . . . an "iPhone-esque" impact that raises the bar and redefines an industry. Something not just evolutionary but truly disruptive.

17.1 OSGi AS AN ENABLER

For OSGi to cross the chasm, it must enable something big that a business wants to buy. Maybe cost reduction, improved responsiveness, and time-to-market benefits will be enough. But, that's easily perceived by many as a rather evolutionary impact. It's not really disruptive.

Possibly, OSGi will flourish in the data center, as organizations seek more adaptable platforms that lend them these benefits. But this doesn't necessarily guarantee that development teams will leverage OSGi to build systems with a modular architecture. Leveraging a platform built atop OSGi is separate from building modular software systems, even though OSGi enables both.

Without something trendy that promises real benefits, it'll get brushed under the carpet like what has happened to many technologically superior solutions. Perhaps it's already happening, with all the hype surrounding the cloud. Or maybe it'll be the cloud that helps OSGi cross the chasm. OSGi doesn't obviously enable the cloud, but OSGi can enable the dynamic and adaptive runtime benefits of the cloud.

But again, this doesn't mean teams will begin leveraging OSGi to design modular software. It only means that the platform itself is adaptable. Of course, there is benefit in that. But, if that's the route that is taken, teams will still continue to develop monolithic applications that lack architecturally resiliency, and the full benefit of OSGi (and modularity) will not be realized.

17.2 THE DISRUPTION

OSGi has the potential to have a much broader impact, affecting everyone from the developer to those working in the data center. So, what might this trend be that will propel OSGi to stardom?

OSGi enables ecosystems!

Now, you're thinking that I've gone off the deep end, perhaps? But, give me a chance to explain.

17.2.1 A BIT OF (RECENT) PLATFORM HISTORY

To start, let's take a brief walk down memory lane—not too far back but far enough so that we can see how important the ecosystem is in today's most successful platforms. And these platforms span a range of markets, from mobile to social media. But, each is successful in large part because of a thriving ecosystem.

17.2.1.1 Apple

In 2007, Apple released its first-generation iPhone. Without question, the device revolutionized the mobile phone industry. Although the device offers a great user experience that has certainly played a role in its surging popularity, people flock to the iPhone today because of the wealth of applications available. Yeah, "there's an app for that."

Apple, recognizing the power of this ecosystem, now delivers the iPad. With fewer preinstalled applications than the iPhone, Apple is counting on the ecosystem to drive adoption. The more consumers who flock to the device, the more developers who flock to the platform to deliver applications. As more applications become available, consumers will buy more iPads. The ecosystem fuels itself. Apple has simply provided the environment for the ecosystem to thrive.

17.2.1.2 Eclipse

In 2003, the Eclipse team was thinking of ways to make Eclipse more dynamic. Its decision to use OSGi to create a rich client platform that supports plug-in architecture was the first step toward the resulting ecosystem we know today. One of the reasons developers use Eclipse is because there are an abundance of plug-ins available that allow them to do their jobs more effectively. Other developers create Eclipse plug-ins because Eclipse is a popular IDE used by many developers. Again, the ecosystem fuels itself. The Eclipse team provided the environment that allows today's Eclipse ecosystem to thrive.

If you're interested, you can read more about the history of Eclipse and OSGi at this website: www.eclipse.org/equinox/documents/transition.html.

17.2.1.3 Hudson

Arguably, Hudson is today's most popular continuous integration server. But it hasn't always been. Before Hudson was CruiseControl. And although CruiseControl did help development teams get started on their path toward continuous integration, it was also unwieldy to use in many ways. With Hudson's plug-in architecture, developers have the ability to extend the tool in ways the original creator couldn't imagine or couldn't find the time to do himself. Kohsuke created Hudson and gave the development community a new platform for continuous integration. With its plug-in architecture, though, he also provided an environment that allows the Hudson ecosystem to thrive.

17.2.1.4 Social Media

Facebook. MySpace. Twitter. These are examples of social media tools with a strong developer community that creates extensions to the platform that users can leverage to enhance the experience. Facebook developers. MySpace developer platform. Twitter API. Each allows the ecosystem to thrive.

17.2.1.5 And Others

It's easy to find other platforms with similar ecosystems. The ease with which WordPress themes and plug-ins can be developed and used to enhance a WordPress website is another example. In fact, many content management systems provide similar capabilities. A large reason why the Firefox and Chrome Web browsers have emerged as the preferred Web browsers is the ease with which add-ons and plug-ins can be installed that extend the capabilities of the browsers. The Atlassian Plugin Framework is another example that uses OSGi, and platforms such as Force.com and SharePoint have built (or are trying to build) similar ecosystems.

17.3 THE POWER OF ECOSYSTEMS

Aside from Eclipse (and Atlassian), none of these other platforms leverage OSGi. Yet, each is wildly successful because of two reasons:

- An environment was created that allowed an ecosystem to form and flourish. This environment includes a platform and a marketplace.
- A group of customers and developers converged on the marketplace and fueled growth of the platform. The result is a self-sustaining ecosystem.

If you look at many of the more popular platforms that have emerged over the past decade, they tend to possess a similar characteristic—a community of individuals dedicated to providing great solutions leveraging the foundation of the platform. OSGi and modularity enable ecosystems on the Java platform.

17.3.1 ECOSYSTEMS AND THE TWO FACETS OF MODULARITY

Chapter 2 talked about the two facets of OSGi: the runtime model and the development model. I also explained how one could possibly see widespread adoption while the other has little impact. A strong ecosystem surrounding OSGi and modularity must leverage both. Developers would create reusable modules, implying they are designing modular software. For development teams to leverage these modules, they must be using a platform that supports the runtime model.

two facets of modularity, 21

17.3.2 CBD HAS ALREADY HAD ITS DAY, YOU SAY?

Now some of you might argue that this sounds a lot like the component-based development (CBD) fad of the 1990s. True . . . to an extent. Certainly, these ideas are not new. But, there are also some striking differences between that which OSGi enables and the CBD fad that has come and largely gone, or whose promise was never fully realized.

Foremost, the CBD fad was focused almost exclusively on visual components, such as ActiveX. Although some attempted to create components for the Java platform, the movement largely failed to go mainstream. Instead, Java EE grew in popularity and, for a number of years, garnered everyone's attention. Why did this happen?

In my opinion, the answer is fairly simple. Even though numerous marketplaces emerged that allowed the consumer and producer to come together to buy and sell components, there was never a suitable component execution environment, that is, an environment that would support dynamic deployment, support for multiple versions, dependency management, and, in general, complete control over all components currently executing within the environment. ActiveX components did have an execution environment (though did not support each of these capabilities), but Java did not. Today, in OSGi, Java has the requisite execution environment!

17.4 THE ECOSYSTEM

It's easy find holes in this idea. To explain why it cannot work. Yet, it's happening elsewhere, so why not on the server . . . in the enterprise? Certainly, there are a variety of different ways such an ecosystem could manifest itself. Possibly multiple ecosystems emerge like what we see in the mobile market today.

But for a moment, imagine the world where you have the ability to easily assemble a platform from prebuilt infrastructure modules that exactly meet the demands of your application. You might purchase these modules, you might choose to use open source modules, or you might build them yourself. Those you don't build you obtain from a module marketplace, possibly deploying them to your (cloud) environment.

When you choose to use a module, it's dynamically deployed to your environment. The modules it depends upon? You're given the option to purchase and deploy them. You develop your software modules using the sound principles and patterns of modular design to ensure loose coupling and high cohesion. As you roll out your business solution modules, you simultaneously deploy the additional infrastructure modules that are needed.

In this marketplace, modules are sourced by multiple vendors. Some large. Some small. Neither the stack nor your applications are monolithic beasts. Instead, they are a composition of collaborating software modules. Your infrastructure isn't necessarily tied to a specific vendor solution. The option always exists for organizations to purchase modules from different providers, easily swapping one provider module out with another.

The ecosystem flourishes. Developers flock to sell their latest creation. Organizations seek to add amazing capabilities to their right-sized environment at a fraction of the cost compared to what they are accustomed to today. The business benefits are real. The technical advantages are real. And the resulting ecosystem is sustainable.

A successful ecosystem demands both the runtime model and the development model. Today, OSGi is the only standard technology that will allow this type of successful ecosystem to form on the Java platform. But, will it happen? We may have a long way to go, but it sure would be cool! And it would be a shame if we lost this opportunity.

17.5 CONCLUSION

Modularity is not new. Nor is OSGi. Unfortunately, few software systems have been designed with either in mind. As the Java platform continues to embrace modularity, developers can leverage powerful techniques that allow them to design software systems that are dynamic, extensible, malleable, reusable, and more. Whether OSGi reigns as the dominant module system on the Java platform or an alternative module system steps in, one thing is certain: Modularity on the Java platform stands to redefine how we develop software systems using Java. Modularity is a core concept necessary for the future of Java application architecture.

SOLID PRINCIPLES OF CLASS DESIGN

The SOLID principles lie at the heart of the object-oriented paradigm. Many of the principles presented here first appeared in Robert Martin's *Agile Software Development: Principles, Patterns, and Practices* (2002), which serves as an excellent companion to this discussion. These principles help you manage dependencies between classes and encourage class cohesion. They are also critical to effective module design using object-oriented techniques.

Note

For a discussion on how the SOLID principle of class design aids the development of modular software applications, see Chapter 4, "Taming the Beast Named Complexity."

The SOLID principles are the following:

- **Single Responsible Principle**: Classes should change for only a single reason.
- **Open Closed Principle**: Classes should be open for extension but closed to modification.
- **Liskov Substitution Principle**: Subclasses should be substitutable for their base classes.
- **Dependency Inversion Principle:** Depend upon abstractions. Do not depend upon concretions.

- **Interface Segregation Principle**: Many specific interfaces are better than a single, general interface.
- **Composite Reuse Principle:** Favor polymorphic composition of objects over inheritance.

I also believe an additional principle is equally important. Sadly, it breaks the acronym. I call this principle the *Composite Reuse Principle*, which is to favor polymorphic composition of objects over inheritance (Knoernschild 2001).

Single Responsibility Principle (SRP)

Classes should change for only a single reason.

The basis for this principle is cohesion. Cohesion represents the measure to which a class performs a single function. Classes that are highly cohesive are easier to understand. But they are also easier to maintain. This is the motivating force behind SRP. If a class has more than one reason to change, then it stands to reason that the responsibilities of that class that are the cause of change should be separated into multiple classes.

Cohesion is not a concept new to objects. In fact, the concept is taught in most introductory programming courses. Ironically, I found that although most developers can easily define cohesion and explain its benefits, few developers actually apply it. Cohesion measures the degree to which an entity does a single thing. Given this definition, it's no surprise that if some entity is responsible for performing only a single thing, most of our entities should be fairly small. Yet, I commonly come across methods that run well over 100 lines of code and classes that run orders of magnitudes larger than that. I struggle to convince myself that either is cohesive. When you're designing a highly cohesive system, you have to think small.

Open Closed Principle (OCP)

Classes should be open for extension, but closed for modification.

The Open Closed Principle (OCP) is undoubtedly the most important of all the SOLID principles. In fact, each of the remaining class principles are derived from OCP. It originated from the work of Bertrand Meyer, who is recognized as an authority on the object-oriented paradigm. OCP states that we should have the ability to add new features to our system without having to modify our set of preexisting classes. As stated previously, one of the benefits of the object-oriented paradigm is to enable us to add new data structures to our system without having to modify the existing system's code base.

Let's look at an example to see how this can be done. Consider a financial institution where we have to accommodate different types of accounts to which individuals can make deposits. Figure A.1 shows a class diagram that illustrates how we might structure a portion of our system. (For the purposes of this discussion, we focus on how the OCP can be used to extend the system.)

In Figure A.1, the `Account` class has a relationship to our `Account-Type` abstract class. In other words, our `Account` class is coupled at the abstract level to the `AccountType` inheritance hierarchy. Because our `Savings` and `Checking` classes each inherit from the `Account-Type` class, we know that through dynamic binding, we can substitute instances of either of these classes wherever the `AccountType` class is referenced. Subsequently, `Savings` and `Checking` can be freely substituted for `AccountType` within the `Account` class. This is the intent of an abstract class and enables us to effectively adhere to OCP by creating a contract between the `Account` class and the `AccountType` descendents. Because our `Account` is not directly coupled to either of the concrete `Savings` or `Checking` classes, we can extend the `Account-Type` class, creating a new class such as `MoneyMarket`, without having to modify our `Account` class. We have achieved OCP and can now extend our system without modifying its existing code base.

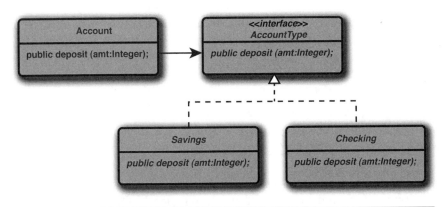

Figure A.1 Open Closed Principle

Therefore, one of the tenets of OCP is to reduce the coupling between classes to the abstract level. Instead of creating relationships between two concrete classes, we create relationships between a concrete class and an abstract class or, in Java, between a concrete class and an interface. When we create an extension of our base class, assuming we adhere to the public methods and their respective signatures defined on the abstract class, we have essentially achieved OCP. Listing A.1 illustrates a simplified version of the Java code for this example, focusing on how we achieve OCP, instead of on the actual method implementations.

Listing A.1 Account Class

```java
public class Account {
    private AccountType _act;
    public Account(String act) {
        try {
            Class c = Class.forName(act);
            this._act = (AccountType) c.newInstance();
        } catch (Exception e) {
            e.printStackTrace();
        }
    }
    public void deposit(int amt) {
        this._act.deposit(amt);
    }
}
```

Here, our `Account` class accepts as an argument to its constructor a `String` representing the class we want to instantiate. It then uses the `Class` class to dynamically create an instance of the appropriate `AccountType` subclass. Note that we don't explicitly refer to either the `Savings` or `Checking` class directly. Listing A.2 shows the `Account-Type` interface.

Listing A.2 AccountType Interface

```java
public interface AccountType  {
    public void deposit(int amt);
}
```

The `AccountType` class serves as the contract between our `Account` class and `AccountType` descendents. The deposit method is the contract. Listing A.3 and Listing A.4 illustrate the Checking-Account and SavingsAccount classes that implement the Account-Type interface.

Listing A.3 CheckingAccount Class

```
public class CheckingAccount extends AccountType {
   public void deposit(int amt) {
      System.out.println();
      System.out.println();
      System.out.println("Amount deposited in " +
         "checking account: " + amt);
      System.out.println();
      System.out.println();
   }
}
```

Listing A.4 SavingsAccount Classes

```
public class SavingsAccount extends AccountType {
   public void deposit(int amt)  {
      System.out.println();
      System.out.println();
      System.out.println("Amount deposited in " +
         "savings account: " + amt);
      System.out.println();
      System.out.println();
   }
}
```

Each AccountType descendent satisfies the contract by providing an implementation for the deposit method. In the real world, the behaviors of the individual deposit methods would be more interesting and, given the preceding design, would be algorithmically different.

LISKOV SUBSTITUTION PRINCIPLE (LSP)

Subclasses should be substitutable for their base classes.

We mentioned in our previous discussion that OCP is the most important of the class category principles. We can think of the Liskov Substitution Principle (LSP) as an extension to OCP. To take advantage of LSP, we must adhere to OCP because violations of LSP are also a violation of OCP, but not vice versa. LSP is the work of Barbara Liskov and is derived from Bertrand Meyer's Design by Contract. In its simplest form, it is difficult to differentiate OCP and LSP, but a subtle difference does exist. OCP is centered around abstract coupling. LSP, while also heavily dependent on abstract coupling, is also heavily dependent on preconditions and post-conditions, which is LSP's relation to Design by Contract, where the concept of preconditions and postconditions was formalized.

A precondition is a contract that must be satisfied before a method can be invoked. A postcondition, on the other hand, must be true upon method completion. If the precondition is not met, the method should not be invoked, and if the postcondition is not met, the method should not return. The relation of preconditions and postconditions has meaning embedded within an inheritance relationship that is not supported within Java, outside of some manual assertions or nonexecutable comments. Because of this, violations of LSP can be difficult to find.

To illustrate LSP and the interrelationship of preconditions and postconditions, we need to consider only how Java's exception handling mechanism works. Consider a method on an abstract class that has the signature shown here:

```
public abstract deposit(int amt) throws
InvalidAmountException
```

Assume in this situation that our `InvalidAmountException` is an exception defined by our application, is inherited from Java's base `Exception` class, and can be thrown if the amount we try to deposit is less than zero. By rule, when overriding this method in a subclass, we cannot throw an exception that exists at a higher level of abstraction than `InvalidAmountException`. Therefore, a method declaration on a concrete subclass such as that shown here is not allowed:

```
public void deposit(int amt) throws Exception
```

This method declaration is not allowed because the `Exception` class thrown in this method is the ancestor of the `InvalidAmount-Exception` thrown previously. Again, we cannot throw an exception in a method on a subclass that exists at a higher level of abstraction than the exception thrown by the base class method we are overriding. On the other hand, reversing these two method signatures would have been perfectly acceptable to the Java compiler. We can throw an exception in an overridden subclass method that is at a lower level of abstraction than the exception thrown in the ancestor. While this does not correspond directly to the concept of preconditions and postconditions, it does capture the essence. Therefore, we can state that any precondition stipulated by a subclass method cannot be stronger than the base class method. Therefore, any postcondition stipulated by a subclass method cannot be weaker than the base class method.

To adhere to LSP in Java, we must make sure that developers define preconditions and postconditions for each of the methods on an abstract class. When defining our subclasses, we must adhere to these preconditions and postconditions. If we do not define preconditions and postconditions for our methods, it becomes virtually impossible to find violations of LSP. Suffice it to say, in the majority of cases, OCP will be our guiding principle.

DEPENDENCY INVERSION PRINCIPLE (DIP)

Depend upon abstractions. Do not depend upon concretions.

The Dependency Inversion Principle (DIP) formalizes the concept of abstract coupling and clearly states that we should couple at the abstract level, not at the concrete level. Abstract coupling is the notion that a class is not coupled to another concrete class, or class that can be instantiated. Instead, the class is coupled to other base, or abstract, classes. In Java, this abstract class can be either a class with the abstract modifier or a Java interface data type. Regardless, this concept is actually the means through which LSP achieves its flexibility, the mechanism required for DIP, and the heart of OCP.

In our own designs, attempting to couple at the abstract level can at times seem like overkill. Pragmatically, we should apply this principle in any situation where we are unsure whether the implementation of a class may change in the future. We have encountered situations during development where we know exactly what needs to be done. Requirements state this very clearly, and the probability of change or extension is quite low. In these situations, adherence to DIP may be more work than the benefit realized.

At this point, there exists a striking similarity between DIP and OCP. In fact, these two principles are closely related. Fundamentally, DIP tells us how we can adhere to OCP. Or, stated differently, if OCP is the desired end, DIP is the means through which we achieve that end. While this statement may seem obvious, we commonly violate DIP in a certain situation and don't even realize it.

When we create an instance of a class in Java, we typically must explicitly reference that object. Only after the instance has been created can we flexibly reference that object via its ancestors or implemented interfaces. Therefore, the moment we reference a class to create it, we have violated DIP and, subsequently, OCP. Recall that in order to adhere to OCP, we must first take advantage of DIP. There are a couple of different ways to resolve this.

The first way to resolve this impasse is to dynamically load the object using the `Class` class and its `newInstance` method. However, this solution can be problematic and somewhat inflexible. Because DIP doesn't allow us to refer to the concrete class explicitly, we must use a `String` representation of the concrete class. For instance, consider the code shown here:

```
Class c = Class.forName("SomeDescendent");
SomeAncestor sa = (SomeAncestor) c.newInstance();
```

In this example, we want to create an instance of the class `Some-Descendent` in the first line but reference it as type `SomeAncestor` in the second line. This was also illustrated in the code samples in the section "Open Closed Principle (OCP)." This is perfectly acceptable, as long as the `SomeDescendent` class is inherited, either directly or indirectly, from the `SomeAncestor` class. If it is not, our application will throw an exception at runtime. Another more obvious problem occurs when we misspell the class of which we want an instance. Yet another, less apparent, obstacle eventually is encountered when taking this approach. Because we reference the class name as a `String`, there isn't any way to pass parameters into the constructor of this class. Java does provides a solution to this problem, but it quickly becomes complex, unwieldy, and error prone.

Another approach to resolving the object creation challenge is to use an object factory. Here, we create a separate class whose only responsibility is to create instances. This way, our original class, where the instance would have previously been created, stays clear of any references to concrete classes, which have been removed and placed in this factory. The only references contained within this class are to abstract, or base, classes. The factory does, however, reference the concrete classes, which is, in fact, a blatant violation of DIP. However, it is an isolated and carefully thought through violation and is therefore acceptable.

Similarly, using a dependency injection framework such as Spring offers the advantage that I do not reference any concrete class in my code but instead reference the class in a configuration file. Spring is the object factory and dependency injection is how the instances are wired together at runtime.

Keep in mind that we may not always need to use an object factory. Along with the flexibility of a factory comes the complexity of a more dynamic collaboration of objects. Concrete references are not always a bad thing. If the class to which we are referring is a stable class, not likely to undergo many changes, using a factory adds unwarranted complexity to our system. If a factory is deemed necessary, the design of the factory itself should be given careful consideration.

INTERFACE SEGREGATION PRINCIPLE

Many specific interfaces are better than a single, general interface.

Simply put, any interface we define should be highly cohesive. In Java, we know that an interface is a reference data type that can have method declarations but no implementation. In essence, an interface is an abstract class with all abstract methods. As we define our interfaces, it becomes important that we clearly understand the role the interface plays within the context of our application. In fact, interfaces provide flexibility: They allow objects to assume the data type of the interface. Subsequently, an interface is simply a role that an object plays at some point throughout its lifetime. It follows, rather logically, that when defining the operation on an interface, we should do so in a manner that does not accommodate multiple roles. Therefore, an interface should be responsible for allowing an object to assume a single role, assuming the class of which that object is an instance implements that interface.

While working on a project recently, an ongoing discussion took place as to how we would implement our data access mechanism. A lot of time was spent designing a flexible framework that would allow uniform access to a variety of different data sources. These backend data sources might come in the form of a relational database, a flat file, or possibly even another proprietary database. Therefore, our goal was not only to provide a common data access mechanism but also to present data to any class acting as a data client in a consistent manner. Doing so would clearly decouple our data clients from the backend data source, making it much easier to port our backend data sources to different platforms without impacting our data clients. Therefore, we decided that all data clients would depend on a single Java interface, depicted in Figure A.2, with the associated methods.

At first glance, the design depicted in Figure A.2 seemed plausible. After further investigation, however, questions were raised as to the cohesion of the `RowSetManager` interface. What if classes implementing this interface were read-only and didn't need insert and update functionality? Also, what if the data client were not interested in retrieving the data but only in iterating its already-retrieved internal data set? Exploring these questions a bit further, and carefully considering ISP, we found that it was meaningful to have a data structure that wasn't even dependent on a retrieve action at all. For instance, we may want to use a data set that was cached in memory and wasn't dependent on an underlying physical data source. This led us to the design shown in Figure A.3.

In Figure A.3, we segregated the responsibilities of our `RowSetManager` into multiple interfaces. Each interface is responsible for allowing a class to adhere to a cohesive set of responsibilities. Now, our application can implement the interfaces necessary to provide the desired set of functionality. We are no longer forced to provide data update behavior if our class is read-only.

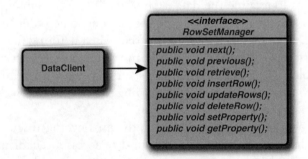

Figure A.2 Violation of Interface Segregation Principle

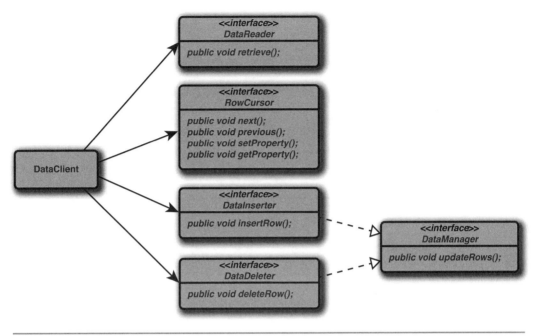

Figure A.3 Compliance to Interface Segregation Principle

COMPOSITE REUSE PRINCIPLE (CRP)

Favor polymorphic composition of objects over inheritance.

The Composite Reuse Principle (CRP) prevents us from making one of the most catastrophic mistakes that contribute to the demise of an object-oriented system: using inheritance as the primary reuse mechanism. The first reference to this principle was in *Design Patterns: Elements of Reusable Object-Oriented Software*. For example, let's turn back to a section of our diagram in Figure A.1. In Figure A.4, we see the `AccountType` hierarchy with a few additional attributes and methods added. In this example, we have added an additional method that calculates the interest for each of our accounts. We have added this method to the ancestor `AccountType` class. This seems to be a good approach, because our `Savings` and `MoneyMarket` classes are each interest-bearing accounts. Our `Checking` class is representative of an account that is not interest bearing. Regardless, we justify this by convincing ourselves that it's better

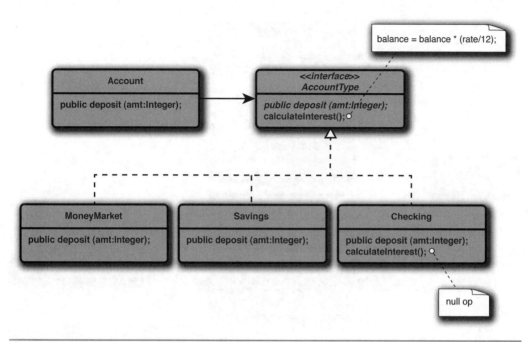

Figure A.4 AccountType hierarchy

to define some default behavior on an ancestor and override it on descendents instead of duplicating the behavior across descendents. We know that we can simply define a null operation on our `Checking` class that doesn't actually calculate interest, and our problem is solved. While we do want to reuse our code, and we can prevent the `Checking` class from calculating interest, our implementation contains a tragic flaw. First, let's discuss the flaw and when it will surface. Then, we'll discuss why this problem has occurred.

Let's consider a couple of new requirements. We need to support the addition of a new account type, called `Stock`. A `Stock` does calculate interest, but the algorithm for doing so is different than the default defined in our ancestor `AccountType`. That's easy to solve. All we have to do is override the `calculateInterest` in our new `Stock` class, just as we did in the `Checking` class, but instead of implementing a null operation, we can implement the appropriate algorithm. This works fine until our business realizes that the `Stock` class is doing extremely well, primarily because of its generous interest calculation mechanism. It's been decided that `MoneyMarket` should calculate interest using the same algorithm as `Stock`, but `Savings` remains the same. How do we solve this problem? We have three choices. First, redefine the `calculateInterest` method on our `AccountType` to implement this new algorithm and define a new method on `Savings` that implements the older method. This option is not ideal because it involves modifying at least two of our existing system classes, which is a blatant violation of OCP. Second, we could simply override `calculateInterest` on our `MoneyMarket` class, copy the code from our `Stock` class, and paste it in our `Money-Market calculateInterest` method. Obviously, this option is not a very flexible solution. Our goal in reuse is not copy and paste. Third, we can define a new class called `InterestCalculator`, define a `calculateInterest` method on this class that implements our new algorithm, and then delegate the calculation of interest from our `Stock` and `MoneyMarket` classes to this new class. So, which option is best?

The third solution is the one we should have used up front. Because we realized that the calculation of interest was not common to all classes, we should not have defined any default behavior in our ancestor class. Doing so in any situation inevitably results in the previously described outcome. Let's now resolve this problem using CRP.

In Figure A.5, we see a depiction of our class structure using CRP. In this example, we have no default behavior defined for `calculateInterest` in our `AccountType` hierarchy. Instead, in our `calculateInterest` methods on both our `MoneyMarket` and `Savings` classes, we defer the calculation of interest to a class that implements the `Interest-Calculator` interface. Now, when we add our `Stock` class, we simply choose the `InterestCalculator` that is applicable for this new class or define a new one if it's needed. If any of our other classes need to redefine their algorithms, we have the ability to do so because we are abstractly coupled to our interface and can substitute any of the classes that implement the interface anywhere the interface is referenced. Therefore, this solution is ultimately flexible in how it enables us to calculate interest. This is an example of CRP. Each of our `MoneyMarket` and `Savings` classes are composed of our `InterestCalculator`, which is the composite. Because we are abstractly coupled, we easily see we can receive polymorphic behavior. Hence, we have used polymorphic composition instead of inheritance to achieve reuse.

You might say at this point, however, that we still have to duplicate some code across the `Stock` and `MoneyMarket` classes. While this is true, the solution still solves our initial problem, which is how

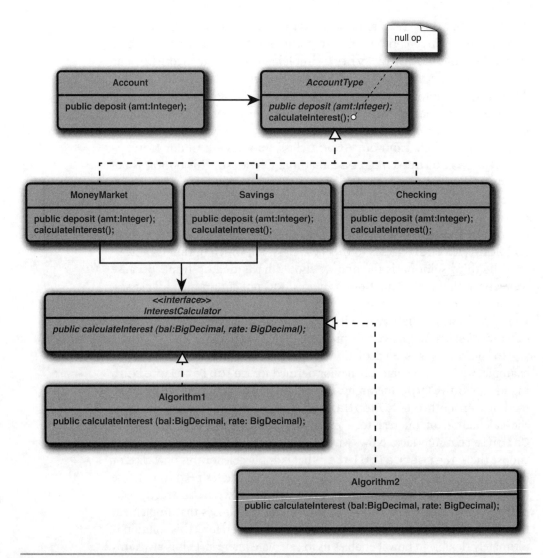

Figure A.5 Refactored AccountType hierarchy

to easily accommodate new interest calculation algorithms. Yet an even more flexible solution is available; it's one that will enable us to be even more dynamic in how we configure our objects with an instance of `InterestCalculator`.

In Figure A.6, we have moved the relationship to `Interest-Calculator` up the inheritance hierarchy into our `AccountType`

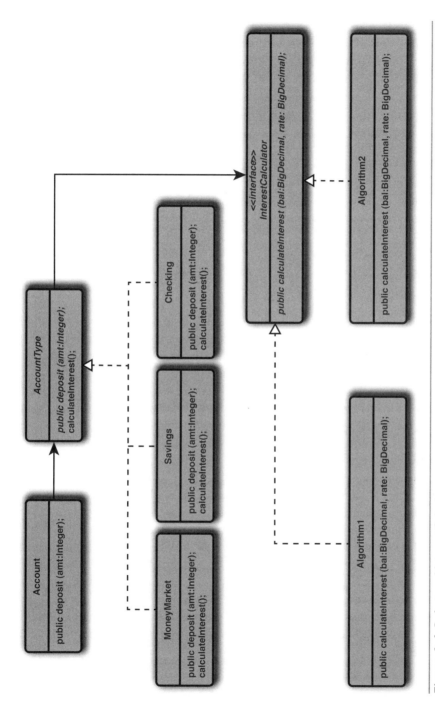

Figure A.6 Refactored InterestCalculator

class. In fact, in this scenario, we are back to using inheritance for reuse, though a bit differently. Our `AccountType` knows that it needs to calculate interest, but it does not know how to actually do it. Therefore, we see a relationship from `AccountType` to our `InterestCalculator`. Because of this relationship, all accounts calculate interest. However, if one of our algorithms is a null object—that is, it's an instance of a class that implements the interface and defines the methods, but the methods have no implementation (Martin 1997)—and we use the null object with the `Savings` class, we can now state that all of our accounts need to calculate interest. This substantiates our use of implementation inheritance. Because each account calculates it differently, we configure each account with the appropriate `InterestCalculator`.

So, how did we fall into the original trap depicted in Figure A.4? The problem lies within the inheritance relationship. Inheritance can be thought of as a generalization over a specialization relationship—that is, a class higher in the inheritance hierarchy is a more general version of those inherited from it. In other words, any ancestor class is a partial descriptor that should define some default characteristics that will be applicable to any class inherited from it. Violating this convention almost always results in the situation described previously. In fact, any time we have to override default behavior defined in an ancestor class, we are saying that the ancestor class is not a more general version of all of its descendents but actually contains descriptor characteristics that make it too specialized to serve as the ancestor of the class in question. Therefore, if we choose to define default behavior on an ancestor, it should be general enough to apply to all of its descendents.

In practice, CRP is applied a bit differently. In fact, it's not uncommon to define a default behavior in an ancestor class. However, we should still accommodate CRP in our relationships. This is easy to see in Figure A.5. We could have easily defined default behavior in our `calculateInterest` method on the `AccountType` class. We still have the flexibility, using CRP, to alter the behaviors of any of our `AccountType` classes because of the relationship to `InterestCalculator`. In this situation, we may even choose to create a null op `InterestCalculator` class that our `Checking` class uses. This way, we even accommodate the likelihood that `Savings` accounts can someday calculate interest. We have ultimate flexibility.

REFERENCES

Martin, Robert C. 2002. *Agile Software Development: Principles, Patterns, and Practices.* Boston: Addison-Wesley.

Knoernschild, Kirk. 2001. *Java Design: Objects, UML, and Process.* Boston: Addison-Wesley.

Martin, Robert C., Dirk Riehle, and Frank Buschmann. 1997. *Pattern Languages of Program Design 3.* Reading, MA: Addison-Wesley.

INDEX

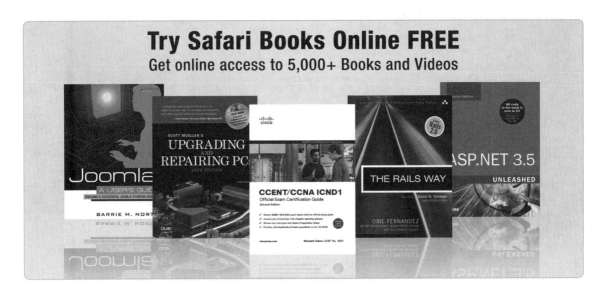

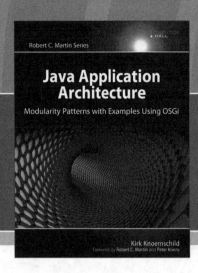

Safari
Books Online

FREE
Online Edition

Your purchase of *Java Application Architecture* includes access to a free online edition for 45 days through the **Safari Books Online** subscription service. Nearly every Prentice Hall book is available online through **Safari Books Online**, along with thousands of books and videos from publishers such as Addison-Wesley Professional, Cisco Press, Exam Cram, IBM Press, O'Reilly Media, Prentice Hall, Que, Sams, and VMware Press.

Safari Books Online is a digital library providing searchable, on-demand access to thousands of technology, digital media, and professional development books and videos from leading publishers. With one monthly or yearly subscription price, you get unlimited access to learning tools and information on topics including mobile app and software development, tips and tricks on using your favorite gadgets, networking, project management, graphic design, and much more.

Activate your FREE Online Edition at
informit.com/safarifree

STEP 1:   Enter the coupon code: EVRNVFA.

STEP 2:   New Safari users, complete the brief registration form.
           Safari subscribers, just log in.

If you have difficulty registering on Safari or accessing the online edition,
please e-mail customer-service@safaribooksonline.com